ARTIFICIAL COMMUNICATION

ARTIFICIAL COMMUNICATION

HOW ALGORITHMS PRODUCE
SOCIAL INTELLIGENCE

ELENA ESPOSITO

THE MIT PRESS   CAMBRIDGE, MASSACHUSETTS   LONDON, ENGLAND

The MIT Press would like to thank the anonymous peer reviewers who provided comments on drafts of this book. The generous work of academic experts is essential for establishing the authority and quality of our publications. We acknowledge with gratitude the contributions of these otherwise uncredited readers.

This book was set in Stone Serif and Avenir by Jen Jackowitz. Printed and bound in the United States of America.

Library of Congress Cataloging-in-Publication Data

Names: Esposito, Elena, author.
Title: Artificial communication : how algorithms produce social intelligence / Elena Esposito.
Description: Cambridge, Massachusetts : The MIT Press, [2022] | Series: Strong ideas series | Includes bibliographical references and index.
Identifiers: LCCN 2021013271 | ISBN 9780262046664 (hardcover)
Subjects: LCSH: Telecommunication—Social aspects. | Artificial intelligence—Social aspects. | Online identities. | Social intelligence.
Classification: LCC HM851 .E765 2022 | DDC 303.48/33—dc23
LC record available at https://lccn.loc.gov/2021013271

10 9 8 7 6 5 4 3 2 1

For Emma

CONTENTS

INTRODUCTION

Algorithms that work with deep learning and big data are getting better and better at doing more and more things: They quickly and accurately produce information, and are learning to drive cars more safely and reliably than humans. They can answer our questions, make conversation, compose music, and read books. And they can even write interesting, appropriate, and—if required—funny texts.

Yet when it comes to observing this progress, we are seldom completely at ease—not only because of our worries about bias, errors, threats to privacy, or malicious uses by corporations and governments. Actually, the better the algorithms become, the more our discomfort increases. A recent article in the *New Yorker* describes one journalist's experience with Smart Compose,[1] a feature of Gmail that suggests endings to your sentences as you type them. The algorithm completed the journalist's emails so appropriately, pertinently, and in line with his style that he found himself learning from the machine not only what he would have written, but also what he should have written (and had not thought to), or could want to write. And he didn't like it at all.

This experience, extremely common in our interactions with supposedly intelligent machines, has been labeled the "uncanny valley":[2] an eerie feeling of discomfort that appears in cases where a machine seems too similar to a human being—or to the observer themself. We want the machine to support our thoughts and behaviors, but when we find what appear to be thoughts and behaviors *in* the machine, we do not feel comfortable. Today, each of us customarily communicates with automated programs (*bots*) with little attention given to their nature—when we buy plane tickets online, when we ask for assistance on the web, when we play video games, and on many other occasions.[3] Nevertheless, when we reflect on or debate the subject of algorithms, we still find ourselves discussing topics such as the possibilities of a machine passing the Turing test,[4] the arrival of a technological "singularity," or the creation of a superintelligence far beyond human abilities.[5] We compare ourselves to machines, and we don't like it if they seem to be winning. In our endeavors to build intelligent machines, we do not just wonder whether we have succeeded, but if the machines are becoming *too* smart.

But is this really what we have to worry about? While we may get an eerie feeling around machines that resemble us a little too closely, should we say that the fundamental risk of algorithms is that they might *compare* or *compete* with human intelligence? This book starts from the hypothesis that analogies between the performance of algorithms and human intelligence are not only unnecessary, but misleading—even if the reasoning behind them appears plausible. Today, after all, many algorithms seem to be able to "think" and communicate. In communication as we know it, our partners have always been human beings, and human beings are endowed with intelligence. If our interlocutor is an algorithm, we impulsively attribute to "him" or "her" the characteristics of a human being. If the machine can communicate autonomously, one thinks, "it must also be intelligent," although perhaps in a different way than humans. On the basis of this analogy, research has focused on the parallels and differences between human intelligence and machine performance, observing their limits and making comparisons.[6] But is it really advisable to continue following this analogy?

That we can communicate with machines, I argue, does not imply that they have their own intelligence that needs to be explained (an explanation that may also require explaining the mysteries of "natural" intelligence), but that, foremost, *communication* is changing. The object of study in this book is not intelligence, which is and remains a mystery, but communication, which we can observe and about which we already know a great deal. For example, we know how communication has changed over centuries and with the evolution of human society. We know that communication has moved from simple interactions between parties sharing physical space to more flexible and inclusive forms, which have also allowed communication with previously inaccessible partners distant in space and time, in increasingly anonymous and impersonal settings.

Within the evolution of communication, the role of human beings has changed profoundly. Today there is no need for partners to be present; there is no need to know who they are and why they communicate, nor to know what they mean and to take it into account. We can read and understand the instruction booklet of a dishwasher without knowing who wrote it and without identifying ourselves with the writer's point of view; we interpret a work of art without being bound to the perspective and intention of the artist.[7] There is no need for most information to be stored in someone's mind (nobody knows the civil code by heart), and in all cases of fiction, we identify with the characters of novels and films knowing that they never existed and that they are not the authors of the communication they carry along. The idea of successful communication as a precise sharing of identical content between the minds of participants has been unrealistic for many centuries, in practice if not in theory. In most cases, issuers and receivers do not know each other, do not know each other's perspectives, contexts, or constraints—and do not need to do so. On the contrary, this lack of transparency allows for otherwise unthinkable degrees of freedom and abstraction.

That communication changes its forms is not new and is not an enigma. Rather, the issue is identifying and understanding the differences and continuities between forms old and new. Today, the autonomy of communication from the cognitive processes of its participants has gone a step further. We need a concept of communication that can take into account the possibility that a communication partner may not be a human being, but instead is an algorithm. The result, already observed today, is a condition in which we have information whose development or genesis we often cannot reconstruct, yet which is nevertheless not arbitrary. The information generated autonomously by algorithms is not random at all and is completely controlled—but not by the processes of the human mind.[8]

How can we control this control, which for us can also be incomprehensible? This is, in my opinion, the real challenge that machine-learning techniques and the use of big data pose to us today.

The chapters of this book elaborate on this perspective while investigating the use of algorithms in different areas of social life. What do we see, not see, or see differently, if we consider the workings of algorithms as communication, rather than intelligence?

The book opens with a discussion on the adequacy of the classic metaphor of artificial intelligence, as well as derivatives such as neural networks, to analyze recent developments in digital technologies and the web. The latest generation of algorithms, which in various forms have given rise to the use of big data and related projects, does not try to artificially reproduce the processes of human intelligence. This, I argue, is neither a renunciation nor a weakness, but the basis of their incomparable efficiency in information processing and in their ability to interact with users. For the first time, machines are able to produce information never before considered by a human mind and act as interesting and competent communication partners—not because they have become intelligent; instead, it is because they no longer try to do so. The processes that drive algorithms are completely different from the processes of the human mind, and in fact no human mind nor combination of human minds could reproduce them, much less understand algorithmic decision-making processes. Yet human intelligence remains indispensable. Self-learning algorithms are able to calculate, combine, and process differences with amazing efficiency, but they are not able to produce them themselves. They find the differences on the web. Through big data, algorithms "feed" on the differences generated (consciously or unconsciously) by individuals and their behavior to produce new, surprising, and potentially instructive information. Algorithmic processes start from the intelligence and unpredictability (from the contingency) of users to rework them and operate intelligently as communication partners, with no need to be intelligent themselves.

The subsequent chapters explore the consequences of this condition in practical work with algorithms. In chapter 2, I trace the proliferation of lists in digitized societies to a fact about lists known since antiquity: they make it possible to manage information one does not understand—possibly producing new information as a result. I analyze use of visualization in the digital humanities in chapter 3 as a technique to make meaningful the results of the incomprehensible procedures of algorithmic text processing. Chapter 4 deals with digital profiling and algorithmic individualization, which implement paradoxical forms of standardized personalization and generalized contextualization, thereby redefining the meaning of "context reference" and "active public." The enigmas inherent in the attempt to realize a technique of forgetting through algorithms ("remembering to forget") are the focus of chapter 5, which discusses the possibility of using algorithms for this purpose precisely because of their peculiar inability to do so. Finally, chapter 6 queries the consequences of digitization on the use of photographs, which today seem to be produced to escape the pressure of the present rather than to preserve experiences as memories.

The book closes with an analysis of algorithmic prediction in chapter 7, which wraps up my exploration by returning to intelligence and its digital forms. In the wake of the increasing lack of transparency of increasingly efficient algorithms, the idea is emerging that machines are incomprehensible primarily because there is nothing to understand—and there is nothing to understand because machines *do not understand*. Algorithms seem intelligent not because they can understand, but because they can predict. As Ilya Sutskever, chief scientist at OpenAI, explicitly states in reference to software for automated writing: "If a machine . . . could have enough data and computing power to perfectly predict . . . that would be the equivalent of understanding."[9]

Prediction is the new horizon of research on artificial forms of intelligence, in a context that radically changes the terms of the question: when you work with algorithms, the issue is not explaining but predicting, not identifying causal relationships but finding correlations, not managing the uncertainty of the future but discovering its structures (patterns). Yet the world remains uncertain, the future remains open, and the use of algorithms must still be explained. It is here, in my opinion, that the issue of control and the challenge of algorithms arise today—of how to manage the impact of their meaning-independent procedures in a global society in which meaning, contingency, and uncertainty are still precious resources.

Bologna, February 2021

1

ARTIFICIAL COMMUNICATION? ALGORITHMS AS INTERACTION PARTNERS

COMMUNICATION WITH ALGORITHMS

Whether algorithms can "think" is still very uncertain.[1] What is more certain is that contemporary algorithms, based on machine learning and big data, can participate in communication. Today's algorithms can act as communication *partners*. Precise estimates are difficult, yet it is claimed that bots are the authors of approximately 50 percent of online traffic.[2] Millions of Twitter users are bots,[3] most fake Facebook accounts are created by automated programs,[4] and at least 40 percent of Wikipedia editing is carried out by computer-controlled accounts.[5] According to an evaluation by the Oxford Internet Institute, highly automated accounts generated close to 25 percent of all Twitter traffic about the 2016 US presidential election.[6] That Google and Facebook are driven by algorithms is well known, with the paradoxical consequence that the "discovery" that human operators guide the selection of news in Facebook's list of tending topics was perceived as a scandal.[7] Automated systems are also used in personalized communication; on Gmail, Smart Reply recognizes emails that require responses and generates perfectly adequate natural language answers on the fly.[8] Spotify's most popular compilation, Discover Weekly, is entirely assembled by an algorithm—as well as its Release Radar, a hyperpersonalized playlist of the latest tracks.[9]

Algorithms can also be the authors of texts and books in traditional printed media. Companies like Narrative Science[10] and Automated Insight[11] have developed algorithms to produce texts that are indistinguishable from those written by human authors: newspaper articles, brochures for commercial products, textbooks, and more. Philip Parker, professor at INSEAD in Fontainebleau, patented a method to automatically produce plausible and informative books, including more than one hundred thousand titles already available on Amazon.com. Robojournalism is regularly used by the Associated Press and many companies like Samsung, Yahoo, Comcast, and others.[12]

Often, moreover, we talk directly with algorithms. We routinely book train tickets, make appointments, and ask for assistance via dialogue with chatbots. Digital personal assistants like Apple's Siri, Amazon's Alexa, or Google Assistant use natural language interfaces to answer new questions, manage calendars, or offer individual suggestions and recommendations. In many cases, these programs seem to know the users better than their human partners and often better than the users themselves,[13] anticipating their needs and demands even before they emerge.

How should we interpret these amazing developments in the communicative performance of algorithms? Communication as we know it normally takes place between humans (or at most between humans and other living beings). If machines now participate in communication, does this mean that machines have become human, or at least that they have learned to reproduce the intelligence of human beings? Are we witnessing the realization of the ideal of an artificial intelligence (AI) that has accompanied the progress of digitization from its beginnings,[14] or are we facing something different that requires a transition to a different way of thinking?

In this chapter, I argue that what we can observe in interactions with algorithms is not necessarily an artificial form of intelligence, but rather an artificial form of communication. Intelligence and communicative capacity are not the same thing. Algorithms are able to act as communication partners—whether they are intelligent or not is another matter. Modern machine-learning algorithms are so efficient not because they have learned to imitate human intelligence and to understand information, but rather because they have abandoned the attempt and the ambition to do so and are oriented toward a different model. Machine-learning algorithms that use big data, I claim, are artificially reproducing not intelligence but communication skills, and they do so by parasitically exploiting the participation of users on the web.

The concept of communication must be reconsidered. Can we still talk of communication when one of the partners has no understanding of the information conveyed? What does this mean for social information processing? In the following pages I try to give an answer to these questions by examining the notion of communication and proposing a concept that does not presuppose any sharing of thoughts between participants. In the final part of the chapter, I show the consequences of the shift from intelligence to communication in the design of algorithms and, in particular, in the idea of autonomous-learning programs.

ARTIFICIAL COMMUNICATION

The protagonists of the current communicative revolution are algorithms, but algorithms by themselves are not new. The concept of the algorithm dates back at least to the Middle Ages, the term itself having roots in the latinization of "al-Khwarīzmī," the name of a Persian mathematician from the ninth century.[15] What is new is the recent exploitation, made possible by the use of big data and machine-learning techniques, of a specific feature of algorithms—their lack of intelligence.

The advantage of algorithms has always been one of not requiring any "creative" thought in their execution.[16] As with computers, they carry out operations in sequence according to precise instructions, proceeding mechanically.[17] In algorithms, and in the digital management of data that relies on them, information processing and mapping have nothing to do with understanding—indeed, in many cases a need for understanding would rather be an obstacle.[18] As the number of elements to be analyzed grows (up to today's incredible scales of petabytes and zettabytes) the operations of these machines become less and less comprehensible[19]— yet their performance not only does not decrease, but gradually becomes more precise and reliable. Digital machines have other ways to test the correctness of their procedures.

The communicative relevance of algorithms is actually related to their independence from understanding. We are facing a way to process data (and to manage information) that is different from human information processing and understanding.[20] My assumption is that this difference is not a liability but instead is the very root of the success of these technologies. Just as human beings first became able to fly when they abandoned the idea of building machines that flap their wings like birds,[21] digital information processing managed to achieve the results that we see today after abandoning the ambition to reproduce in digital form the processes of the human mind. Now that they no longer try to resemble our consciousness, algorithms have become more and more able to act as competent communication partners, responding appropriately to our requests and providing information neither constructed nor reconstructable by a human mind.[22]

This is already evident in our practical use of algorithms, but not always in our theorizing about them. The metaphors used in the field of big data and machine learning retain a reference to the human mind and its processes. Take, for example, the widespread idea that recent procedures of deep learning are so effective because they are based on biological neural networks, replicating the functioning of the human brain. As most researchers admit,[23] however, we still know very little about the workings of our brains, which makes the analogy quite curious—does it make sense to take our ignorance as a model?[24] If machines no longer try to understand meaning as happens in the human mind, shouldn't we find a different, more fitting, metaphor?

Recent approaches to big data are very different from the programs of AI research from the 1970s and 1980s, which aimed to reproduce the processes of human intelligence, by imitation or by analogy ("strong" or "weak" AI, respectively), with a machine.[25] This is no longer the case. As some AI designers explicitly declare, "We do not try and copy intelligence"[26]—for this would be too heavy a burden. Translation programs do not try to understand the documents they translate, and their designers do not rely on any theory of language learning.[27] Algorithms translate texts from Chinese without knowing Chinese, and their programmers do not know it either. Spell checkers correct typographical errors in any language, knowing neither these languages nor their (varying) conventions. Digital assistants operate with words without understanding what words mean, and text-producing algorithms "don't reason like people in order to write like people."[28] Examples multiply across all areas in which algorithms are the most successful. Algorithms competing with human players in chess, poker, and Go have no knowledge of the games nor of the subtleties of human strategies.[29] Recommendation programs using collaborative filtering know absolutely nothing about the movies, songs, or books they suggest, yet operate as reliable tastemakers.[30] Computer-based personality judgments work "automatically and without involving human socio-cognitive skills."[31]

These programs are reproducing not intelligence but rather communicative competence. What makes algorithms socially relevant and useful is their ability to act as partners in communicative practices that produce and circulate information, independently of their intelligence. Could we say that machine-learning programs realize not an artificial intelligence but a kind of artificial communication, providing human beings with unforeseen and unpredictable information? Maybe our society as a whole becomes "smarter" not because it artificially reproduces intelligence, but because it creates a new form of communication using data in a different way.

That the focus of the web is on communication rather than on intelligence is confirmed by the rampant success of social media, which had not been foreseen in any model of digital evolution. The web today is organized more through contacts, links, tweets, and likes than by meaningful connections between content and between sites[32]—it is driven by communication, not by meaning and understanding.[33] Every link (every communicative behavior) is treated as a like, and "liking" and "being like" have also been equated.[34] Everything that happens online is used as a fact and thus becomes a fact, having consequences and producing information.

CAN WE COMMUNICATE WITH PARTNERS THAT DO NOT THINK?

If we are to examine communicative competence, and as such to shift our reference from (artificial) intelligence to (artificial) communication, we must start asking different questions. The focus is no longer on the participants (on whether they are human or not, and what it means to be human in a digital world);[35] it is on the process of producing information.

Is what happens in the interaction with algorithms on the web "communication," or do we need to modify the concept? Does it still make sense to speak of communication when data processing is performed by a machine that does not understand the content being communicated? Are the users of web services communicating, and if so, with whom? The answers to these questions depend on our concept of communication, and the concept should be powerful enough to also cover interactions with machines.

Most concepts of communication require that the mental processes of its participants converge on some common content. According to the Latin root of the term "communication" (*communicatio*), it is assumed that partners have the same thought in common, or at least part of it. Communication happens if, at the end of the process, the receiver gets at least some of the information that the issuer put into the channel. Even considering noise and differences in coding/decoding, interpretation and competence, the idea is that in a successful communication, some element of the identity of information must be preserved.[36] The problem with this approach, however, is that in the interaction with machines, we are dealing with a situation in which one communication partner is an algorithm that does not understand content, meaning, or interpretation. It deals only with data.[37] A user, therefore, shares no information (not even partially) with their interlocutor, because the interlocutor does not know any information. Can we still say that they are communicating?[38] Are we dealing with an "aberrant" condition, or with an unprecedented form of communication?[39]

My argument in the following sections follows Niklas Luhmann's theory of social systems and his notion of communication.[40] I claim that the very reasons why Luhmann's approach has been criticized (and often misunderstood) are now the very reasons that make it particularly appropriate to deal with novel aspects of digital communication. Luhmann explicitly refused to define communication in reference to conscious subjects. The concepts of subject and individual, he argued, act only as empty formulas for a very complex phenomenon that falls within the competence of psychology and does not directly interest sociologists or communication theorists.[41] The objects of sociology are not subjects but communications, in which the thoughts of the participating individuals (which are and remain indispensable) are not the constituent elements. Luhmann's theory of communication, therefore, distances itself from psychic processes and their communicative role, thereby breaking with this tradition in sociology.

That Luhmann's concept of communication is not based on psychic content and requires no sharing of thoughts among participants becomes a great advantage when dealing with algorithms that do not think. In all forms of communication, Luhmann argues, information is different for everyone and always relative to a specific observer.[42] But a common identity of information among participants is itself not required for communication.

Luhmann's simple yet very effective innovation is to define communication starting from the receiver, rather than from the issuer. According to his approach, communication comes about not when somebody says something,[43] but when somebody understands that someone said something. One can write entire books and make elaborate speeches, but if no one reads or listens or even notices it, there was no real communication. Yet if a receiver understands information that (they believe) someone uttered, communication takes place—whatever this information is to the receiver, and whatever the issuer had in mind (or indeed did not have in mind). I do not have to enter Proust's mind to understand À la recherche du temps perdu—an understanding that I may gain in another language and experience a hundred years after the work was written. I only have to understand his communication—in my way, and according to my thoughts. The information I get from Proust's work will inevitably be different from Proust's thoughts, which makes communication an endless, fascinating process of discovery.

Since information is always relative to the observer, the receiver always obtains information that is different from what the utterer had in mind.[44] The thoughts of the participants are not part of communication itself, leading to an infinite variety of individual understandings. The task of sociology and of communication theory is to analyze how this diversity of understandings can still produce forms of coordination.[45] Even without a shared understanding, not every interpretation is socially acceptable, and explicit misunderstandings are an exception, rather than the rule.

The fundamental power of this notion of communication, as concerns our focus on algorithms, pertains to the fact that, in its noninclusion of the thoughts of participants,[46] such a notion could in principle extend to participants that do not think (such as algorithms). If we start from the perspective of the receiver, what counts is whether they take something to be a communication partner. Since in communication the receiver attributes the information obtained to their counterpart, however, the partner is normally a human being;[47] we do not normally communicate with machines, to which this kind of information is not attributed.

This does not mean that machines cannot be informative, however. We habitually gather information from objects in the world and from machines—our watches, for example, tell us what time it is—but we do not attribute the information to the watch. Our watch informs us about the time, but only because it was constructed by someone in order to convey that information. It does not develop its own way of dealing with time and does not decide itself how to calculate it. We do not communicate with our watch. Yet algorithms are confronting us with an unprecedented situation. From algorithms we get information that often was not planned or available in advance and was unknown to the programmers themselves. Self-learning digital programs autonomously develop their procedures and identify patterns, which they use to produce their answers to our requests. In conversations with digital personal assistants or social bots, for example, the information we get did not exist before we formulated our request and is produced by the machine expressly to respond to that request. Nobody knew that information in advance or decided how to produce it—the algorithm generated it itself. The production of information can be attributed only to an interactive partner, as in communication—but in this case the partner is not a human being, but a machine.

When we interact with algorithms, then, do we communicate with them? Does their role in communication require us to consider them as possible partners? It is a tricky matter. The issue of communication with machines and the current relevance of the Turing test depend on the answer to this question. The problem here is not whether the person is or is not aware of dealing with a machine, for doing so is now an everyday occurrence, and one where such a question is usually not relevant. Today our counterparts are often bots (in online services, video games, social media) even if we are not aware of it—and when we are aware, as with personal assistants, we do not normally care.[48] What matters is whether the interaction from which we gather our information has the features of a relationship with a contingent, autonomous partner.

VIRTUAL CONTINGENCY

Contingency implies selection and uncertainty. It means that there are a number of possible options to choose from, and our decisions could always be different.[49] However, algorithms by definition do not know uncertainty; they do not choose between possibilities, nor are they creative, being designed to follow the instructions that program their behavior. In this sense, algorithms are not contingent—which is why they can operate so efficiently and reliably. Just like traditional machines, we expect algorithms to be neither unpredictable nor idiosyncratic, even when they deliver information. Different watches should all indicate the same time to all users, if they work properly. As von Foerster observed, if the outcome of a traditional machine becomes unpredictable, we do not think that it is creative or original—we think that it is broken.[50] We do not care about the moods nor the perspectives of machines, only about their results. We repair them precisely to restore their predictability.

Recent algorithms, however, are different: their semblance of contingency is an essential feature. Even if these machines follow a completely determined course, we want their outcomes to be unpredictable, and to produce something we do not yet know—that is, new information appropriate to a given interaction with a user. The expected outcome is not predicted by anyone and, in the case of self-learning algorithms, could not be predicted—that's why we use algorithms, and why they appear creative. The dilemma faced by designers, therefore, is to build machines that are creative yet controlled at the same time—to program the production of unpredicted outcomes. Even if the machine is completely determined, its behavior should appear contingent and react to the contingency of the user. Cozmo, for example, a real-life toy robot based on a series of machine-learning algorithms,[51] is "programmed to be unpredictable" without being simply random.[52] Cozmo's behavior must appear responsive and appropriate to the user, otherwise it is no fun. A personal assistant like Alexa should respond appropriately to the user's requests, producing new and relevant information in the course of the interaction. The paradoxical purpose of programming intelligent algorithms is to build unpredictable machines in a controlled way. The goal is a controlled lack of control.[53]

How can an algorithm act as a contingent partner in an interaction? In some cases, the contingency of a machine is simply the projection of the contingency of its user. This happens, for example, with the robotic toys studied by Sherry Turkle that work well as communication partners because children or elderly people interacting with them project onto them their own contingency.[54] This always happens with dolls and puppets, with which children play as if the toys understand and respond to their behavior. What is reflected in the performance of robotic toys—and what makes them more fun than traditional dolls—is not the ability to understand but the ability to "perform understanding" in elaborate and seemingly reactive ways.[55]

Self-learning algorithms go further and do something more enigmatic. When a user interacts with a learning algorithm,[56] they face a contingency that is not of their making—although it also does not belong to the machine. The perspective that the machine presents is still a reflected perspective—because the algorithm inevitably does not possess its own contingency—although one which does not simply reflect the perspective of the user. Instead, what the algorithm reflects and represents is the perspectives of *other* observers; what the user observes through the machine is the outcome of the processing of other users' observation. I call *virtual contingency* the ability of algorithms to use the contingency of users as a means of acting as competent communication partners.

GOOGLIZATION

Where do algorithms find the contingency they reflect? How do they access the external perspectives they elaborate and present to their communication partners? To be able to participate in communication, algorithms must be on the web.[57] As smart and sophisticated as algorithms can be, artificial communication would not be possible without the web—a power only realized once algorithms were taken online. The path-breaking effect of the "participatory web" (Web 2.0, and possibly 3.0)[58] was not so much customization, but rather an inclusion and exploitation of virtual contingency.[59] Algorithms parasitically "feed" on contributions by users and actively use them to increase the complexity of their own behavior—along with the complexity of their communicative capacities. In interactions with learning algorithms, I claim, users experience an (artificial) form of unpredictability and reflexivity. Such interactions artificially reproduce the conditions of communication.

The prototype of this approach is Google, and this is also the reason for its success. The breakthrough came in 1998 with the introduction of link analysis in the World Wide Web.[60] Previously, information retrieval took place by way of searching through a limited, unlinked, static collection of documents. The organization and categorization of information were entrusted to specialists such as librarians, journal editors, or experts in various fields. Link analysis, instead, extends to the web and introduces a form of information retrieval that becomes huge, dynamic (unlike traditional documents, web pages are constantly changing their content), hyperlinked, yet above all, self-organized. The structure is decided not by experts but by the dynamics of the web. And it is incomparably more efficient.

The design of Google's PageRank algorithm marked a conceptual turn, "inventing" the internet as we know it today.[61] Its authors, and later owners of the company, describe it as starting from the idea of exploiting the link structure of the web as a large hypertext system.[62] The key insight was to determine which pages are important and for whom, disregarding the content of the pages themselves. To appropriately decide the ranking of pages responding to users' requests, the idea was to use information that is external to the web pages themselves and which rather refer to what other users did in their previous activity. In other words, to decide which pages are important, PageRank does not look to see what the pages say or how they say it, but instead looks at how often they were linked to and by whom. The ranking is based on the number of *backlinks* to the pages (how many times they have been pointed to by other websites) and on their importance—where the "importance" of backlinks depends itself on how many links they in turn have. The definition of "relevance" is openly circular: a page has high rank if the sum of the ranks of its backlinks is high,[63] including both the case of a page with many not particularly authoritative backlinks and the case of a page with a few highly linked backlinks.

The genius of PageRank's innovation lies in relinquishing the goal of understanding what the page says and relying solely on the structure and the dynamics of communication. Google's creators did not try to come up with a great organizational scheme for the web based on experienced and competent consultants, as did competing search engines like Altavista and Yahoo.[64] They did not try to understand and build an algorithm that understands; instead, "they got everyone else to do it for them" by surfing the net and making connections.[65] Content comes into play later, as a result and not as a premise. Google uses the links to learn not only how important a page is, but also what it is about. If the links to a given page use a certain sentence, the system infers that the sentence accurately describes that page and takes this into account for later searches. The algorithm is designed to apprehend and reflect the choices made by users,[66] activating a recursive loop in which the users use the algorithm to get the information, their searches modify the algorithm, and the algorithm then impinges on their subsequent searches for information. What the programmers design is only the algorithm's ability to self-modify. What and how the algorithm selects depend on how users are using it.

This system has been developed further to take into account factors beyond popularity, such as users' click behavior, reading time, and patterns of query reformulation.[67] As Google declares in the InsideSearch pages of its website, algorithms today rely on more than two hundred signals and clues referring to "things like the terms in websites, the freshness of content, your region."[68] The company produced a "Knowledge Graph" that provides a semantic connection between billions of entities and allows for more rapid and appropriate responses, also including information and results not yet thought of by anyone. The "intelligence" of the system, however, derives from its use of previous user activity and from sources of information already available on the web, from Wikipedia to databases of common knowledge. As John Gianandrea, director of engineering at Google, declared: when one is googling "Einstein," "We're not trying to tell you what's important about Einstein—we're trying to tell you about what humanity is looking for when they search."[69] The intelligence of the system is the intelligence of the users that the algorithm exploits to direct and organize its own behavior.

Google has become the symbol of an approach that can be found in other successful projects on the web.[70] Since 2003 the term "googlization" has been employed to describe the spread, in more and more applications and contexts, of a model that does not rely on traditional status makers like editors or experts, but "feeds" on the dynamics of the web to organize its operations and even itself.[71] Vaidhyanathan argues that the web is guided by a "googlization of everything" that takes advantage of the operations performed by users to produce a condition in which "Google works for us because it seems to read our minds."[72] In reality, Google does not need such powers. Rather, Google merely uses the *results* of what we had in mind in order to produce that which we did not.

Google, along with other systems that work in the same way, feeds on the information provided by users to produce new information, which is introduced into the circuit of communication. It is this information that users obtain from their interactions with algorithms, and which can only be attributed to the algorithms themselves. When speaking of interactions with algorithms, it makes no sense to refer only to the perspective of those who entered the data, because they could not know precisely how the data would be used. Similarly, it makes no sense to refer to the perspective of what the algorithm itself meant, because it did not *mean* anything. Constraints and orientation depend not on intentions but on programs, which are normally inaccessible.[73]

Algorithms make selections and choices based on criteria that are not random, instead reflecting and elaborating upon the indeterminacy of their participants. Users receive contingent responses that react to their contingency using the contingency of other users. While they do not directly communicate with this assortment of other users, the result of this interaction is a specific answer to a specific question which would not exist if other users were not also engaged in communication. Google and similar models appear to communicate with their users, and are able to do so precisely because they do not try to understand content. They do not artificially reproduce intelligence, but directly engage in communication. In light of this, are we dealing with a new form of communication?

WHAT ALGORITHMS LEARN

If interaction with learning algorithms is communication, we are dealing with a form of artificial communication. By "artificial" here I mean more than a communication that was produced by someone, since all communication would be artificial in this sense.[74] A communication is artificial when it involves an entity—the algorithm—that has been built and programmed to act as a communication partner by someone who does not participate in the communication. It is communication with an artificial partner.[75]

Considering artificial communication more closely can help us to explore the enigmatic ability of algorithms to learn. Recent algorithms using big data can learn to recognize images never encountered before, carry on conversations about unknown topics, analyze medical data and formulate diagnoses, as well as anticipate the behavior, the reasoning, and also the wishes of users. On the basis of their ability, we can (or will soon be able to) ride self-driving cars, translate online phone calls from one language to another in real time, and use digital assistants to deliver the information we need at any given moment. But what do learning algorithms learn? And who teaches them?

Self-learning algorithms can apparently learn by themselves. Whether supervised, semi-supervised or unsupervised, learning algorithms decide autonomously how to learn and what to learn. They are able to use data to learn functions they have not specifically been programmed for.[76] Their programmers only design a set of procedures that should allow the machine to develop its own way to solve a task, or even (in the case of unsupervised learning) to determine its own task, finding structures in data such as groupings or clusters. The programmers do not know what the machine is learning, instead they teach it to learn autonomously.

This is not an easy task, especially if it is an explicit goal. Michael Warner, a Carnegie Mellon–trained robotic researcher, claims that in many situations where you invoke machine learning, you do so "because you do not really understand what the system should do."[77] The programmers give indications that the learner will use in its own way, and then see if the result is satisfactory. When a learning algorithm is expected to learn to play a game, for example, the programmers do not teach it the moves, or even the rules of the game. The machine makes random moves, and after a number of attempts, the programmers tell it if it has won or lost. The learning algorithm uses these "reinforcements" to calculate in its own way an evaluation function that indicates which moves to make—without making predictions, without a game strategy, without "thinking" and without imagining the perspective of its opponent.[78] Nobody knows what the machine learned, or how it did so, but the processes involved produce amazing performances, such as defeating the most qualified champions of games like chess or Go. As the programmers of AlphaGo, the computing system built by Google to play Go, put it: "Our goal is to beat the best human players, not just to mimic them."[79]

AlphaGo learned to become an outstanding Go player and beat the best players in the world. For this purpose it did not learn to play the game *like* human players (or better). In fact, the algorithm did not *learn* Go—it learned to *participate in* Go, taking advantage of the moves of other participants to develop and refine its own moves. AlphaGo was originally trained with data from a server that allowed people to play against each other on the internet. The players were all amateurs and their skills were rather coarse, but the program refined these skills enormously by playing millions of games against itself. AlphaGo and other game-oriented algorithms learn via self-play, refining their skills with a trial-and- error process.[80] The system learns "not just from human moves, but from moves generated by multiple versions of itself."[81]

These procedures confirm the hypothesis that algorithms learn not to think but to participate in communication, that is, to (artificially) develop an autonomous perspective that allows them to react appropriately and generate information in their interaction with other participants. What AlphaGo thinks or does not think is irrelevant to its performance. It is competent, reactive and creative—and can also be surprising. It is a perfect game partner even and precisely because it does not think like a human player. Through training, algorithms do not become more intelligent; they just learn to play better. The programmers themselves do not understand the "reasoning" of the algorithm. When the programmers indicate that the algorithm is "wrong," they merely signal that there is an error, without indicating what it is. The algorithm uses these reinforcements to direct its own behavior, which becomes more and more refined and effective—and less and less comprehensible.[82]

LEARNING TO LEARN FROM MACHINES

Learning algorithms learn to participate in communication, and they can do so because they do not need to understand what people have in mind. For the same reason, people can themselves learn from their interactions with learning algorithms, even if they don't understand them.

An example is the legendary move 37 in the game of March 2016 between Lee Sedol, one of the world's top Go players, and the algorithm AlphaGo. The move was described by observers as absolutely surprising and unpredictable. "It was not a human move" and couldn't have come to any human mind.[83] It was actually produced by an algorithm that does not have a mind, yet it allowed AlphaGo to win the game and then the match. Later, this incomprehensible move triggered a process of learning by human players that profoundly transformed the practice of the game. Revisiting move 37, Go players found it to be brilliant, and took it as a clue to rethink their game strategies, dramatically improving them—thereby learning from AlphaGo.[84] Following this revision, Lee Sedol himself produced the celebrated, highly unlikely (1 in 10,000) move 78 ("The Touch of God") in his fourth game with AlphaGo, the game he was able to win.[85]

Lee Sedol defeated the algorithm by reinterpreting with human skills a move that no human being could have devised. The incomprehensible behavior of AlphaGo highlighted possibilities that could be processed by human players in their own way to produce a meaningful result. It is likely that the algorithm later incorporated move 78 in its procedures and learned to manage the move and its consequences;[86] however, it would not have been able to do this without the human being that devised it. No algorithm, however advanced its ability to self-learn, can generate possibilities that are not implicit in the data supplied.[87] No algorithm can independently generate contingency, but algorithms can process human-generated contingency in unprecedented ways, ways that might generate further possibilities and further contingency in interactions with human beings.

Even and especially if the algorithm is not an alter ego, if it does not follow a strategy, and if it does not understand our reasoning, human users can still learn from their interactions with an algorithm to develop their own strategies. Not through understandable algorithms that can trigger understandable processes, but through obtaining and using clues that no one could have imagined, thereby changing their way of observing. People using their intelligence to learn from non-intelligent machines is an opportunity for increasing the complexity of communication. In the case of Go, it was a matter of game strategy, yet the same mechanisms can be applied to designing social algorithms in general.[88]

Yet relying on black boxes is not reassuring, especially when one knows that their operations are not immune from biases and errors of various kinds.[89] The recent branch of research on "explainable AI" attempts to respond to this concern by looking for procedures that enable machines to provide explanations of their operations.[90] But explaining incomprehensible processes seems a hopeless task. As Weinberger claims, it would amount to someone seeking to force AI "to be artificially stupid enough that we can understand how it comes up with its conclusion."[91] Yet algorithms as communication partners can be explainable without being understandable.[92] The requirement would be that they have sufficient communicative competence to respond to requests for clarification from their interlocutors in an appropriate, comprehensible, and controllable way. What users understand by way of an explanation of the machine does not have to be the finer processes of the machine. This actually happens often in human explanations as well, insofar as they offer clues to make sense of a communication without giving access to the psychic processes of the partner—and is the direction in which the design of advanced algorithms is currently moving.[93]

CONCLUSION

Interactions with algorithms are a challenge for sociology and communications theory. Whether one decides that they are a specific form of communication and that the concept of communication should be amended accordingly, or one decides that algorithms are not communication partners, the task of communication theory is still to adequately describe the development of these digital processes. We must be able to show how interactions with algorithms affect communication in society in general and to provide insights that can help to direct the work of those who design and write algorithms.[94]

In more and more areas, the familiar reference to (artificial) intelligence becomes unhelpful, whether these are cases in which communications are attributed to things (e.g., the Internet of Things) or cases in which communications are treated as things (e.g., the digital humanities). Does this mean that we are moving toward a state of widespread intelligence where there will be no separation between things and people, between intelligent algorithms and the minds involved in communication?[95] I argue instead that these developments require a shift from references to intelligence to references to communication. What algorithms are reproducing is not the intelligence of people but the informativity of communication. When new forms of communication combine the performances of algorithms with the performances of people, algorithms are not confused with people, nor do they become intelligent. The difference between the operations of algorithms and human thought gives rise to new ways of dealing with data and producing information in the circuit of communication.

The following chapters test this claim by describing and analyzing various cases of communication with algorithms—each under different conditions and with very diverse consequences.

2

ORGANIZING WITHOUT UNDERSTANDING: LISTS IN ANCIENT AND DIGITAL CULTURES

A WEB OF LISTS

When algorithms talk to us, they do so in lists[1]—not always, but far more often than was the case before, in press or mass media communications. Algorithms seem to be retrieving an ancient way of communicating that societies had overlooked for thousands of years. Why is this happening? We will see that it is at least partly the result of the ways in which lists are a "natural" way for algorithms to communicate with us. And we will see that our common way of organizing information and dealing with news has become more and more affected by our communication with machines that do not think like us.

The web, labeled by Umberto Eco "The Mother of All Lists,"[2] apparently "thinks" in the form of lists.[3] In the digital world, the pervasive form of the list seems to be the preferred manner of organizing information, reproduced recursively at various levels of organization.[4] Lists multiply. The algorithms directing the web are lists of instructions; databases are lists of data that search engines process to provide further lists of websites; and services like Amazon and TripAdvisor deliver lists of products and restaurants, while News Feed constantly offers updated lists of friends' Facebook activities. Forms of communication in traditional media are furthermore affected by this shift: articles are written more and more often in the manner of a "listicle," that is, as a list, and there are entire websites, such as Listverse, containing nothing but listicles.[5]

The web works on the basis of lists to produce further lists, and then a second order of lists helps to direct our search for information—also by way of lists: for example, BuzzFeed and other services manifest themselves as lists of newsworthy lists. Lists are managed through lists, with their ultimate form being the ubiquitous top-ten lists that seem to have become one of the primary forms by which newer generations are organizing information. A prophetic, though parodic, example of this might be found in the character of Rob Fleming in Nick Hornby's novel *High Fidelity*, who reflects on himself and the world through the practice of compiling top-five lists of all of the elements of his personal life and self-image.

Why are lists multiplying exponentially in our digital society? Why does the web seem to have an affinity with the form of the list, which previously had a long history in ancient civilization, before being supplemented and then gradually replaced by other more efficient methods for data management?

In this chapter I explore the practice of using lists in digital societies, where this form of informational organization is not only on the web but, in the last few decades, has become a more general and ubiquitous mode of evaluation for objects and services. This phenomenon can be found everywhere in ratings and rankings: university rankings; financial ratings; ratings of restaurants, hospitals, and prisons; rankings of states; rankings of movies, books—of virtually everything, deeply affecting practices of observation and self-observation in all areas of society.[6] Is there something common to these forms, given their parallel ascent in contemporary culture—and do they all have the same effect? What are the differences (and relationships) between lists, ratings, and rankings? What is the specificity of the list compared to other forms of sequential organization?

To answer these questions, I first describe and distinguish flat, evaluative, and hierarchical lists. I then trace the historical evolution of the form of the list and its progressive generalization in Western civilization, which led to increasingly structured forms of content organization. In a subsequent step, I specifically address the web and digital data processing, and ask why the form of the list is spreading at this moment, especially in the last three decades since algorithms have begun to become active participants in social communication. What is the relationship between lists, the web, and algorithms—the central tools of web information processing?

LISTING, RATING, RANKING

Lists are everywhere, and occur in different forms: there are simple *lists* (friend lists on Facebook), there are *ratings* (lists of evaluated items like restaurants or financial assets with corresponding metrics—stars, alphabetic letters, hearts), and there are *rankings* organized as lists of objects in hierarchical order (the "100 Best Colleges in the US"). They are all lists, but not all lists are rankings, nor even ratings. Furthermore, not all ratings are rankings. What, then, is the difference?

Ratings have an evaluative component, in the sense that they attribute scores—about the solvency of companies, the reliability of nations, the quality of restaurants, wines, or movies, and so on—such as AAA, Ba2, three stars, or two glasses. In many cases, ratings are created without the intention of comparison—they only evaluate, assigning scores to individual objects in their specificity. The assessment is focused on single items, because every scientific article, every firm, every wine, every object is— strictly speaking—unique and distinct from every other one. What these raw scores offer is a multiplicity of singular judgments. In classic guides like *Michelin*, the various features of restaurants were initially dealt with separately: the quality of materials and preparation, for example, but also originality, atmosphere, view, and many other factors that cannot be sensibly aggregated into a single measure.[7]

Rankings, instead, compare the listed items. They establish a hierarchy, typically from first to tenth place (such as the items on the first page of Google search results), although they also may run up to the fiftieth or two-hundredth rank, and so on: the ten best restaurants in London, the top fifty universities less than fifty years old, the best two hundred sci-fi movies of all time. Each entry has a unique position that is higher or lower than the previous one, and this positional information is delivered by the ranking. One's attention is focused on the comparison much more than on the characteristics of the items, which tend to disappear from view. The users of rankings look at who's up and who's down, rather than their independent properties. The ranking primarily describes the mutual relationships between a number of entities, rather than the performance of each individual one.[8]

Simple *lists*, on the other hand, have no evaluative component, nor do they need to have an order—something clearly shown by the much-quoted list of animals in Borges's Chinese encyclopedia (animals that belong to the emperor, embalmed ones, suckling pigs, mermaids, fabulous ones, stray dogs, and so on, including "those included in the present classification," and "others"),[9] but also by most of our daily shopping lists. Usually there is no reason why milk might be listed before apples or dishwasher detergent or eggs, and the list can be read from the bottom to the top without losing any information. Lists are extremely flexible and extremely fungible, and they usually require contextual or interpretive additions in order to become useful[10]—for example, the layout of the store where we do our shopping, or groupings by the user (dairy products, fruits, household cleaners).

When did these different forms (ratings, rankings, and lists) become such a fundamental part of the organization of society? What made them possible? What are the relationships between them? When and how do evaluative and hierarchical forms combine with the simple sequence of the list?

WRITING, CONTEXT, AND ABSTRACTION

Flat lists are an ancient form, typical of civilizations in times of early writing practices, especially those practicing nonalphabetic techniques—in Mesopotamia, among the Sumerians, and in the archaic civilizations of Egypt and China.[11] While lists also exist in oral discourse, they are infrequent in face-to-face communication.

The conditions of oral communication do not favor the use of lists, because lists require an initial step of abstraction and decontextualization. The space of the list is not our immediate physical space. Participants in face-to-face conversations are, instead, always immersed in a context and in an ongoing situation. They share the same space and the same time—here and now. In primary orality, when all communications were face-to-face, no awareness of contextual factors and their variability was required because there was no need to observe them: one only communicated with people who were simultaneously in the same place, knew it, and knew each other.[12] Context was taken for granted and communication was characterized by a low level of abstraction.[13]

Writing introduced a substantial intellectual break with the conditions of orality; it required writers and readers to distance themselves from the concrete context of an ongoing situation and to record content for a different condition in time and space—with the advantages and the freedom connected with this detachment, yet also with its related complexity. The form of the list helped in this move. Lists abstract their objects from the present situation and place them in a different frame, together with the other listed items. Lists break the "natural unity of the perceptual world";[14] they require an act of distancing and introduce a discontinuity between the listed items and everything else, and of the listed objects from each other. Thinking in the form of lists supports the intellectual attitude introduced by writing and requires the support of written records.

Archaeological research shows that at the beginnings of writing, especially nonalphabetic writing, lists were very common.[15] Ancient written documents practically never had a narrative form and did not reproduce discourse—this would happen much later. These documents were rather drawn up in the form of lists. From the perspective of sociological communication theory, this is completely plausible. People did not write what they said, nor did they write in order to communicate with absent partners—they wrote for administrative and economic purposes. Lists were written to record sales and purchases, rentals, loans, marriage bonds, wills—not to communicate with someone but to define content and to remember it, just as we do with our own notes and shopping lists. But ancient lists collected the most heterogeneous of materials. Mesopotamian cuneiform lists include plants, animals, artifacts, professions, titles of officials, toponyms, body parts, and foodstuffs—each in an order about as adventurous as Borges's Chinese list of animals. In Weinberger's terminology, ancient lists were *miscellaneous*, including piles of items without a predetermined classification or categories defined in advance.[16] As with all flat lists, these ancient records could be read either downward or upward, since the order did not provide any additional information.[17]

Despite the lack of an unequivocal order (or because of it), the production of lists marked a significant step in the organization of knowledge.[18] Lists require that we abandon our implicit adherence to an immediate context and that we observe the recorded items in a detached way,[19] but do not necessarily imply the further abstract conceptual tools necessary to build an alternative context.[20] According to Goody, advanced abstraction and recontextualization were the consequence, not the precondition, of written lists; abstraction came later. When items are listed in a column (or in the multiple columns of a table), an observer can notice correspondences and similarities that escape the zoomed-in focus one has when absorbed in a context, or combine objects according to patterns and structures. They can be grouped, opposed, or rearranged. This can give rise to a deeper analysis of correlations and correspondences that can eventually lead to more abstract forms of conceptualization of content. As Doležalová observes, "An idea is not necessarily the driving force in compiling a list, but may emerge from it."[21] To make use of a list, you don't have to understand an abstract organizing principle–rather you develop one in dealing with the list.

The advantages of this nonabstract organization of content primarily concern forms of writing that are not completely phonetic. With accomplished phoneticity, that is, with the use of the alphabet since the eighth century BCE, detachment from context was perfected and new forms of abstraction became possible (and needed). While pictographic writing is only accessible to a reader who already knows the meaning of its signs, and syllabic writing requires the addition of vowels by a reader able to make the appropriate integrations,[22] reading an alphabetic text does not require such contextual information. With the alphabet, if a reader knows the rules of how a language should be read, it is possible to read texts about previously unknown topics and issues, because the texts themselves provide all the information required for communication.[23] In linguistic terms, the co-text takes the place of the context.[24] Only then could the context of the writer be fully uncoupled from the context of the reader. Time and space for the text do not coincide with the coordinates of the location of its readers, who must be able to manage this separation, while the writer must take into account contextual differences in order to produce an understandable text. Writers and readers must be able to master a world of abstract references (a date, a toponym) independent from any reference to their immediate situation (yesterday, over the hill).

According to Havelock, these performances were the background of the beginnings of abstract thought in Western civilization,[25] which led to the progressive marginalization of lists as relatively concrete forms of ordering. Western consciousness, he argues, was born when a notion like "justice" became a universal concept and no longer coincided with a list of examples: Agamemnon is just, Hector is just, and so on. Eco claims that a rise in abstraction led to a switch from definitions according to properties (which Aristotle called definition *per accidens*) to definitions according to essences, which require a more detached analysis of an object.[26] Plato, who first defined concepts in terms of a thing's abstract essence, despised lists, which he claimed merely enumerate a "swarm" of examples.[27] Aristotle then notoriously introduced an organization of ideas by abstract categories,[28] which provide a frame of reference that replaces immediate contexts. Metaphysics rejects the form of the list. An abstract understanding of the world comes before its observation.

Havelock's interpretation might be controversial, but scholars agree that the form of the list, widespread in the ancient world,[29] became progressively less common after the introduction of alphabetic writing. Lists can still be found in epic poems like the *Iliad* (as in the famous catalog of ships),[30] or in many passages of the Old Testament—which in fact were composed orally before the introduction of the alphabet. In written texts of Western culture, the form of the list was gradually supplemented by more complex arrangements—tree structures or classification systems— producing an order that goes beyond the simple juxtaposition of objects and beyond the rhetorical forms of accumulation and enumeration.

Lists do not disappear in this process, but take on other functions, confirming the remarkable flexibility of their form.[31] The recording of data in lists was a prerequisite for their manipulation and for the development of forms of calculation, like divinatory arithmetic in Chinese and Mesopotamian civilization,[32] eventually leading to algebra and to other abstract computations. While ancient "miscellaneous" lists from the fourth and third millennia BCE did not have an order, since the middle of the second millennium BCE, more specific forms of organization came into being. These forms refer to the meaning of the words (following the parts of the human body from the head to the feet, or according to spatial orientation), or to the form of the signs (e.g., according to the initial letter or to the acrographic principle—i.e., graphic similarity). Once data are objectified in writing, they can be observed from a distance and it becomes almost inevitable to identify other organizational criteria. With the increase in abstraction of social semantics, more and more complex classifications followed. Lists tended to develop toward organized series like ratings and rankings. In the form of Porphyry's tree,[33] eventually, the hierarchical arrangement in abstract categories remained for thousands of years the basic scheme for the organization of knowledge.[34]

LISTING MACHINES

Jumping forward several centuries, the complexification of the order of knowledge introduces the next step of the argument in this chapter: why are lists multiplying in the digital world, and what is their relationship with the logic and the operational mode of algorithmic data processing?

As argued above, research on the ancient uses of writing shows that lists are an effective way to manage complexity with limited abstraction capability. Lists were very common in ancient cultures that started recording and organizing data. A big advantage of the organization of data into lists is that they do not need abstraction nor reflection about the sorted objects or the organizing activity. Miscellaneous lists make it possible to generate an order without a predefined ordering criterion, without going into the details of the listed items, and without really knowing them.[35] They yield an order almost automatically, even if one doesn't understand what one is ordering.

Modern societies, of course, are very capable of abstraction, but not ubiquitously. The algorithms that process data on the web do not work with abstraction, which is their main asset. Algorithms merely calculate. This has always been the case;[36] but the lack of abstraction becomes more and more relevant with the development of sophisticated procedures like self-learning algorithms working with big data, as with the recent machines that seem to be able to act as competent communication partners.[37] In projects based on algorithms, lists are recognized as "very useful devices."[38] And algorithms produce the pervasive lists we find on the web and in digital data processing. Why?

The power and the efficiency of algorithms depend on their ability to calculate without abstraction. The impressive accomplishments of self-learning algorithms in recent years have been achieved using programming techniques that explicitly give up on the idea or even on the ambition of artificially reproducing the forms of human intelligence. Algorithms do not reason the way we do in order to do what we do with abstract reasoning. This can explain, as in ancient prealphabetic cultures, the preference for the form of the list, which becomes informative without requiring abstraction in its production and in its use.

According to David Weinberger, the digital age is introducing a "new order of order," changing the shape of our knowledge.[39] The system for organizing the world no longer coincides with the system for understanding it—as had been true for the human reasoning incorporated into the model of Porphyry's tree. Instead of specifying organizational categories ahead of time in the form of structured trees, a revolution has occurred in tagging content that uses "piles of leaves" without a predefined order[40]—in practice, flat lists with no ordering principle, from which a previously unknown order can emerge. Self-organizing taxonomies, for example, emerge as "folks-onomies." The order resulting from the miscellaneous collection of unselected, uncontrolled big data (and metadata) has no underlying principle and is flexible, dynamic, and inevitably ambiguous (and thus "messy"), yet still provides a frame that makes it possible to deal with the data.

Algorithms sort data and discover patterns without understanding the elements sorted, offering them up to meaningful interpretation—that is, algorithms "add context back."[41] Meaning and understanding, if they arise, emerge from the algorithmic organization of the data, and are not its premise. Systems for image recognition, for instance, "discover" faces of cats in the materials they analyze, but not because they have a concept of "cat," which would serve as a means of understanding and recognizing its instances.[42] These algorithms, used by Flickr and Instagram, instead work with piles of data and metadata, identifying patterns without any

humanly understandable reason.[43] The outcomes of algorithmic processing, however, can become meaningful to the users, with outcomes often
presented themselves in the form of a list. Algorithms work with lists to
produce lists.

From the perspective of the user, meaning must be produced out of
an order that has been produced independently of meaning. That's why
lists are so effective. Think, for example, of the success of listicles. With
increases in the uses of automation and exorbitant availability of data,
the role of algorithms in the management of materials in publishing and
journalism is becoming increasingly important. All kinds of editorial
decisions are outsourced to the algorithms—such as those guiding Facebook News Feed, Chartbeat, or others.[44] Their products are lists, which are
deeply affecting the production of news. Buzzfeed was the first to realize
and explicitly exploit this form of organization, cramming into its lists
news items that were detected algorithmically within reports published
elsewhere, and publishing them as such.

The outcome is the listicle, which is easy to write (being produced by
machines), and is similarly easy to read. Readers are met with a sequence
of topics with no connection to each other and no argumentative order.
People like listicles. They read and consume them as they prefer, stopping when it suits them and freely building their own order—without in
turn losing or distorting the sense of the list, given that it has no sense
to distort. The sense can be produced as a consequence of the list. Poole
attributes the rampant success of listicles to this ease.[45]

For this reason, when in March 2014 the *New York Times* decided to get
closer to its readers, it started running more listicles. Not only book, restaurant, and movie recommendations,[46] but also political comments and
takeaways from relevant events or inquiries are presented as sequences of
points, in articles such as "Midterm Election Results: 4 Key Takeaways,"
"Damage Control at Facebook: 6 Takeaways from the Times's Investigation," and "Five Takeaways from Our New China Project."[47] This evolution
is transforming the landscape of contemporary journalism with complex
feedback loops.[48] Whereas traditional newspapers such as the *New York
Times* are increasingly resorting to the algorithmic forms of the list, highly
automated sites are discovering the need to take care of and monitor the
workings of algorithms by approaching the practices and methods of

traditional journalism: BuzzFeed created BuzzFeedNews, Facebook introduced News Feed, Google offers Google News.

This has happened significantly in journalism, but not only journalism. Top-ten lists are multiplying on the web and becoming a specific form of information dissemination. In many cases they are not pure lists because a hierarchical ordering is involved: these lists not only include a set number of entries, they also ascend or descend in orders of magnitude ("1 to 10: The Best Vegan Restaurants in Trastevere"). But even these hierarchical orderings are produced by algorithms without understanding and without abstraction, drawing on indications and forming calculations based on the behavior and preferences of users (likes, retweets, and backlinks).[49]

CONCLUSION

As in ancient Mesopotamia, in our digital civilization lists produce arrangements that can generate specific forms of information and information management, including the recent booming proliferation of ratings and hierarchical rankings. This poses a challenge to theoretical description. To investigate these developments we might need a revised version of the *Listenwissenschaft* ("science of lists")[50] developed to deal with Babylonian lists and their evolution. A proper scientific observation of the organization of the web would need to be updated to fit the features of our digital environment.

This raises new questions. The discussion about information processing on the web would have to deal with the social effects of the organization of data in lists. One should explore what happens when our digital society observes itself and the observations of its members according to the processes of algorithms that do not think—as in current journalism. The selection and organization of news is guided not by human reasoning but by formal patterns computationally drawn by the behavior of the users. What does the form of the list make visible and what does it obscure, when its production does not use abstraction and merely reproduces, reorganizes, and amplifies the abstract processes and the selections of the users? How does an awareness of the features and consequences of lists contribute to properly describing digital information management?

3

READING IMAGES: VISUALIZATION AND INTERPRETATION IN DIGITAL TEXT ANALYSIS

NONLINGUISTIC LITERARY ANALYSIS

We typically communicate through language, but often we also communicate with images. How we get information from pictures, however, is different from how we process texts in ways that become crucial when our communication partner is an algorithm. Visualization helps us make sense of the processes of computers and use them to get new information—even and especially when the materials they deal with are not images. This is shown by the field explicitly dedicated to the study of texts: literary analysis. The most recent and innovative research does not use "literary" tools. Instead of reading texts, literary scholars visualize them, utilizing images rather than language.[1]

As Franco Moretti and Oleg Sobchuk put it: "If there is one feature that immediately distinguishes the digital humanities (DH) from the 'other' humanities, data visualization has to be it."[2] DH experts who apply computational techniques to expand the scope and the capabilities of textual analysis are obtaining information with innovative categories and tools— and raising unprecedented issues, such as in studies of the "loudness" of voices in literary texts or of the relationship between the lengths of titles of novels and the size of the market.[3] But the results of this literary analysis are not gained by reading literary texts and are not expressed in literary form. They are not spoken or written—they are shown.[4]

Visualization tools are crucial to the work of the DH, especially in studies involving large amounts of data.[5] According to Gitelman and Jackson, "Data are mobilized graphically."[6] Franco Moretti's "distant" reading transforms texts into "maps, graphs, trees."[7] The patterns identified by algorithms are translated into spatial configurations that transform the complex topology of digital processing into two-dimensional (and possibly three-dimensional) images.[8] The corresponding techniques are gaining more and more momentum, moving "out of the realm of an exotic research specialty and into the mainstream of user interface application design."[9] Münster and Terras propose the phrase "visual digital humanities" as a novel umbrella term in the field.[10]

A theoretical analysis of this trend is still not available.[11] Why has the textual discipline par excellence, literary analysis, moved toward visual tools?[12] My argument in this chapter is that visualization is an answer to the opacity of algorithmic procedures and a way to make them productive. Instead of explaining ("answering the 'why' question"),[13] the digital humanities are devising other ways to deal with the incomprehensibility of digital processes and to exploit it in interactions with human users. Visualization is a powerful, increasingly widespread, solution.

EXPLORING IMAGES

In itself, there is nothing new in the use of images for communicative purposes. Compared to language (oral or written communication), images have the great advantage of communicating a lot of information at once, if in a less analytic way.[14] As Ware points out, among the greatest benefits of visualization are the sheer quantity of information that can be rapidly interpreted, and the possibility of perceiving emergent properties that were not anticipated.[15] Think of the difference between describing a landscape verbally and presenting a postcard like the image shown in figure 3.1.

A linguistic description takes much longer (one can say only one thing at a time) and includes only the information explicitly taken into account. If you forget to say that there are flowers in front of the house or

Figure 3.1

that the chimney is made of bricks, your interlocutor cannot know it. An image, on the other hand, transmits a great deal of information in a single moment, even information of which neither the sender nor the receiver was aware.[16] Even if the recipient does not actively engage with it, upon seeing the image, they know that the tree is to the left of the house and that there are clouds in the sky. Likewise, visualization can be used to generate for the receiver information that the sender themself did not know.

With or without a reference text, pictures have always been used in narrations and explanations to carry out two distinct functions: showing information that is already available and making it possible to produce new information. These two functions correspond respectively to the roles of images as *illustrations* and as *visualizations*, which are also central in digital processes.

Illustrations can directly convey information or support a linguistic text (oral or written) to make the communication of information more immediate and persuasive.[17] Illustrating a linguistic text with images, communication takes advantage of both registers: the explicitness of language and the diffusiveness of visual perception.

Images, however, can also be used to autonomously produce information, as a way of "using vision to think."[18] This is the case specifically indicated by visualization that I address in this chapter. *Visualizations* are used as a "medium for human interaction with the data"[19]—not, as with illustrations, to more efficiently convey already available information, but to create new information. One shows an image, and sees what one gets from it (if one gets something). The image activates a "hypothesis generation process" that could not happen through verbal means.[20] Visualization is particularly useful to create knowledge in an interaction with a viewer—not to transmit information but to explore it.[21] This happens with maps, diagrams, tables, graphs, charts, and with all devices that present visual encodings of data in order to obtain further information.

Visualization is not a tool unique to the humanities. The DH borrows it from the natural sciences, which uses visualization for analytical purposes. It is also an ancient technique to obtain information from data.[22] Spatial (bi-, tri-, and today also poly-dimensional) representations allow for the identification of connections and relationships that could not be grasped otherwise. The natural sciences has always done so, exploring and manipulating images, patterns, radiographies, and models.[23] With the intervention of computers, however, the use of visualization has become more complex, and today we distinguish at least three different ways of using images for exploratory purposes. Here I will call them "scientific visualization," "information visualization," and "digital visualization."

Scientific visualization or "scivis" has a long tradition and uses representations to show "physically based" forms.[24] Scientific visualizations are bound to the "a priori based spatial layout of the real physical object,"[25] which is reproduced in a simplified way through a model, a schema, or a two-dimensional image in order to be explored more easily—think of a map or a geometric drawing. Faithfulness to the world is a requisite. An x-ray plate shows an image of the internal organs to allow diagnosis. A map refers to a territory and reproduces its structure, though not its complexity, and this simplicity is what makes the map so useful for the purpose of orientation. Obviously, the use of images requires skills to interpret them, which may be greatly refined. Even when employing abstract and highly elaborate images, however, scientific visualizations always do so to make visible a structure that exists, but could not be directly perceived.

Information visualization or "infovis" starts from these practices, but differs because it is unbound from the layout of the objects.[26] It is a surprisingly recent invention, introduced in the second half of the eighteenth century to enable use of graphics as "instruments for reasoning about quantitative information."[27] The purpose of information visualization is understanding, not representation—gaining "insight, not pictures."[28] Envisioning information has been described as a "cognitive art" that employs abstract, nonrepresentational images to show information, not objects.[29] In information visualization, the graphical models may represent concepts and relationships that do not necessarily have a counterpart in the physical world[30]—time series, frequency of diseases, movements of stock prices, distribution of criminal behavior across generations. The result is the widespread presence of graphs, diagrams, histograms, pie charts, scatterplots, which do not resemble their objects.

The data on which the information is based are quantified and expressed visually with points, circles, rectangles, ascending and descending lines, to allow free exploration and analysis. For example, the evolution of the most common science-fiction themes over time—quite complex and not spatial—can be presented with the lines of a graph.[31] This makes it possible to see immediately how the popularity of aliens, space travel, robots, and time travel has changed from 1970 to 2009. Geometry and topology are used to express key differences in data with visible signs and with their location in space.[32] Exploring the images, the user can develop new ideas.

Since the 1990s the use of information visualization has increased greatly, along with the rise of desktop 2D graphics software and the use of personal computers by designers, and has been further enhanced in the 2000s as a consequence of big data and new high-level programming languages—from which the current DH approaches derive. Analysis focuses on "processes or datasets that are either too large, or too complex, to be fully understood by a single (static) image."[33] According to Manovich, the use of computers has led to a specific variant of information visualization that can be called *digital visualization*.[34] Here a new agent intervenes in the process and allows for endeavors that would not be possible otherwise: this new agent, which explores data and produces information, is in this case the computer itself. Algorithms do not just show patterns—they find them. Via its digital forms, which involve the autonomous intervention of algorithms in the management and processing of data, visualization changes its object and its purpose.[35]

The central innovation here is, in my view, that the use of computer-supported visual representations of data is accompanied, explicitly or implicitly, by the promise or the hope to, in Alexandru Telea's words, "discover the unknown."[36] Through digital visualization we can obtain knowledge that we were not looking for.[37] The autonomous work of algorithms is expected to identify structures (or patterns) in the data without the intervention of the researcher. Visualizing the patterns, then, algorithms can show something the researchers were not searching for, thereby broadening their interpretive horizon.[38] What is displayed is not the structure of the objects of a study, nor a simplified representation of the available data, but the configurations autonomously "discovered" by the algorithms, which are offered to interpretation and exploration. The interpretation may then lead to new information.

For literary studies the possibility of using images to produce information opens up new horizons of exploration. Therefore, visualization is taking on a central role in the digital humanities, as today scholars combine the reading of images with the reading of texts.

VISUAL PROVOCATIONS

How does textual analysis change when one uses digital techniques? Why is visualization attaining such a central role in literary studies? The reason lies in the management of incomprehensible materials. DH scholars make extensive use of algorithms to process texts—a process that produces its own texts, though ones that are impenetrable to human readers[39]—and to work with corpora too large or too small for human analysis. DH programs analyze hundreds of texts or single words and characters within a text.[40] The unprecedented challenge in managing the results of the working of algorithms is to make informative the outcomes of processes that are often opaque to the human mind.[41]

In response to this challenge, experts in literary studies have begun to systematically turn to visualization, which is becoming the fundamental tool for a new form of textual analysis. This analysis is based on the coordinated contribution of human readers oriented toward meaning, and of algorithmic procedures that do not know and do not use meaning.[42] Text-processing machines do not think like us and in general do not think at all: "The computer "reads" (processes) the text as a meaningless string of characters."[43] As David Weinberger says, "To imagine thinking the way computers think . . . is to imagine not thinking at all."[44] The task of digital visualization is to make these incomprehensible processes informative to human readers; its "critical question" is about the best way to transform data into something that people can understand.[45]

Digital visualization techniques can be seen as exploration tools that allow users to investigate patterns and obtain information—including information that was not there before. Its purpose, for example, can be to "visualize uncertainty" in the patterns that algorithms identify in processed texts.[46] This is accomplished not by communicating the meanings that patterns and configurations have for the authors of the text (who were not aware of them), nor by communicating the meanings identified in these patterns and configurations by algorithms (for whom texts do not have meaning). Algorithms, after all, certainly do not perceive uncertainty. Instead, visualizations are required because nobody knows what the information generated by algorithmic procedures *is*. Patterns are defined, and information is generated (if it is generated) in interactions with a user who explores the resulting images.

This produces specific challenges. Informative openness is a big advantage of using images, yet at the same time it is a liability the DH have to deal with. Visualization can yield previously unknown information, but one cannot know in advance if and how the visualization will be informative.[47] One doesn't know if the user will get information, nor what it will be. Starting from the same data, many alternative views can be produced, which can be more or less informative for the reader.[48] A visualization designer always has to face the dilemma of "choosing from a multitude of data processing possibilities and an even greater choice of potential visualization options," which is exacerbated by the fact that the purpose is to identify only the visualizations that can produce "interpretable visual patterns"—that is, those that can be meaningful to the users.[49]

The same data can be illuminating or incomprehensible depending on the technique used. A bubbleline can highlight relationships that are not recognizable in a graph, in a word cloud, or in a histogram, even if the data they visualize do not change.[50] Behrisch and colleagues show the complexity of choosing from available options to decide how to visualize high-dimensional data.[51] A scatter plot, for example, enables one to see clearly if two variables are correlated, but risks producing visual clutter if large numbers of items need to be displayed. Parallel coordinates and radial visualization, on the other hand, enable analysts to explore patterns across a large set of dimensions, and matrix representations can show patterns at a local and a global level of detail—but a wrong ordering for a specific task may hide the patterns instead of revealing them. Similar considerations apply to all available techniques. Visualization is always an open and problematic process.[52]

In their use of visualization, DH experts are dealing with these problems. Today there are effective tools to support researchers. For example, the text reading and analysis environment, Voyant, allows users to process corpora of texts by producing many different views: graphs, bubblelines, correlations, mandalas, cirrus, scatterplots, links, DreamScapes, looms, knots, trends, and many others.[53] The data underlying the different views are the same, although the resulting images are very different. It is up to the researcher to experiment with the different visualizations and find out what they show—if they show something. Galloway observes that "data have no necessary visual form."[54] Visualization is the contingent translation of a mathematical structure into a visual form, and can thus vary in what forms are taken. Even if absolutely controlled, none of them is right or wrong, because "data have no necessary information,"[55] and "this is information that does not have any obvious spatial mapping."[56] Visualization is correct if it works, and this depends on the situation and on the researcher.

Algorithms themselves produce not the results of text analysis, but rather "provocations" that serve as "surprising observations that can challenge existing assumptions."[57] The visualizations they show can trigger hypotheses generation,[58] but the interpretation is up to the scholar dealing with the texts, who can accept the provocation and modify their perspective starting from the "proposals" autonomously generated by machines—or not. Provocations can work or not work—can generate information or not. If a provocation succeeds, the result is a new form of text analysis, which cannot be attributed only to the researcher but presupposes the active contribution both of the machine processing the materials and of the reader interpreting the results. Using digital visualization, texts can yield information with procedures very different from our familiar reading practices, thus, requiring a reflection on the notion of reading and its forms.[59]

READING, NON-READING, DISTANT READING

The use of algorithms in textual analysis makes it possible to obtain information with methods very different from our established reading practice. Should the application of digital procedures to texts be considered a new way of reading? When one interprets digital images instead of linguistic sentences, is one reading? Who reads, and what?

The answers to these questions depend on what is meant by reading, and in the DH, there is an active debate on the notion of reading and the contribution of algorithms. We are certainly dealing with innovative and potentially very productive methods to manage written materials, which pose a challenge to the established models of literary analysis and criticism.[60] It is not clear, however, if they are still a form of reading. A leading proponent of expanding our understanding of reading, Franco Moretti, is intentionally ambiguous in this regard. Moretti introduced the very successful term "distant reading" to describe a form of text analysis so different from our familiar practices of reading that it requires "a little pact with the devil: we know how to read texts, now let's learn how not to read them."[61] When someone reads at a distance using the visualizations produced by machines, then, do they read or not?

In literary debate the question remains open, with a peculiar notion of reading that "is not 'really' reading" and explicitly includes its negation.[62] In the context of this debate, the ambiguity seems to have a reason. The focus of the discussion lies in the opposition between human *close reading*, dealing with a limited number of texts studied in detail (a "canon"),[63] and *distant reading*, as an analysis of units that are "much smaller or much larger than the text: devices, themes, tropes—or genres and systems."[64]

This requires digital processing of extended corpora that could not be analyzed by a human reader. Consider Franco Moretti's analysis of British novels from 1740 to 1850, which deals with seven thousand titles,[65] and Lev Manovich's survey on Japanese manga, which works with one million images.[66] Algorithmic reading is, first of all, distanced from reading the canon, from close reading. Distant reading is non-reading in the sense of not being close up—it's about "zooming out" instead of "zooming in."

Outside of this debate, however, distant reading can also be interpreted as unrelated to reading altogether. Algorithms do not read and do not need to read—this is how they gain their specificity and advantage. Algorithmic text processing is different (distant) from reading on at least two levels: in its relationship with documents and in its management of meaning.

First, the *object* of reading changes. Whereas close reading interprets the text without dissolving its structure, distant reading does the exact opposite.[67] The traditional notion of reading has a "documentcentric" attitude bound to the unity of the text as a book or an article.[68] A text as a document is a "communicative event: written by someone, in specific circumstances, to convey a specific meaning. . . . A text is meant to address us, to 'speak' to us." The corpora addressed by distant reading, instead, "are not 'communicative events'"; corpora "do not speak to us"[69]—hence they are not properly documents. If we want to keep corpora as texts, the concept of "text" must be modified, uncoupling it from a restricted reference to individual documents.

The digital humanities are moving in this direction. According to Matthew Kirschenbaum, the materials of algorithmic processing are not documents such as books or articles: "in today's .txtual condition . . . a 'primary record' can no longer be assumed to be coterminous with . . . a 'physical object.' "[70] Electronic texts are independent from material supports, that is, from books or newspapers that bind communication to the specific objects circulating the texts. Katherine Hayles points out that in electronic reading, recording media do not coincide with transmission media.[71] The text circulates and is produced independently from the constraints of the book.[72] Machine-reading devices use materials available on the web to produce their own computational objects, drawing them indifferently from populations of documents, or from individual lines, nouns or letters.[73] This does not mean that a text is produced arbitrarily; rather, it means that its unity no longer depends on the boundaries of the book associated with the author's perspective. It is no longer "document-centric," but depends instead on the constraints of the programs governing the work of algorithms.[74]

This is relevant not so much because we can read a novel in an electronic format on a Kindle or because the novel can include hyperlinks, but because, through data mining and visualization techniques, we can deal with texts that are different from the ones transmitted by books. The stability of printed text is lost in the "processuality" of electronic texts.[75] What makes a text a text is not the unity of communication related to the intention of the issuer, but its *addressability*[76]–that is, the possibility of being adopted by the machine as a "provisional unity" in its operations. A text is instead what the algorithm processes *as text* at different layers of analysis: analyses of characters, words, lines, works, and of genres.[77] As Whitmore puts it: "Textuality is massive addressability."[78]

This transformation is connected with a second dimension of "distance" in distant reading: distance *from meaning*. The current way we read has the goal of getting meanings from texts. However, as Moretti says, "Corpora . . . have no meaning in the usual sense of the word."[79] The meaning of programs is what they do.[80] Human interpretations referring to meaning provide the starting point for digital processing,[81] but machines do not understand meaning, and their analysis must be independent from the interpretation of each individual researcher[82]—and strictly speaking from a reference to individuals and their meanings.[83] Distant reading moves to a "scopic vision" that is not bound to a single point of view.[84]

Algorithms use meanings as sources of difference that can be combined with one another in a meta-management that does not need to understand the meaning nor the perspective of the author.[85] Silke Schwandt argues that computers are semantically blind.[86] Algorithms recognize what a text is about not because they understand its words or interpret the text's meaning, but because they deal with meanings as *things*, identifying formal aspects such as the use of "mine" as an erotic term in Emily Dickinson's texts or the structure of the title of gothic novels.[87] Meaning is connected to other meanings in order to reveal patterns; but patterns themselves do not necessarily have a meaning and are not the result of an interpretation.

ALGORITHMIC READING IS NOT ALGORITHMS READING

What, then, does reading mean today, if we want to take into account the contributions of algorithms to this activity? If "machines can read,"[88] they still read in a different way than human beings, doing so "second hand . . . without a single direct textual reading."[89] Algorithms do not do the same things that humans do, but better. Their ability to deal with big corpora is not only a quantitative change: "When we work on 200,000 novels instead of 200, we are not doing the same thing, 1,000 times bigger; we are doing a different thing."[90] Dealing with huge corpora, instead of reading, one counts things; instead of interpreting, one builds graphs, maps, and trees.[91] Instead of understanding meaning, one develops a topological analysis that allows pattern visualization "at a distance" that would have escaped the view of traditional close reading. This zoomed out perspective on texts,[92] which are not themselves read, becomes a "condition of knowledge."[93]

Instead of reading texts, DH scholars often observe visualizations—analyzing images rather than interpreting sentences. They could not deal with such materials without the contribution of algorithms. Should we then modify our notion of reading to also include these different things done by algorithms? Like many others, Katherine Hayles thinks that we should.[94] She argues that we need to expand our understanding of reading and admit a broader repertoire of reading strategies that includes hyperreading as computer-assisted reading, in which linear reading is accompanied by the exploration of links, by search queries, skimming, filtering by keywords and various other electronic management modes.[95] This understanding should also include *authentic* machine reading, whereby algorithms use digital (possibly unsupervised) methodologies to discover patterns and structures in texts without having had any initial hypothesis.[96] The option in this case is to expand the notion of reading, assuming a porous boundary between human interpretation and machine pattern recognition.[97] In this interpretation, reading overlaps with modeling, gaming, role playing, adapting, translating, rendering, and simulating.[98]

In my opinion, however, this understanding of reading risks becoming so extensive that the notion loses all usefulness. Confronted with the challenge of describing the many complex forms of information processing in our digital societies, we should, instead, hold onto and combine their differences, rather than efface these distinctions in broad notions. The use of algorithmic techniques in the DH prefigures a mode of dealing with texts that does not erase but—on the contrary—accentuates and exploits the differences between different modes of using written materials.[99] Instead of a porous boundary, we are dealing with a particularly sharp one. According to Katherine Hayles, "Saying computers cannot read is . . . merely species chauvinism."[100] I prefer the opposite strategy of explicitly claiming that computers do not read and—more crucially— that precisely for this reason, they contribute to reading.

As argued in chapter 1, computers are becoming increasingly effective partners in information processing not because their capabilities resemble ours, but because they are learning to work in more and more distinct ways than humans performing similar tasks. It seems to me that anthropocentric shortsightedness (species chauvinism) occurs today not in denying that machines can be like human beings, but rather in claiming that machines can only be recognized and appreciated for how well they emulate human activities. Human reading does not need to be the standard by which we understand how algorithms process texts. The debate on distant reading shows that they do something different; therefore, combining algorithmic processing and human reading produces a new and powerful way of analyzing texts. Algorithms' innovative and extremely productive contribution to the production of information relies on their participation in artificial communication.

Instead of reading, Moretti notes, algorithms recognize patterns.[101] The difference between algorithmic text processing and reading is highlighted in visualization practices. Algorithms do not read and do not interpret, but instead identify and present patterns to be interpreted. By presenting patterns through visualization, algorithms can make it possible to read otherwise inaccessible texts, such as Gertrude Stein's "The Making of Americans," or to obtain information from corpora that include thousands of texts.[102]

Here the groundbreaking innovation in literary analysis, which marks its difference to conventional reading practices, is in my opinion not simply a dependence on machines and, in general, on non-human devices such as algorithms. With respect to our familiar media, the central innovation is that algorithms are *noisy* media. All other media—whether printed on paper or broadcast over radio waves moving through the air—should be as "silent" as possible, in the sense of transmitting information in a neutral way in which the media themselves are imperceptible. If a medium is perceived in a received communication, as when printed words are not sharp or an image on the screen is blurred, it produces noise—that is, a disturbance that should be minimized.[103] Digital media can follow this model and practically eliminate transmission noise—for example, in digital music reproduction. But digital technology can also be used differently in communication, making the receiver aware of the active role of the machine and its contribution to the generation of content. The debate over distant reading shows it: "Noise is not an obstacle to interpretation, but its aim."[104]

In distant reading, machine intervention radicalizes McLuhan's formula of "the medium is the message":[105] computers are expected to intervene very noisily on content. They should autonomously produce information that differs from that delivered by the participants and which is often completely new. This is a radical innovation, clearly separating digital textual analysis from human forms of reading. While human beings used to be the only ones able to produce information, now digitally supported nonhuman textual analyses produce patterns that can generate new information and enable an unprecedented management of texts.

Nevertheless, algorithms themselves do not read, and reading cannot be accomplished without interpretation. Algorithms only produce patterns, which by themselves are not meaningful, and are generally overabundant. Working with large data sets, such as the corpora on which distant reading is practiced, it is inevitable to find patterns—indeed, to find too many.[106] Algorithms do not need to understand meanings and can work "semantically blind"— "drawing unexpected paths through a documentary space that is distinguished by its overall incomprehensibility."[107]

Without interpretation, however, these incomprehensible patterns are useless.[108] This in my opinion is why visualization, with its different techniques, is becoming central: it permits the use of the "blind reasoning power of computers" to explore patterns and to render them meaningful, and furthermore provides the basis of a new way to analyze text using algorithmic "provocations."[109]

If and when provocations by algorithms are accepted, the resulting textual analysis is a far more complex form of reading. The aim, according to Jessop, is "to support interpretive scholarships by allowing areas or relationships of interest to be identified within large volumes of texts."[110] The interpretation is produced by a human reader, although through ways and potentialities that would not be possible without the autonomous contributions of algorithms. What remains is no longer traditional reading. A scatterplot analyzing the distribution of word forms in a corpus of texts can generate clusters that are not based on interpretation, but can significantly modify interpretive reading—for example, finding connections between words and groups of words in a way that could not be detected by any human observer and thus raising new questions. In these cases, the machine operates as a partner making proposals that can direct interpretation in unexplored directions.[111]

By combining the differing capabilities of human reading and algorithmic processing of texts, one of the most significant methodological innovations of the digital humanities is emerging: an *algorithmic reading* that does not coincide with our traditional interpretive reading and does not imply that algorithms themselves read. It is still a form of reading because it starts from texts and produces interpretations, but in a new, powerful way that relies on the active, autonomous role of algorithms that do not themselves interpret.[112] It uses the difference between interpretive reading and algorithmic text processing without opposing or assimilating either.

CONCLUSION

Algorithmic text processing is not in continuity with human meaning-oriented reading.[113] Computers don't read, they count. Machines don't understand meaning, they process data. In the DH, literary analysis using algorithms needs to find a way to make meaningful the results of processes that do not rely on understanding meaning and that are often not in themselves understandable. Instead of trying to interpret them, DH scholars turn to visualization, which can make it possible to obtain from texts information nobody yet knew nor understood—in a manner distinct from both reading and illustration. To analyze written texts, scholars in the DH also observe machine-produced images. The outcome is a new, powerful way of reading texts that relies on practices that are effective precisely because they are not forms of reading. With the contribution of algorithms, digital culture provides us with a form of textual communication that can be enormously informative and even creative—if we accept that the intelligent processes that understand and interpret text are only one component at play in the production of information.

4

GETTING PERSONAL WITH ALGORITHMS

ANONYMOUS PERSONALIZATION

If the web is a communication medium, today it is not a *mass* medium in the traditional sense. Broadcast mass media communication is standardized (providing the same content for each user) and generalized (addressing everyone). What appears on the screen of our computer or smartphone, or what our personal assistant tells us, instead, is different from what anyone else receives. We are addressed by name and informed about restaurants and happenings in our surroundings, or about sporting events that may interest us; we are notified of our appointments, of traffic conditions on the routes we take, or of birthdays of friends and relatives; we receive music playlists and movie suggestions matching our tastes. We come to know what happens in the world through the tailored format of our news feed, and when we look for information, Google presents us with results especially selected for us—as well as with a multitude of commercial ads that are supposed to specifically meet our wishes.

Whereas mass media communication is anonymous, communications on the web are increasingly personalized. Being personally addressed by machines, however, is different from being personally addressed by actual persons. Algorithms do not know us nor do they understand us, yet profiling techniques make it possible to provide each user (a reader, a viewer) with targeted information related to their interests and needs. In both cases (analog and digital), the outcome is a specific message for a single recipient; but algorithmically constructed profiles have very different compositions from the kinds of personalization used by human communication partners—and very different results. A lively debate is currently investigating the forms that this difference takes in digital communication.[1] Alexa calling us by our name, to which we respond by asking her for advice, is not the same as a conversation with a friend or colleague—but in what ways, and with what consequences? Does this form of "de-massification" in media create space or expand it for the self-realization and individualization of users? Could it be doing the opposite?[2]

The participation of algorithms in communication raises new issues concerning the role of those on the receiving end, and the meaning of personalization in general. Is communication personalized if the receiver actively intervenes in and shapes this process, or shall we speak of personalization as something that directly addresses the individual context or perspective of the receiver? In the first case, the user themself personalizes the message they receive; in the second case, this message is personalized by someone or something else. Are we personalizing or are we personalized? Or perhaps depersonalized?

In traditional mass media communication, the difference between the two options is elusive, since the different dimensions of personalization mentioned are, for these media, overlapping—if not absent entirely. All mass communications are standardized (they cannot be changed by the users, who passively receive them) and generalized (they do not refer to the context or the perspective of any one receiver). On the web, however, algorithms can affect personalization in both directions, addressing different communications to groups of users with different interests, or with consideration of the concrete situation of each receiver. To investigate this hypothesis, I focus in this chapter on two different (and potentially complementary) forms of "de-massification" used in algorithmic profiling: the identification of specific groups of users through behavioral profiling and collaborative filtering, and the addressing of situations of single users through context-oriented systems. The outcome, I argue, is an unprecedented combination of profiling and active intervention by individuals, a state of affairs which is further defined and discussed in the last section of the chapter.

THE WEB OF INDIVIDUALS

Our media world was transformed in the early 2000s by the arrival of Web 2.0,[3] a technological innovation that led quickly and seemingly spontaneously to a cascade of further innovations in communication and practices of identity. The initial change itself was somewhat minor—the infrastructure of the web remained the same as it had been for "Web 1.0," being based on the TCP/IP communication protocols—but the programming technologies used to create documents altered more radically. Moving beyond the then-standard HTML, which is used to produce static hypertext documents, programmers began to also use tools such as Ajax and Adobe Flex, which allowed for the creation of more dynamic pages, open to the contributions and interventions of their visitors. The result was disruptive, as it soon became clear that Web 2.0 had brought with it unprecedented forms of participation and openness that themselves quickly gave way to previously unthinkable forms of communication, including: the contemporary universe of UGC (user-generated content), which involves blogs, wikis, and more modern content-sharing services like YouTube or Flickr; the proliferation of tags (indices of content through keywords); the multiplication of aggregators like Google News and the Huffington Post; and, of course, the entirety of what we now know as social media.

Many applications that used to run on the user's computer are now run on web servers that allow for *cloud computing*, which is the dissolution of the web into a nebula of computers and interconnected archives accessible to everyone through computing devices that are themselves almost devoid of software and data. As was observed more than a decade ago,[4] this move transformed the World Wide Web into a World Wide Computer, one that harnesses its processing power and data from each of its interconnected devices in an eternally fluid, continuous process of updates and revisions (i.e., it is "permanently beta").[5]

This turbulent universe was given names such as the "participatory web," underlining the unprecedented involvement of users, and the expectation that this would cancel the distinction between sender and receiver. Emblematic of this approach is the figure of the "prosumer," who at the same time, and by the same means, uploads and downloads content. This began in the early 2000s with communication protocols for peer-to-peer sharing such as BitTorrent and eMule, in which a "swarm" of hosts can upload to/download from each other simultaneously. Users who download files containing songs or video clips can at the same time offer their files (and by extension the use of their storage capacity) to other users.

The move from participation to individualization came soon after, a shift that led *Time* magazine to proclaim "You" its person of the year in 2006. It was widely believed that, through user participation, the web would allow everyone a more fully developed, individual experience online—a uniqueness that had hitherto been impossible due to technical and other constraints. Web 2.0, open to all, would be a world of unsurpassed individualization. Wasik speaks of this in terms of a "celebration of the self": individuals can configure their media world to their liking and according to personal interests, in a manner that best expresses individuality.[6]

It seemed then that we would soon be rid of the outmoded category of the passive consumer. In the new "architecture of participation," no one would be *just* a consumer anymore.[7] A more independent and active model of the individual would emerge,[8] marking the "end of the couch potato era" that characterized mass culture.[9] According to this interpretation, the open and interactive World Wide Computer would overcome the asymmetries of broadcast media, in which the position of its (many) receivers was neatly separated from that of its (few) broadcasters, and "downloads" (onto televisions, radios, etc.) were immensely more numerous than uploads.

This interpretation assumed the active role of participants would transform all familiar forms of communication. Journalism would move from a lecture model to that of a conversation or seminar, which would involve the audience configuring, selecting and often actively producing the news.[10] The one-to-one marketing model would establish a learning relationship between producers and consumers, who would get "exactly what they want—when, where, and how they want it."[11] Advertisements, which in their traditional forms had suffered a progressive loss of effectiveness, would move toward targeted ads, including personalized banners on web pages oriented toward users' individual interests, tastes, and preferences. Indeed, in the most advanced forms of direct marketing, consumers would voluntarily produce their own ads for themselves by interacting with games and virtual worlds made available by companies.[12] Static narration and fiction would evolve toward the new generation of interactive stories, steered by choices made by their audiences.[13]

Is that what happened? After almost two decades of experience, we can see that these predictions have been confirmed and refuted at the same time. There have been transformations, yet their consequences are more complex than expected—and in many cases different altogether.[14] Today's news media are certainly more personalized and decentralized, but also hampered by forms of users' isolation like filter bubbles and echo chambers, not to mention the unavoidable issue of fake news.[15] Online advertising is affected by a growing "banner blindness" in which users, instead of looking at customized ads, try to avoid or ignore them.[16]

Traditional forms of fiction, instead of disappearing, have multiplied in the new model of on-demand streaming services which, while allowing users to experiment with how they consume media, almost never allow for direct audience intervention as a story progresses. Interactivity in fiction, although technically possible,[17] remains rare. The case of the Ukrainian TV series *Servant of the People*, instead, shows an intertwining of fiction and reality that goes beyond the familiar condition in which observing reality is unconsciously influenced by mirroring in fiction, with real consequences. In the *Servant of the People* model, the consequences are conscious and deliberate: the members of the audience (who are Ukrainian voters) choose to make the fiction real. The series presents the vicissitudes of a high school history teacher who is indifferent to politics, yet ends up elected president of the republic. After three seasons of the TV series, the actor who plays the protagonist, Volodymyr Zelensky, was elected president of Ukraine in spring 2019, leading a party with the same name as the series. In a sense, Ukrainian voters decided to enter the mirror.

PERSONALIZATION AND STANDARDIZATION

The future often holds surprises, but in hindsight, we can see that predictions from the early years of Web 2.0 were significantly misguided. Prognosticators assumed that active personalization was preferable and would be looked for wherever possible, while standardization (having the same communication for everyone) would only ever occur due to technical constraints of earlier media, and was destined to disappear with digital progress. According to this view, the audience would always want to be proactive in shaping its media world, and had become passive "couch potatoes" only because the medium did not allow for anything else. Technological innovations related to digitization would finally offer the possibility of satisfying the desire of citizens to always be creative and original, as active users wanting personalized communication.

It didn't happen that way. Today we see that the possibilities of personalization did not eliminate standardized communication. Instead, new combinations of activity and passivity and individualization and anonymity in audiences were to arise. The presumed contrast between personalization and standardization, however suggestive, proved to be too simple an explanation. Personalization is not always useful, or even desirable, and the medium of standardized communication can still provide creative, autonomous offerings.

Standardized broadcast media, which does not allow for intervention by the individual, also has the power to select the topics that will become a common object of attention. In making the same message available to all members of their audience, they let everyone know what others know.[18] The issues discussed in traditional mass media can be taken for granted regardless of the opinions, orientations, and idiosyncrasies of each individual. This minimum reference is the basis for the establishment of a public sphere and a collective reference. As a consequence of this mass media, I would argue, people are not only informed about the issues that interest them and that they would actively look for, but also about topics they have little to no interest in—and this is an amazing performance.

The standardized communication of mass media, moreover, can offer ample space for personal configuration. The individual reader of a book can decide for themself the rhythm, the speed and the order of reading; they can slow down or accelerate, go back, start from the end, or skip passages, and compare the text with other texts that confirm, contradict, or integrate it. In doing so, each reader produces a specific communication, corresponding to their characteristics, interests, and knowledge, and different from that of any other reader.

Personalized communication can be oppressive, while standardized communications, which are the same for everyone, can allow individualized users to be active and autonomous—something we can clearly see today. Whereas mass media communication does not require that we grasp and develop the variety of approaches between individual autonomy and collective reference, the intervention of algorithms has the effect of unfolding the complexity of possible communicative forms with the diverse combinations of anonymity and personalization that we observe today: filter bubbles, selfies, flash mobs, influencers, social media, targeted shopping, reverse profiling, avatars, and many other unprecedented patterns. To analyze this variety we need a more articulated range of dimensions, expressing on the one hand a reference to the individual context of the receiver (or the lack thereof), and expressing on the other hand the receiver's active intervention (or the lack thereof).

PROFILING: CONTEXTUAL OR BEHAVIORAL?

In our digital society the configuration of communication is changing. Unprecedented forms of communication relying on the active role of algorithms are being tested, and the media landscape of society is transforming. In the following pages I explore these recent developments, with reference to the concept of virtual contingency introduced in chapter 1. The concept indicates the ability of algorithms to exploit the behavior and unpredictability of users to learn and act on communication in complex and appropriate ways. Algorithms, which are not, and must not be, intelligent, use big data to feed on the intelligence of users and to learn to act as smart and engaging communication partners—and also to address individual communications to each of us. In digital communication, I argue, virtual contingency produces an unprecedented interweaving between activities of users and generalized references, yielding innovative configurations.

From the perspective of the user, traditional mass media communication could be personalized only if audience members actively intervened and configured the messages. If the communication one got was to differ from that of others, one had to take steps to personalize it. Instead, algorithms today can take charge of this process. In many web services, each user receives content or messages different from what others are receiving—without "doing" anything in the conventional sense. Personalization of communication does not necessarily require active receivers anymore.[19]

From the perspective of the sender, traditional mass media communication was either directed toward everyone—being general and non-contextual—or it targeted a specific person at a precise moment in time in a manner that was ill-suited for other recipients. Today's algorithms, instead, can provide specific references through completely automated, generalized procedures that do not even require personal information such as names or addresses. Awareness of this possibility spread in the general public during a case in which the retailer Target, in identifying a pregnant woman before her parents knew about it, showed that it is possible to reconstruct precise information about a person using only anonymous data available on the web.[20] Communication can be addressed to everyone, and yet can also refer to the specific context of each receiver.

Traditional distinctions implode in this process. New forms of digital communication seem to produce a paradoxical form of mass personalization and generalized individualization—specific and local, for everybody, everywhere.[21] The paradox, however, is resolved if one considers the new agents participating in communication: algorithms. To describe and explain the resulting forms of communication, we need to account for their active role.

In fact, profiling techniques that rely on algorithmic procedures are developing new ways of dealing with individuals. They can address individuals as tokens of a class ("you and others like you"), or they can refer to them on the basis of their specific activity and context ("where you are and what you do"). The corresponding forms of personalization are very different.

With automated recommendations, for example, systems based on *behavioral profiling* are distinguished from *context-oriented* systems.[22] The former target a user's active participation on the web as representative of their interests, while matching these to the interests of other users rated as similar to them. Developing classic statistical segmentation techniques, these systems focus on increasingly restricted groups, ultimately targeting the individual. The availability of huge quantities of data from different sources makes it possible to segment a group more and more, ideally going as far as ending up with a segment of one. Through big data and virtual contingency, algorithms use prior behaviors of users and the behaviors of others to provide information that matches (or is assumed to match) one's specific interests on the basis of past choices and of the interests of "you and others like you."

In context-oriented systems, on the other hand, the focus is on the situation and the intent of individual users.[23] If you are looking for food in Naples in summer, you get recommendations for pizza and salad.[24] Here too the algorithms use huge amounts of data, yet these data are generated within a given context, provided by various sensors (from smartphones, The Internet of Things, etc.) and by other local sources. In this kind of system, "context may include the time of the day, the location of the user, the device used to access information or the companion with whom an activity is undertaken."[25] A user receives recommendations based on what is occurring around them in the moment and on what they are trying to accomplish—that is, based on "your situation" instead of that of "others like you."[26]

Of course, profiling techniques can combine both systems to target their users.[27] Nevertheless, the two approaches are conceptually different—and in both cases, receivers can adopt a passive or an active attitude. To understand the forms and social consequences of algorithmic profiling, we must distinguish the corresponding possibilities in a new frame of reference.[28]

FORMS OF DIGITAL COMMUNICATION

The table below presents my proposal for describing digital communication along two dimensions of profiling, according to the activity of a

Table 4.1

		contextual profiling	
		Yes	No
behavioral profiling	Yes	algorithmic individualization	collaborative filtering
	No	context-orientation	reverse personalization

group of users (*behavioral profiling*), and according to the specific situation of the single user (*contextual profiling*).

Let's start with purely behavioral profiling—represented here by the top right corner of the table—which selects communications addressed to the members of a group identified through *collaborative filtering* (for "people like you"). Each user shares these communications with other people in different situations, as was the case in broadcast mass media.[29] Communications are generalized, although in this digital form, not to everyone. When the single user gets a news feed, for example, the generalized components of algorithmic communication no longer refer to the public as a whole, but only to one segment—those people connected with that user by profiling techniques. The generalized reference is thus not the general public.

This issue is widely discussed in the debate on filter bubbles. The expression, introduced by Eli Pariser in *The Filter Bubble: What the Internet Is Hiding from You*, is based on observations of the participatory web, and in particular on innovations introduced by Google in 2009. Since at least 2009, Google has not been delivering the same search results to everyone, but provides information specifically referring to the perspective of those people the algorithm connects a user with. As a result of the filters operating on the web at all levels (with Google, and also with Facebook, Twitter, and all kinds of digital aggregators), the individual audience member is isolated in a sort of cultural bubble preventing her from accessing information that does not agree with her perspective. One does not have to pay anymore (with money or attention) for information that does not hold personal interest: no more overviews of markets in which they lack investments, results for sports that they do not follow, gossip and culture news for which they do not care, and so on. As

Herrman observes, in these services, filter bubbles are not an unintended consequence.[30] On the contrary, they are the point, corresponding to the idealized end of massified media promised by services such as PointCast in the late 1990s: the narrowing of broadcast communication down to a single user.

These kinds of personalized news feeds and aggregators are rising in use, yet generalized media seems destined to remain. In fact, Freewheel's 2018 Video Marketplace Report shows that 58 percent of video consumers in the US and Europe still get their content on TV screens (digital or otherwise), and that premium video services are increasing in popularity and importance compared to user-generated content.[31] Traditional news media, such as broadsheet papers and magazines, also continue to exist. Indeed, some newspapers such as the *New York Times* and the *Washington Post* have been increasing readerships—though often through digital versions with new features and services.[32]

It would appear that the generalization function of the traditional mass media remains fundamental and has not been fulfilled by individualized news feeds. We are still interested in knowing what others know, getting information that might not interest us personally. In fact, in many cases the most aware and informed citizens find it attractive to go beyond individualized content. Internet companies that offer personalized news services, such as Facebook and Buzzfeed, have recently been moving toward the model of traditional journalism, including having editorial offices with dedicated staff.[33] The result is, of course, not a move back to the broadcast model, but one toward new combinations of the activity of algorithms and the passivity of users. Indeed, in some cases, specific "anti-isolation" services are proposed whose functions introduce personalized newsfeed content from political perspectives deemed contrary to one's own ideologies (such as left-wing or right-wing), with the explicit purpose of mitigating political polarization.[34] Filters themselves are filtered against bubbles.

Returning to the table above, at the bottom left corner, we find the inverse to purely behavioral profiling in purely contextual profiling, in which the individual user receives messages tailored to their specific situation in space and time. Actively exploiting *context-orientation*, users can configure their communication and experiment with innovative ways of observation and self-observation.[35]

The ubiquitous phenomenon of selfies, for example, demonstrates one way in which the presentation of self in public can be transformed using digital techniques.[36] A selfie is not simply a photograph of oneself, like one might create using a timer on an analog camera. The automatic timer records the image from the perspective of someone else observing us: we see how an "other" sees us. In most cases, instead, the selfie is produced by way of a specific function offered by the smartphone that uses photo software to invert the image so that it looks like what one would normally see in a mirror.[37] The selfie then records the self-image that each of us sees in the mirror, rather than an external image, and this image is immediately posted on the web and shared with others.

Selfies are a typical example of social photographs—"everyday images taken to be shared"[38]—and are used to create a digital equivalent of the presentation of self that occurs in real face-to-face interactions.[39] We build our identity by seeing ourselves through the eyes of others, yet now what others see of us is the image we choose to present, one often processed with software tools: I "see me showing you me."[40] The user of these digital technologies actively configures a self-presentation, which becomes the basis of external observations (likes, tags, followers and other forms of digital feedback) from which the user learns who they are.

How does this condition affect the constitution of personality? Strands of research are already exploring this question in sectors relying most heavily on digital communication. A study by Formilan and Stark, for example, addresses the interesting phenomenon that electronic artists will often have many aliases—up to a dozen or more.[41] These aliases, with which an artist makes themself known to their public, are different from traditional pseudonyms, stage names, or the masks that, according to Erving Goffman, we wear to present the different aspects of our individuality. Like everyone else, electronic artists possess an individuality, even if it involves multiple representations, and are aware of it. Through their aliases, however, they experiment with alternative digital identity constructions that do not fully belong to them since their audience contributes in constructing them.

Aliases are "projected identities," "trial balloons" launched into the digital world in order to produce feedback that artists can acknowledge and elaborate upon. Through their aliases, artists learn who they are from their interactions with audiences—a process of continuous curation that leads digital identities to change, consolidate, or even disappear. There is nothing authentic either at the beginning or at the end of this process of mirroring and differentiation, insofar as, in more than one case, the artists decide to take their given name as their alias or one of their aliases.[42] Jesse Abayomi (real name), known in the electronic music scene as Zone 3 and Iroko, finally chose Abayomi as an additional alias,[43] reached through an identification path involving his audience. It is as authentic as any of his other aliases[44]—or as any of the so-called white labels under which electronic artists release tracks with anonymous identities. Digital audiences can also take advantage of the intervention of algorithms in communication to actively experiment with innovative forms of belonging and detachment, recognition and rejection.

The two types of profiling discussed can be combined into forms of *algorithmic individualization*—top left in the table—yielding communications that are both contextualized (according to the situation of the receiver), and personalized (referring to their individual behavior and the behavior of similar people). Particularly since the adoption of sophisticated machine-learning techniques, the intervention of algorithms makes it possible to offer to each user a specific message, one that matches their interests and is tailored to their specific context. Anyone registered in Facebook automatically receives personally contextualized content when accessing their personal web page, alongside the posts of digital friends. The same happens in online music, e-commerce recommendations, e-learning, news, and tourism systems, including advertising and various forms of targeted offers.[45] Two users doing the same search on the same site get different individualized answers on their screens, referring to their interests, their behavior, their location and their moment in time—without any active intervention involved.

This "real-time individualization" of a site to suit a visitor's unique needs relies on the use of contextual data *and* on segmentation of the universe of users based on increasingly detailed information produced with behavioral profiling.[46] It is a kind of individualization in which the receivers are no more active than the couch potatoes addressed by generalist media, yet they get a personalized communication tailored to their situation, tastes, and inclinations. Users do not personalize, they are personalized.

We are dealing with a form of web communication that combines context-oriented and behavioral profiling, a form that does not depend on user intervention, yet is contextualized and different for everyone. Several researchers have been investigating this, using labels like "new algorithmic identity," "data subjects," and "algorithmic individualization."[47] Nothing is personal in these forms of personalization.[48] Our identifications do not rely on our essential features or on the inherent characteristics by which we recognize ourselves. The focus shifts to our history of interactions with the web, and to identifications that are rather "made for us" through statistical models based on sensors and on web use.[49] Even if these digital identities start from the active behavior of users on the web, the role of their subjects ends up in a form of "interpassivity" in which individuals are "enacted" as "data doubles" they do not control.[50] The resulting form of individuality is deeply different from the modern one in which everyone actively observes, tests, and recognizes his or her specificity: "on personalized platforms there are in fact no individuals, but only ways of seeing people as individuals."[51]

Accomplished algorithmic individualization could be seen as the full realization of the fantasy of the participatory web of the 2000s, which promised to acknowledge the uniqueness of each user. Now that we inhabit a properly individualized web, we have come to understand that, in addition to the advantages it provides in everyday life, this technology also has many dark sides.[52] As Pariser argues, having access to information often no longer means having access to a shared world, and instead involves an increasingly sophisticated exploration of a more or less extended individualized world.[53] Without a common point of reference, we would not know what others know or do not know—nor indeed would we be able to judge our own ignorance on the matter. The problem is not so much the management of knowledge but the management of "un-knowledge."[54]

In the personalized web each user accesses their own specific content: a user sees things that many others do not see, while often not seeing the things that others do.[55] Individualization not only affects the way the world is presented to the observer, it also modifies the world itself. Realizing this effect can trigger feelings of rejection, transforming what was otherwise a sense of empowerment into one of passivity and impotence. Users tend to think, "This is creepy" instead of "This is helpful."[56] In these cases, individualized communication does not make you feel unique and productive, but isolated and "massified."

People often take action against the excessive interventions of algorithms, yet they also often do so by resorting to *other* algorithms. In the last few years, the use of ad-blocking software—specific forms of algorithms that protect users from web page advertisements—has been spreading rapidly.[57] This creates a paradoxical condition in which the individualization of users tends to block the very conditions that make this possible.[58] Ad blockers, in fact, operate by preventing cookies, pop-ups, embedded video and audio, and especially those tracking devices that detect data related to the individual user. The individualized user of the participatory web, then, blocks the very production of big data that feeds the virtual contingency of the algorithms, blocking the individualization of communication.

In opposition to algorithmic individualization, where particular combinations of different profiling techniques produce a situation of passive user customization, web communication may still enable users to individuate themselves on their own terms.[59] Owing to the decentralized and open nature of much of the web, many of the profiling tools used by algorithms are observable for users, who exploit them to create a sort of *reverse personalization*—represented here in the bottom right corner of the table—in which they actively configure their communication.

One example of this comes from influencers on the web who address an audience that is also expert and watchful.[60] The audience of the participatory web is active users who dig into the web and discover the rules behind the behavior of its participants (senders and receivers)—and therefore also of themselves as users of the medium: as Wasik puts it, "the participants become their own show."[61] In many cases users deal with the web knowing that the relationship is shaped according to the data of "people like them," and stage this circularity. "Tribes" on the web experiment with the ways in which they observe themselves. Typical digitally triggered phenomena such as flash mobs—as originally described by their inventor, and carried out—lacked content, as participants were aware.[62] The point of the show was no show at all, "pure scenes," where the participants observed themselves observing the event.

In the same way, prosumers who upload content on the web are largely not amateurs and do not naively transfer their personal data such as holiday memories onto YouTube without observing how they will be observed. The declared goal of the vastly successful social networking service TikTok is to stimulate and support users' creativity, freeing them from technological difficulties and offering a place where everyone can become active participants.[63] The basic challenge of these services is how to get people to engage with them.[64] These users are mostly people acutely aware of being observed, who act on the basis of a meta-understanding of digital communication and its mechanisms. The result is a mass communication in which "the consumer himself is the Big Brother," using refined tools to observe himself, others, and their interventions in communication.[65]

These innovative developments are highly revealing about the meaning and forms of users' active interventions in communication—and also about the reasons for the failure of certain connected projects that had raised high expectations. Interactive fiction, for example, in which the reader/viewer was expected to contribute to help determining the course of a story, had little success after initial curiosity wore off. Audiences do not seem interested in deciding the plot of novels or movies, even (and precisely) if these readers/viewers can be deeply affected when the story does not go as they wished. Since the modern period, in fact, the value of fiction essentially lies in observing the observation of others, entrusting an invisible author with the creation of a narrated world, its events, and its characters. As such, it is an invented world, and we know it.

Precisely because it is not real, fiction allows us to do something that in "real reality" is impossible: to observe others as if we could read their mind.[66] Audience members want to observe how others observe, thereby experimenting with perspectives different from their own, and potentially learning to observe themselves and their own perspective.[67] For this purpose, the separation of the fictional world from the real world must be maintained, and with it also the impossibility of intervening directly in the plot. You cannot enter the mirror if you want to be reflected in it.

This kind of fiction still has a fundamental function, although now a new combination is emerging that takes advantage of the intervention of algorithms and that reshapes the distinction between the narrated world and the lived world. Video games, one of the most influential forms of digital communication, use algorithms to offer the users the possibility of active intervention in the game world, developing a highly innovative "grammar of fun."[68] Through virtual contingency, video games go beyond the modern model of storytelling and reading, yielding an active experience for the gamer while still enabling their entry into the mirror of fiction.[69]

Video games, as with novels, can be designed from the perspective of a character involved in their depicted events (first-person point of view—or POV) or from an external perspective (third-person POV).[70] But the player of a first-person POV video game does not only observe the world through someone else's eyes. Contrary to the basic rule of fiction and the centrality of its perspective, the player also acts in the (virtual) world and lives a particularly immersive game experience[71]—shooting, hiding, running away from enemies. However, they cannot see themself in the game; typically, the only part of an avatar's body that the player can see is their hands.[72] In a third-person POV, though, the player can see the whole body of their character from a perspective above and behind the avatar. In a game shifting back and forth from first- to third-person POV, a player who identifies with and acts through an avatar can also observe their virtual self through the eyes of another. For the first time, the video game offers a space in which the observer sees with the eyes of another not only the world, but also themself and their own behavior. In the form of the avatar, according to Waggoner the player experiences a "virtual identity" that allows them to be "both self and not-self," "other and not other at the same time."[73]

CONCLUSION

Communication mediated by algorithms learning from the behavior of users is modifying from within our established forms of standardization and personalization. In addition to the modern distinction between individual and collective (or private and public) references, a new equivalent of the public sphere is taking shape:[74] one that follows users' choices, then processes and multiplies them, and then re-presents them in a form that requires new choices. The result is an unprecedented configuration of activity and passivity in relations between issuers and recipients, which can be exploited by both parties.

5

ALGORITHMIC MEMORY AND THE RIGHT TO BE FORGOTTEN

REMEMBERING TO FORGET

On March 13, 2014,[1] the European Court of Justice issued a judgment in favor of the plaintiff on case C-131/12 about the right of citizens to request the removal from web search results of the links associated with their name, understood as the "right to be forgotten."[2] The ruling directly addresses the role of algorithms in the processing of social information, and raises a lively debate around the consequences of digitalization for memory.

The judgment reacted to a complaint lodged by a Spanish citizen against Google. The company was accused of infringing upon his privacy rights because its search engine made his personal data accessible to everyone on the web, even if the event they referred to had been resolved for a number of years and the matter had become irrelevant. The court was asked to judge whether individual citizens should have the right to make their personal information untraceable (the right to be forgotten: § 20) after a certain time simply because they wish it ("without it being necessary . . . that the inclusion of the information in question . . . causes prejudice to the data subject": ruling C-131/12, §100). The court also had to decide whether Google should be held responsible for the processing of personal data, and should be forced to suppress links to web pages

containing information on the person in question, even if that information remains available—lawfully published—on web pages where it is
hosted.

The problem to which the European Court responded with its ruling
is related to the unprecedented role of algorithms in the production of
social memory. On the web, data processing uses algorithms, which act
on enormous amounts of data, with no apparent limit to their processing
and storage capability. Making information accessible to everyone with
an internet connection, the web intensifies the problem of the *droit à
l'oubli* (right to be forgotten) which has a long legal tradition emerging
out of French law. This right protects the will of a citizen who has been
convicted of a criminal act and has paid the debt to society to no longer
be remembered for those past facts, and to be able to build a new life and
a new public image. The right to be forgotten is directly connected with
the ability to keep one's future open—a right to reinvention that protects
the future of the person from a colonization by the past.[3] The nineteenth-
century philosopher Friedrich Nietzsche knew it very well when he spoke
of the "need of oblivion for life" as even more important than the ability
to remember[4]—because without forgetting, one would remain bound to
an eternal presence of the past that does not allow for building a different
future. Without forgetting, you cannot plan nor can you hope.

This is certainly plausible. The judgment of the European Court recognizes this right for European citizens and forces Google to remove links
to the personal data of those who request it—unless that information
has public relevance. However, with search engines giving access to the
voluminous data available online, the right to be forgotten protected by
the European Court becomes much more extensive than the classic right
to be forgotten, both materially and socially: it concerns any act (especially those inconsequential on the penal level yet relevant for image and
reputation) and includes any person (not only criminals but each of us,
particularly teenagers).

The forgetting of anyone, though, also affects the forgetting of others—
such as those who are involved in the same event and may not want it
to be forgotten, or those who may become affected in the future or have
an interest in similar events and want to preserve access to the relevant
information. The protection of individual forgetting collides with the

right to information and with the creation of a reliable shared public sphere.[5]

The ruling of the European Court states that the right to privacy overrules the public interest in finding personal information, unless the person holds a public role (§97). The issue is extremely controversial and fits into the open debate about the definition and limits of privacy in web society.[6]

The solution proposed by the European Court, however, also raises practical implementation problems, due to the active role of algorithms. The judgment considers Google accountable and responsible for the excess of memory in our digital world,[7] on the basis of a principle that holds that the responsible entity is "the natural or legal person" who "determines the purposes and means of the processing of personal data . . . whether or not by automatic means" (§4). Google, on the contrary, claims that it cannot be held responsible because the processing of data is performed by the search engine, and the company "has no knowledge of those data and does not exercise control over the data" (§22). Can the autonomy of the operation of algorithms relieve the company from the responsibility for data management?

The European Court denies this, although it distinguishes the processing of data by Google from the processing by publishers and journalists. Even if Google does not direct data processing, search engine activity makes data accessible to internet users, including those who would not have otherwise found some particular page (§36). It also allows users to get a "structured overview" of the information relating to a person, "enabling them to establish a more or less detailed profile" (§37). This affects the privacy of the persons concerned in different and more incisive ways than merely publishing the information. The processing of data by Google is more subtle but more dangerous than that carried out by publishers and journalists; therefore, the company is charged with suppressing links to people who require those pages to be forgotten, even if the publication is lawful and the information remains available.[8]

This decision implies, without making it explicit, a specific definition of social memory and forgetting. Is memory the ability to store information in an archive, even if it is inaccessible? Or does it depend on the ability to find the information when you need it? Is computer memory storage or remembering?[9] Ascribing to Google the management of the right to oblivion implies a clear choice: data are considered forgotten if they are made difficult to find, while social memory should be preserved by the storage of data in the pages of newspapers and in other archives.

David Drummond, general counsel of Google, commenting on the judgment of the European Court, complained that it puts Google in a sort of no man's land,[10] without any of the protections that legislation provides to media, archives, and other communication tools.[11] The ruling does not consider the specificity of the company and does not comment on its claims regarding the unprecedented autonomy of the operation of algorithms. Google acts on data without knowing and without controlling it; thus, it is neither a library, a catalog, a newspaper, a newsstand, nor a service provider. Google is a search engine.

Search engines are not active in the same way as newspapers, publishers, and libraries, which select and organize the information to be disclosed. Search engines are purely passive intermediaries that merely provide access to materials they did not choose and do not know. The information that users receive in response to their requests is organized, selected, and ranked in a way that had not been previously decided by anyone and cannot be attributed to anything other than the search engine. Search engines give access to information they produced themselves.[12] But how do algorithms produce and manage it?

DATA-DRIVEN AGENCY

Contemporary legislation collides with the new forms of agency in the digital world.[13] The actor that selected and produced the additional information—the ranking—in Google is an algorithm such as PageRank that uses the available signals to produce information that was foreseen neither by its programmers, nor by content authors or search users. The information produced, if it was known to anyone, was known only to the algorithm itself—yet does it make sense to say that the algorithm *knows* it? And does it make sense to hold an algorithm accountable?

As discussed in chapter 1, algorithms deal with data in a different way than humans. Whereas human information processing refers to meaning, machine-learning practices allow algorithms to produce information that does not start from meaningful elements. Algorithms do not process information, they only process data. *Data* by themselves are not meaningful. They are just numbers and figures, digital digits that only become significant when processed and presented in a context, producing information. Information requires data, but data is not enough to have information. The same data (e.g., about stock market movements) can be informative or not for different people in different contexts. Referring to Bateson's definition of "information" as a "difference that makes a difference,"[14] we can say that data are differences (stock prices going up/ stock prices going down) that become informative when they matter to someone in a given moment (who, e.g., decides to sell assets, or chooses not to invest).

Algorithms only process differences, from whatever source and with whatever meaning. They need only the data that they get from the web, deriving them from what we think and also from what we do without thinking and without being aware of it. Digital machines are able to identify in the materials circulating on the web patterns and correlations that no human being has identified, processing them in such a way as to be informative for their users. Human beings, however, need information. When communicated to users, the results of algorithmic processing generate information and have consequences,[15] but outgoing information does not need incoming information: the revolutionary communicative meaning of big data is its ability to produce information from data that is not itself information. In Mireille Hildebrandt's words, "We have moved from an information society to a data-driven society."[16]

THE MEMORY OF A WEB-BASED SOCIETY

Whereas in the past the problem of memory was the inability to remember, now the problem of social memory is increasingly connected to the inability to forget.[17] Especially since the spread of Web 2.0, with its virtually unlimited capacity to store and process data, the web seems to allow for a form of perfect remembering. Indeed, our society seems to be able to remember everything.[18] The default value that holds automatically unless you opt out, which demands neither energy nor attention, is now remembering—not forgetting.[19] It's become much easier and cheaper to remember; remembering has become the norm. We decide to forget only as an exception, if it becomes necessary.

Think of our everyday practices on the web while dealing with texts, pictures, and emails. We lack the time to choose and to forget. By not making the decision to preserve anything, we habitually preserve *everything*, as the machine invites us to do. To choose and to decide to forget requires more attention and time. Usually there is no need to eliminate content, thanks to the availability of powerful techniques for searching out interesting information in the mass of data as and when the need arises—for example, in locating a particular message among a cache of saved emails. We therefore remember everything, recording it in the spaces (in the cloud) of a web which by itself does not have any procedure to forget.[20] The judgment of the European Court reflects this approach: the problem is the accessibility of citizens' data in the indelible archives of the web, and the law wants to create the ability of the web to forget (and the possibility that citizens be forgotten).[21]

But does it make sense to say that the web has a limitless memory, or even that it has a memory? The difficulties in implementing an effective regulation of forgetting are related to the fact that memory is not just storage, and efficiency in memory is not equivalent to unlimited data. Memory implies focusing on and selecting data to produce information that refers to a meaningful context. Memory thus requires both the ability to remember *and* the ability to forget.

This double nature of memory— remembering requires forgetting —is not always adequately taken into account. In common parlance and even in a large part of the scientific literature on the topic, memory ostensibly refers to the management of *remembering*. Increasing memory is understood as an increase in the number of memories or as strengthening the ability to remember. In this view, forgetting appears only as the passive negation of memory;[22] if remembering increases, forgetting decreases, and vice versa. The opposite idea, that *forgetting* is a key component of memory, required for abstraction and reflection, is not new, although it has always remained in the shadows. From Themistocles in the sixth century BCE onward, there have always been voices claiming that the ability to forget is even more important than the ability to remember.[23]

Remembering and forgetting, they argue, are the two sides of memory, each essential for its functioning.[24]

This changes our understanding of forgetting. From this perspective, it is not simply erasure of data but an active mechanism that inhibits the memorization of all but a few stimuli, enabling one to focus one's attention and to autonomously organize information in accordance with one's own processes.[25] Forgetting is needed to focus on something and use past experience (that is, remembering) to act in a flexible, context-appropriate manner, rather than either starting from scratch each time or, indeed, always doing the same thing whenever a similar situation occurs.[26]

The web, which stores all data in a kind of eternal present, is not able to forget, yet is also not even able to properly remember.[27] In dealing with data, algorithms behave like the mnemonist studied by Luria,[28] or like people living with hypermnesia, who cannot forget.[29] Like these individuals, algorithms are not able to activate the mechanism that distinguishes what they are interested in remembering from what they are not. However, memory is actually remembering *and* forgetting. Algorithms do not properly remember and do not properly forget; they merely calculate.

When algorithms allow us to forget (as they indeed do—we get from Google, for example, selective lists of links to sites that may interest us), they do it not because they learn to forget, but because their procedures "import" selections made by users to guide their own behavior.[30] The criteria for deciding which sites are relevant and should appear first in a list of search results are not produced by the algorithm and are not even decided from the beginning by programmers; instead, they are derived from the choices of previous users. A website is considered relevant to the algorithm if many web users connected to it many times.[31] The algorithm forgets what had been forgotten by users.[32]

FORGETTING WITHOUT REMEMBERING

How can we deal with a social memory driven by algorithms? How can we ensure both the preservation of the past and the openness of the future, when the agents that manage data move in an eternal present, without remembering and without forgetting?

The most evident influence of digital media has been a shift away from problems of analog memory. Traditional societies were always concerned with protecting the ability to remember (storing and retrieving data), while today we are primarily concerned with protecting the ability to forget.[33] But the two sides of memory have an interesting asymmetry, known since ancient times. You can decide to enhance remembering, and with *ars memoriae* we have for thousands of years developed elaborate techniques to do so.[34] But we do not have an *ars oblivionalis*—an art of forgetting—that would be an effective technique to enhance the ability to get rid of memories.[35] If you want to forget and decide to enhance that process, the most immediate effect is the opposite of the one intended because this draws attention to the content at stake, further cementing the initial memory.[36] For the web it is called the "Streisand effect," similar to the one known and widely studied about censorship—the reason why one should usually refrain from suing defamatory articles, to avoid spreading the news even more: politicians, actors, and all public figures know it very well. Remembering to forget is paradoxical, and deciding to make something be forgotten, almost impossible.

On the web, this kind of boomerang effect has been observed. Reputation management sites on the web (e.g., reputation.com) warn that attempts to remove content are often counterproductive.[37] Once a request to "forget" has been accepted by Google, and a search on that particular person is performed, among the results appears a warning that certain contents have been removed in the name of the right to be forgotten. The obvious consequence is an increase in curiosity and interest in that content. Sites quickly emerged (like hiddenfromgoogle.com) that collect the links removed by virtue of this right to oblivion. Wikipedia has also released a list of links to articles that Google has removed from its search engine in accordance with the "right to be forgotten."[38] Ironically, these "reminders" of the contents that the law requires be forgotten are perfectly legal because the ruling prohibits only the retaining of links to particular pages, and not to the contents of the pages themselves. Those pages continue to be available on newspaper websites or other sources that had diffused them.

Hindering remembering is not enough to induce forgetting. The paradox of remembering to forget must be circumvented in an indirect, more

complex way. The practice of using memory techniques (mnemotechnics) itself recognized that in order to reinforce forgetting, one should
rather multiply the range of available memories.[39] If one increases memories by number, each piece of information is lost in the mass and becomes
difficult to find, to the point where it becomes lost as if it were forgotten.
This practice had never been able to yield a genuine technique (an *ars
oblivionalis*) because of the limits of the human capacity to store and process data (to remember), which would be overloaded by such an unmanageable mass of memories. To be able to forget, we would have to give up
the ability to remember. Algorithms, however, do not have this problem
because of their virtually unlimited capacity for managing data, which,
while being the basis of their excessive remembering, can also be used to
reinforce forgetting.

Thus, to control forgetting on the web in a manner specific to algorithmic memory, one could adopt a procedure directly opposed to the practice of deleting content or making them unavailable. This is the direction
some recent techniques for protecting privacy is going, which is often
understood as protecting forgetting. Strategies of obfuscation have been
designed to produce misleading, false, or ambiguous data parallel to each
transaction on the web[40]—in practice, multiplying the production of
information to hinder a meaningful contextualization. If, together with
every search for information on the web, or together with any input of
information on social media like Facebook, a dedicated software program
produces a mass of other entirely irrelevant operations, it will be difficult
to select and focus on relevant information—that is, to remember.[41]

These techniques, however, require a prior selection of the memories
you want to forget, for which the obfuscation process is activated. Yet
in many cases, one may want to forget memories that one had never
thought needed to be forgotten, and these are the cases targeted by the
legislation about the right to be forgotten.[42] There are services that adopt
the same approach to produce an equivalent of forgetting after the fact.
They act directly on Google's search results through the multiplication of
information. When a person has been publicly shamed on the web, the
service produces sites laden with fictitious or irrelevant information, with
the explicit purpose of pushing the sensitive information in question so
far down the search results that it effectively vanishes.[43] For example, the

service ReputationDefender starts from the assumption that "deleting is impossible."[44] To combat negative or undesired items about a person, it generates a wide range of unique, positive, high-quality content about that person and push it up in the search results. As a result, "negative material gets dumped down to pages where nobody will see it."

The idea is not to erase memories but to enhance forgetting. When the algorithm multiplies data, it does not pay attention to this process—it doesn't "remember" it. The multiplication of memories goes on in the machine without meaning and without understanding. This proliferation makes each datum more marginal, lost in the mass. As in forgetting, it becomes increasingly difficult to find and to use, thereby fulfilling the right to oblivion. The factual conditions of forgetting are carried out without having to activate remembering, bypassing in a sense the paradox of *ars oblivionalis*.

But artificial memory, as both remembering and forgetting, requires constant maintenance. Mnemotechnics work only by taking due care of and maintaining the palaces and caves of memory.[45] Memory athletes should not stop training.[46] Similarly, an effective artificial forgetting must always be renewed because Google constantly changes its algorithms and its targets.[47] Forgetting does not happen once and for all, as an erasure of memories. You must reverse engineer Google and continue to renew forgetting as an active process, producing more and different memories with different strategies.

DATA-DRIVEN MEMORY

These forgetting strategies are ingenious, yet address the issue of forgetting from the perspective of information management—of how it is possible to forget information available to search engines. They adopt the same approach as the European Court of Justice. But algorithms do not work with information. They work with data, creating different problems.

The legislation on the right to be forgotten addresses the indexing of pages in a search engine. When the request of a citizen is accepted, this indexing is blocked, and Google is not allowed to provide a link when a search is made, even if the data remain available in their original location (e.g., the digital archive of a newspaper). Google cannot deliver the information to the users answering their query. It is like blocking the use of a library catalog, while at the same time preserving the books and other materials. This solution corresponds to the legislative attempt to combine the protection of forgetting with the parallel need to protect memory. As Viviane Reding, the European Commission's vice president, said, "It is clear that the right to be forgotten cannot amount to a right of the total erasure of history."[48] To preserve the openness of the future, one would not want to lose the past. All data are still stored at the respective sites, although the "forgotten" items are no longer accessible via Google search. The ruling acts on remembering, not on memory. This of course leaves the users exposed to the boomerang effect of forgetting, since the original pages continue to be available on the web and can become accessible (can be remembered) with different search tools, or even with google.com on any of its sites outside Europe.

But there are deeper, more fundamental problems. Google's indexing, as with the catalog of a library, delivers information. The algorithm itself, however, "feeds" on data, which are much more diffuse and much more extensive than the information understood and thought by someone at some time.[49] Algorithms derive data from the information available in materials online (texts, documents, videos, blogs, files of all types), and from the information provided by users: their requests, recommendations, comments, chats. Algorithms are also able to extract data from information about information: the metadata that describe content and properties of each document, such as their title, creator, subject, description, publisher, contributors, type, format, identifier, source, language, and much more. Each of these bits of data refer to a different context than the original information, a context of which the author is usually unaware and had not explicitly intended to communicate. The Internet of Things and other forms of ambient intelligence also produce a multitude of data that individuals are not aware of, monitoring their behavior, their location, their movements, and their relationships.

Moreover, and most importantly, algorithms are able to use all these data for a variety of secondary uses which are largely independent of the intent or the original context for which they were produced, processing them to find correlations and patterns by performing calculations that the human mind could not realize nor understand, but which become informative. Such secondary uses of data also make it possible to gain information relevant for the profiling and surveillance of citizens.

In these processes, algorithms use the "data exhaust" or the "data shadows" generated as a by-product of people's activities on the web and, increasingly, in the world at large.[50] It is a sort of data afterlife that goes far beyond the representational quality of numbers and of information and depends on the autonomous activity of algorithms.[51] Each difference makes a difference in many different ways, becoming increasingly independent from the original information. Algorithms use data to produce information that cannot be attributed to any human being. In a way, algorithms remember memories that had never been thought by anyone.

This is a great opportunity for the social management of information; however, it is also a grave threat to the freedom of self-determination of individuals and to the possibility of an open future. Information may be rendered inaccessible to indexing in accordance with the right to be forgotten, while data continue to be remembered and used by the algorithms to produce different information.[52] Moreover, the implementation of the right to be forgotten itself involves collecting lots of metadata about which personal data is being used for what purpose. This process reveals personal preferences that, albeit anonymized, can be exploited by others for profiling.[53]

CONCLUSION

Can one remember without forgetting? In order to remember better, is it necessary to forget less, or does the efficiency of memory depend on the ability to coordinate two different and correlated abilities, the ability to remember and the ability to forget? These questions cannot be answered without taking into account the information and communication technologies available at any given time, starting from the powerful and revolutionary tool of writing. For many centuries, increasingly refined technologies such as printing and systems for information storage had to deal first and foremost with the problem of reinforcing the ability to remember, removing from sight the related problem of the ability to forget, a problem with information use that has accompanied Western civilization since it began in ancient Greece.

Today, digital techniques bring forgetting to the forefront. The memory of our society is entrusted not only to texts and archived materials, but also to the tools that make it possible to access and distribute individual's content on the web—that is, to the algorithms that participate in communication. With their contribution, we can find, store, and access a quantity and variety of content that previously would have been unthinkable, creating a form of memory that remembers very much. This memory, however, does not seem to forget enough, unless a regulation—like the one pursued by the European Court of Justice—forces it to do so.

Finding the right balance is not easy. The attempt to create a digital form of forgetting brings out all the puzzles and paradoxes that had been latent for so many centuries: in the human form of memory, in order to reinforce forgetting, one must first remember—remember to forget. But algorithms that create the problem can help solve it. Digital tools remember so well because they work differently from human intelligence. And for the same reason they can forget differently: they can forget without remembering. Algorithms participating in communication can implement, for the first time, the classical insight that it might be possible to reinforce forgetting—not by erasing memories but by multiplying them. This requires a radical change in perspective. It does not solve all the problems of digital memory and of the difficulty in controlling the continuous production of an excess of data, but moves these problems to a different and much more effective level: from the reference frame of individuals to that of communication.

6

FORGETTING PICTURES

PHOTOGRAPHIC EXPERIENCE

After a four-hour hike down into the Grand Canyon and anticipating a longer ascent, my partner and I were standing at Plateau Point, admiring the spectacular view of the Colorado River below. Within a few minutes, a young tourist came down the trail, turned to ask us to take her photo, and immediately retraced her path without stopping to take in the breathtaking vista. Where did that image of an unobserved landscape end up? Who looks at it and why? What is the meaning of extensive digital images constantly being produced and posted online? What does this use reveal about the relationship of our society with time, experience, and representation?

In his presentation of the project *Le Supermarché des Images* (*The Supermarket of Images*[1]), Peter Szendy writes that "we live in a world that is increasingly saturated with images"—there are too many, and there is not space for all of them. Back in 2011, in his installation *Photography in Abundance*, Erik Kessels stacked a room with a million photos that had been uploaded to Flickr in twenty-four hours, showing this in a tangible way.[2] When does the abundance of images become excessive, to the point of saturation? Compared to previous eras, how is our social space overloaded as if it "can no longer contain the images that constitute it"?[3]

As Susan Sontag remarked almost fifty years ago, "just about every-thing has been photographed."[4] We have since moved into an era of "ubiquitous photography"[5]—a condition in which immediate sensory experience (of being in a place and seeing something: this, here and now) is directly overlapped with an image. The spread of camera phones, how-ever, brings in an additional dimension. The smartphone photograph not only fixes the moment in a stable and reproducible way, but typi-cally also enters it into the fluid circuit of images on the web—through Instagram, Facebook, or even the ephemeral production of images on Snapchat, which are generated to intentionally be deleted as soon as they have been viewed.

Why do we do this? How is our experience affected by photography, and how does photographing itself become an experience? Perhaps digi-tal photographs are taken and distributed in order to escape the pressure that our "risk society" puts on the present.[6] At the same time the artistic world is using digital images to experiment with unprecedented forms of immersion in direct experience. Escape and immersion. No one ever said communication was simple.

IMAGES TO REMEMBER

Several studies have pointed out the shift from memorization to com-munication as the primary use of photography in the digital age.[7] In our analog tradition, the production of images was first of all a form of conser-vation and memorization.[8] People took pictures in order to remember the few scenes and the few experiences that were worth preserving. Aspects of the world were reproduced in an image that captured a moment in the inevitable passage of time, a moment that would otherwise be borne into oblivion and dissolution.

Yet the production of images did not record *the* world but rather a *point of view* on the world. As Panofsky observed in 1927, what the image froze and preserved was the perspective of the painter who painted it or the observer who took the picture, saving from oblivion someone's point of view about a moment.[9] The world was always preserved as the memory of someone, even while things changed, and time passed. And as one cannot remember everything, so the number of possible images was limited, and selection was needed. Too many memories, even if we could preserve them, did not serve as a good memory because they would be easily confused and impossible to manage. Just as with memories, for the analog world there could be "too many" images, and a risk of producing a saturation point.[10]

Time passes today as well, but an abundance of images favors a different way of managing transience and presence in the digital age. What changes with a constant production of images at almost no cost and with the possibility of virtually unlimited storage? We can ostensibly reproduce everything and, in theory, keep these reproductions forever because digital images are stored in cloud services, in a virtual form that does not require physical space or much user expense. The images can also be recalled on a whim when we want to remember them. In the form of a digital image, apparently nothing is lost. If there is an excess of images in the digital world, the problem is not simply their large number.

Storage and retrieval were in fact the two big challenges that people traditionally had to cope with to not lose memories: to be able to preserve them and be able to find them in the maze of mnemonic spaces that risked becoming crowded and unmanageable.[11] Both are solved by digital technology, which offers practically inexhaustible storage spaces and retrieval tools that allow us to find all of what we stored without the content getting lost within an excess of memories[12]—even the memories we had not remembered. Using tags on Instagram, for example, we can find all the images we stored, and also tagged aspects that we did not notice at the time but that were marked by others.[13] Moreover, recent machine-learning techniques have developed algorithms that can autonomously produce their own tags, to manage the past from perspectives no one has yet thought of and generate new information. Is this the reason why we photograph everything: to preserve experience and reinforce memory? To deepen our relationship with things by withdrawing them from oblivion, to be able to go back and review them later?

Observation of digital practices for producing and managing images reveals that the opposite is true. As with the tourist in the Grand Canyon, in many cases, we do not take photographs to deepen experience—we do it to withdraw from experience.[14] We do not produce images to preserve the present—we produce them to escape the present. This is a basic difference between the traditional relationship with images and the new digital mode—and is perhaps the reason for the excess of images in our web society.

THE RISK OF THE PRESENT

A digital user equipped with a smartphone often does not experience a moment, but reproduces it. Before looking at the world, they photograph it. Instead of facing the vastness and the risks of an experience, the digital user freezes it in an image and posts it on the web. We all know it: many visitors in exhibitions do not stop and look at a painting, absorbing the multiplicity of perspectives contained in the work of art, together with the specificity of the location in the room, the light, the space, the position, and the present moment—they do not expose themselves to these experiences. Instead of looking, the digital user takes photographs, and they do the same in front of a sunset, a landscape, a dish in a restaurant. As Susan Sontag already remarked, "Images are able to usurp reality."[15] Why do people do it? It would be simplistic to dismiss these practices as superficial and frivolous. Such widespread behaviors signal a deeper change of perspective and horizon, a new cultural approach that must be taken seriously.

Digital tourists are not stupid nor ignorant, yet have a different relationship with images and their management. They do not produce an image to preserve it from the course of time—they produce it to escape the present. This attitude can be traced back to the "risk society" that overloads the present with responsibility for the construction of the future.[16] "Risk" in this sense is not a future condition, but a problem of the present, generated when many possibilities are available and we ask ourselves today if and how the future we will have to face depends on our current behavior. What I do (or do not do) today will have consequences, and tomorrow I will either regret these actions or reap the advantages they bring. If I speculate on the stock exchange, I can lose my money or make substantial gains, and depending on either, tomorrow I will be afflicted or happy. The problem is that now I do not know the future and I cannot know how things will turn out—I only know that the blame (or the merit) will fall on my behavior today, and that I have to decide now.

The awareness of risk as a dependence of the future on the present is now widespread in every area of our private and social lives, from our intimate relationships (it is up to us to decide whether to marry and who to marry, but we cannot know if our marriage will be a happy one); to professional choices (it is up to us to decide what to study and which career to undertake, a decision which can have a variety of positive or negative outcomes); to managing money (do we want to invest in the stock market or not?). The risk awareness places an enormous pressure on the present, which is already observed as a future past.[17] This approach also burdens our experiences with uncertainty and widening anxiety—why am I here now, doing this, when I could be doing otherwise and when these choices affect my future? As O'Doherty writes: "Direct experience might kill us."[18] It would be nice to escape this anxiety and pressure, without withdrawing entirely from the world and from experience.

Instead, perhaps, we could take a photograph—indeed, we take a lot of them. The elaboration of the present is entrusted to its reproduction (it is not the task of the present) and referred to others—the others with whom the web connects us.[19] Photographs become "social photos," simply "taken to be shared."[20] Producing an image, in fact, is not usually done to be stored, but to be posted. Snapchat is the exemplar of this digital use of images, of taking a picture solely to put it on the web, that is, to show it to others. This is the form of reproduction carried out in the digital world: the aim is social multiplication, not temporal preservation. The image is not produced to see it better nor to be able to review it later, but to let others see it. And after they have seen it, it can be removed from circulation, as is true of Snapchat.

Digital users do not look at things and do not directly live experiences— they curate experiences for sharing with others and to show themselves observing them, appearing to build an identity in doing so.[21] The sense of the image becomes an "I see" shown to others—and only then can one see. Experience is produced through mediation and lived by reflection, observing one's observation observed by others—and in this way it becomes interesting and meaningful, unburdened from the weight of the present and from individual responsibility for the construction of the future.

TIME-SPECIFIC EXPERIENCE

Is the outcome an excess of images? Not necessarily, because the web's algorithms are perfectly able to take care of them, selecting the images that become relevant and keeping the others in an indefinite virtuality that accommodates everything. The consequence, however, might be a transformation of direct experience: the immediate space of the here-and-now changes its meaning, and traditional forms no longer work in the same way—possibly supplemented by hybrid modes such as flash mobs, where the participants observe themselves observing the event.[22] The management and preparation of experience are also changing in all forms of involvement that require that which has become the most anachronistic resource: the physical presence of participants in a specific place at a specific time—at concerts, conferences, theatrical performances, and (for images) a new form of art exhibits.

Faced with the excess of images reproduced and circulated online, the organizers of exhibitions have progressively modified structure and meaning in recent years. Already in the twentieth century, the experience offered by exhibitions has been less and less about contemplating a painting or work of art (which can also be reproduced with very high resolution), nor about seeing a sequence of works in chronological order (e.g., from Cimabue to Jackson Pollock), or about works organized according to abstract criteria such as thematic or stylistic affinity. Exhibitions offer rather a contextual experience, a participation in the extended present of the "white cube" of the museum or the gallery, a specific space removed from feeling pressure about time and anxiety about the future.[23] The visitor must be physically there and must perceive the moment with an otherwise unknown intensity and reflexivity. They are not asked to fix their attention on a single work of art but to participate in a broader experience generated by a contemporary exposure to different (often heterogeneous) works and by the works' mutual relationships in the exhibition space—something that cannot be reproduced in an image and cannot be posted on the web. The experience is not about getting to see the *Mona Lisa* or another work of art, but perceiving the spatial arrangement of the room, the light at that time of day, the volumes, the references and harmonies between all exhibited objects.

The contextuality of artistic experience was radicalized in the 1970s with the experimentation of space-bound exhibitions: *site-specific* works like Robert Smithson's *Spiral Jetty*—a 1,500-foot-long, fifteen-foot-wide counterclockwise coil of mud and rocks unfolding from the shore of the Great Salt Lake in Utah[24]—or Daniel Buren's installations integrating contemporary art into historic buildings. Art objects were linked to a specific place inside or outside the museum and could not be moved without losing their meaning. "To remove the work is to destroy it," noted Richard Serra about his *Tilted Arc*.

In a further step of contextualization, some curators are now experimenting with forms of time-bound exhibitions in which visual art (as in the theater) dictates the time of viewing by visitors, which cannot be changed without altering the meaning.[25] Several innovative curational experiments by Hans Ulrich Obrist, for example, are conceived as temporal rather than spatial experiences.[26] The most advanced are supposedly his *Marathons*, twenty-four-hour-long hybrid combinations of conversations, performances, presentations, and experiments. The emptying of present experience linked to the excess of images in digital society is reflected here in its opposite: a rediscovery and replanning of contextual presence in the moment of the exhibition.

Time bound as in theater is, however, it is not yet *time-specific* in the sense of a reflective awareness of temporal context. An authentic, innovative time-specific experience is instead being produced precisely in connection with the excess of digital images, and precisely using photographs. Christian Marclay's video-installation *The Clock* shows this in an exemplary way: it consists of a twenty-four hour-long montage of thousands of images of clocks in movies or on television, combined in such a way that the time shown on the screen always exactly coincides with the current moment of viewing, with the present time of the spectator.[27] Seeing on the screen the images of distant places and moments synchronized with the present, Marclay says, "you're constantly reminded of what time it is, " so that "*The Clock* has the ability to make us present in the moment."[28] The viewers who observe the perspective of others reproduced by the images on the screen are led to reflect on their own perspective and their current context—reversing the tendency to digitally escape the present and their contextual experience.

The realization of these kinds of works, however, is possible only with the support of a new powerful cultural technology. It requires exploiting the exorbitant number of digital pictures available today, from which Marclay could extract the images of watches for all twenty-four hours of the installation. Contrary to the reproduction and consumption of photographs and videos on the web, in this case the excess of images is not intended to escape the present and move away from experience. On the contrary, in the artistic event, images of distant experiences are used to immerse the participants in their immediate experience with unprecedented intensity.

CONCLUSION

The abundance of images in our digital society offers both the option of escaping the present and of immersing oneself in it; more generally, it offers the possibility to explore combinations of presence and absence in dizzying and complex ways. As we already saw in the relationships between remembering and forgetting, personalization and anonymity, creativity and "massification," in many cases the differences generated by digital technology can be understood not as oppositions, but as distinctions whose two sides exist together and bind each other[29]—without the desire to escape the present producing an abundance of digital images, new forms of reflective awareness of the present in exhibitions would not exist either. Whereas the "ubiquity of social photographs threatens our ability to really live in the moment," it also generates "a sensual expression of and engagement with the moment."[30] The saturation of images in the digital world invokes a new relationship between memory and experience, immediacy and detachment, image and vision.

7

THE FUTURE OF PREDICTION: FROM STATISTICAL UNCERTAINTY TO ALGORITHMIC FORECASTS

THE UNCERTAINTY OF THE OPEN FUTURE

The spread of learning algorithms is changing the meaning and forms of prediction, affecting the image of the future and the way to deal with it in the present. Whereas in the current view, the future is seen as open and unknowable because it does not yet exist and depends on present actions and expectations, today's predictive algorithms claim to foresee the future.[1] This claim is both exciting and frightening. It may lead to optimization of the use of resources and to targeted and effective prevention and planning, yet also may bind the future with preemptive policies based on existing patterns.[2] In any case, it breaks with the current idea of the future and management of uncertainty. My point in this chapter is that algorithmic prediction is very different from the idea of prediction that has established itself in modern society since the eighteenth century, oriented and guided by the calculus of probability; that is, it differs from the mathematical treatment of chance that began with the work of Blaise Pascal and Pierre de Fermat in the second half of the seventeenth century.[3] Whereas probability calculus offers a rational way to deal with uncertainty,[4] algorithms claim to provide an individual score for individual persons or singular events.

As studies on the emergence of statistics in the late seventeenth century show, forms of prediction change over time and have important consequences for society. When, as is currently happening, the forecasting agent is an algorithm and not a human being, processes and criteria are different, and results and problems change as well. Algorithmic prediction produces outcomes that would be impossible for a human being to generate, even if equipped with the tools of statistics; yet it also raises different problems that our society has to manage. This chapter aims to investigate these recent developments from a broader social perspective.

We'll see that while machine-learning systems are statistical engines, these systems and statistics are increasingly diverging. In fact, some algorithms, though products of the most advanced scientific practices, bear a surprising resemblance to some of the structures of the magical and divinatory mentality of ancient societies, which today are seen as directly opposed to science. Divination assumed that the future could be known in advance, even if human beings normally could not see it. For centuries instead, scientists of modern society have used statistical tools to manage the future's uncertainty. While machine learning inherits the tools of statistics, it tries, like divination, to foresee future events.[5]

DIVINATORY ASPECTS OF ALGORITHMIC PREDICTION

The task of algorithms is to predict the future. Amit Singhal, the former head of Google Search, explicitly stated this in 2013:[6] that from now on, the primary function of search engines will be anticipating—predicting which information we will need rather than answering queries we have made. The objective of AI, claimed Kitchin, "is more to predict than to understand the world. Prediction trumps explanation."[7] Many projects that previously used digital tools for the purpose of managing information to explain phenomena now have turned to prediction.[8] The goal of precision medicine, for example, is often to guide prognosis and effective treatment, even when the cause of the disease is still unknown. The move of algorithms from explanation to prediction, however, deeply modifies the meaning and the premises of prediction, together with the use of statistics.

Statistical methods can be used for causal explanation, as is currently the case in many areas of research, particularly in the social sciences.[9] A theory suggests hypotheses that are tested with probabilistic tools. Statistics, however, can also be used for empirical prediction. In the first case the aim is finding the "true" model, while in the second case, the goal is finding the best predictive model, with the two goals failing to always overlap. Shmueli shows that in the practice of statistical modeling, the difference between "explaining" and "predicting" is often hidden by a common misconception: if one can explain, it is assumed one can predict.[10] Predictive capability is subordinated to the ability to explain. Instead, the two are different and should be evaluated separately. In the use of models, the indiscrimination between explanation and prediction can lead to serious consequences. For example in the financial crisis of 2007–2008, economists and governmental agencies relied upon the capital asset pricing model (CAPM), which had been evaluated in terms of its explanatory power. But that capacity was not matched by its predictive power, which turned out to be far lower. This worsened the crisis in palpable ways.

Today, however, the availability of very high computing capacity and huge amounts of data generates new possibilities for using statistical tools primarily for predictive purposes. This does not mean, as claimed by some controversial positions in the debate about big data, that explanation has become superfluous and the search for causality obsolete.[11] Instead, it highlights the possibility and the need to distinguish the two goals and to analyze the scientific specificity of prediction, with its forms, its procedures, and its problems—that are different from those of causal explanation.

The modern scientific approach was developed in a time in which science aimed at explaining general results. Even if one can never apply a generalization from a specific finding to other, different cases (the philosopher David Hume's classic problem of induction), probability calculus provides a stringent method and a rational basis for extrapolating from an inevitably circumscribed set of observations to a generalization about all cases.[12] Modern scientific procedures are based on a limited number of carefully selected data, the *experimental* data gathered during sampling that is processed to test the hypothesis formulated by a theory. Collecting all data is not possible, and in the statistical approach, it is not even necessary because one only needs an appropriate sample large enough to be representative. The data, in a sense, are in the service of the theory, that is, serve to validate the hypothesis that explains the phenomena.

Digital procedures work differently in that they rely on enormous amounts of data and on sufficient computing capacity to manage them. Algorithms use *all* data that can be accessed,[13] without "cleaning them up" to correct inaccurate or biased records and without selecting data points, which usually thereby include a myriad of secondary data collected for other purposes. Algorithms that recommend medical procedures, for example, not only use the patients' medical records, but also data from their credit histories, from their relationships with acquaintances, or from their buying habits. The data in this case come before the theory, in the sense that a hypothesis, if formulated, is guided by them. One does not know what one is looking for, but sees what emerges from the data, which are largely unstructured. In the elaboration of the data, one does not look for causal relationships that confirm the hypothesis (because there is no hypothesis); instead, the search is for associations and correlations, for patterns whose detection discloses underlying structures and should make it possible to formulate effective predictions.[14] On the basis of the patterns, one should be able to predict future developments, even if one cannot necessarily explain them. Predictive modeling differs from explanatory modeling.

Models that do not explain often cannot be explained, and the consequence is the much-debated nontransparency of algorithms.[15] While the hypothesis guiding the explicatory approach must be understandable, in predictive modeling, transparency is of secondary importance: one should focus on "predictive accuracy first, then try to understand."[16] Algorithmic methods such as neural networks or random forests are often not interpretable, yet they make it possible to work with heterogeneous data and formulate effective forecasts. One can predict without understanding.[17]

Digital procedures are extremely innovative and their results are often astonishing. Yet a surprising aspect emerges: some features of the predictive use of machine-learning algorithms resemble an ancient, prescientific logic.[18] The terms used in algorithmic prediction ("correlations," "patterns"), the idea of predictions independent of causal relationships, the reference to structures inaccessible to human reasoning, all have ancient and complex traditions in divinatory societies, as in the Middle East and Greece, and as developed in very elaborate ways in Chinese culture.[19] Like algorithms, divinatory procedures were guided by precise techniques that rigidly provided a number of steps to be taken.[20] In both cases there are programs that, unlike scientific practices, do not attempt to explain or understand phenomena, but just try to deal with them.[21]

Like the procedures of machine-learning algorithms, the structures at the basis of divination in ancient times were obscure to the human mind.[22] Divinatory societies relied on the assumption that the world was governed by a cosmic logic and by a basic order that human beings, with their limited capacities, were not able to grasp,[23] just as today we cannot fully understand the procedures of algorithms. Divinatory rationality was not of a scientific but of a ritualistic kind,[24] with the aim not of providing explanations but of managing a "total knowledge" that remained inaccessible.[25] As with algorithms, the goal was not to understand the phenomena but to get directions for action and decision.

The whole universe was taken as infinitely significant, articulated in an inexhaustible network of correspondences.[26] Just as the four seasons corresponded to the four compass points, and the history of a country to its topography, so the life of an individual corresponded to his or her body and his or her fate was inscribed in the order of things. The underlying *correlations* could be captured by identifying configurations and *patterns* in different phenomena: the walnut maple has the same shape as the human brain, the sky is the mirror image of the earth below it, the malformations in newborn humans resemble ominous terrestrial events. These phenomena were all "saying the same thing";[27] therefore, by analyzing patterns in accessible phenomena, divinatory observers believed they could gain indications about correlated, inaccessible ones. From patterns in the liver of sacrificial animals or the flight of birds, with divinatory techniques, one could draw conclusions about the divine plans for the future and directions on the decisions to be taken, without understanding the reason or claiming to explain it.[28]

For many nowadays, the idea that one can make decisions on the basis of the configurations of the liver of a lamb or of the starry sky seems absurd; but the comparison with divinatory practices can enlighten the way in which current algorithmic predictive practices rely upon intricate, barely visible webs of connections.

MANAGING FUTURE UNCERTAINTY

Despite their striking structural similarities, a basic difference separates algorithmic and divinatory procedures: the underlying concept of time. When can a prediction be trusted and what does its credibility rely on? In the ancient divinatory worldview, the idea of anticipating the future was plausible because of the assumption that it was possible to see its structure in advance. The challenge was how. In various forms, in ancient times the basic distinction was between divine temporality and the temporality of human beings. In Mesopotamia the gods used signs to indicate future events to humans.[29] In Greece the gods were placed in eternity (*aeternitas*), while human beings were bound to time (*tempus*).[30] Seen from the divine perspective, the unknowable future appeared no less structured than the past, but human beings could not access it.[31]

In this ancient view, divination was rational, existing as a complex of procedures and techniques that made it possible to "give shape to an amorphous future."[32] To rely on oracles was not superstition and fantasy because of the assumption that the future had a structure already in the present, even if human beings could not know it. The indications one got from omens were uncertain, not because the relationship between the future and the present was uncertain, but because humans could not be sure to properly understand a higher perspective that as a whole remained inaccessible. Divinatory responses were enigmatic and required interpretation. If the verdict turned out to be incorrect, the interpretation was wrong, not the prediction.[33]

This way of seeing time has its consistency and plausibility, but it is not that of the modern world nor of contemporary societies. Our concept of time presents the future as an open field, which today cannot be known either by humans or by any hypothetical superior entity, because it does not yet exist.[34] The future is not a given, but a horizon of the present that moves away as we approach it and can never be reached. What we can know about the future is not the future, but only the present image of the future: our expectations and the information on which they are based. On the basis of these data, which exist and are observable, we can investigate and gather more detailed and reliable information. The prediction takes the form of *planning*: preparing the present to face in a controlled way a future that is always obscure. Because we cannot know in advance what will happen tomorrow, we calculate and manage our present uncertainty. Since the early modern age, the tool for dealing with the uncertainty of the future, instead of divination, has primarily been the *calculus of probabilities*.[35] The calculus does not promise to reveal what will happen tomorrow, but to calculate the probability of a particular future based on how much requisite knowledge we have now in the present (e.g., 40 percent or 27 percent). This enables us to decide something rationally even in face of uncertainty (i.e., even if things can disappoint our expectation).

The approach of statistics was developed in contrast to the divinatory tradition, and its empirical experimental approach became the basis of the scientific and technological attitude of modernity. Instead of interpreting signs, one gathers data; instead of discovering correlations, one notes empirical regularities. This approach was enormously successful, leading to the impressive development of scientific research. Now, however, this very research is producing the advanced techniques of machine learning and algorithmic prediction. These techniques, using statistical tools derived from probability calculus, can be used for prediction, thereby contradicting the assumption of the open, unpredictable future.[36] In ancient times the structure of the future appeared unknowable to humans but not to the gods; today the future appears to be unknowable to humans, yet should be accessible to algorithms.[37] How are algorithmic prediction and probabilistic tradition connected and distinguished?

AVERAGES VERSUS INDIVIDUAL PREDICTION

The key to the smartness of algorithms and all they can do, including make predictions, is the techniques that make it possible for machine-learning systems to autonomously develop the ability to process data and produce their own information. To do this, algorithms need examples of tasks to fulfill, and the web offers a lot of them. If a software program is able to learn, those examples can be used to train algorithms in a more and more accurate and differentiated way. The diversity of contexts on the web becomes the resource for learning and increasing the performance of algorithms.

How do machines learn from examples? To develop this ability, the programmers in machine learning use the tools of statistics.[38] In fact, statistics and probability calculus addressed for centuries the problem of learning from data and produced a number of computational tools to extract information: regression, classification, correlation, and so on. Now machine learning inherits and adopts them, yet uses data in a different way. The goal of statistics is to manage present uncertainty. It addresses the knowledge (or lack of knowledge) of the present, maintaining and confirming the insuperable barrier between the present moment and the open future. Machine learning, instead, addresses the future and has the goal of predicting it. The difference between the two approaches produces a curious relationship of closeness and opposition between machine learning and the tradition of statistics, two formally almost identical cultures that are progressively diverging.[39] Even if they use the same tools, the attitude of machine-learning programmers is very different from that of statisticians, as their problems are different from the ones raised by the "avalanche of numbers" in the nineteenth century.[40]

Statistics wants to contribute to knowing the world by activating a procedure that matches the classical Galilean method: inserting past data into the model and then using it to predict future data, thus verifying the accuracy of the model and eventually correcting it. The goal is explanation: when you do statistics, you want to infer the process by which the data were generated. For machine learning, on the contrary, the purpose is not to explain the phenomena elaborating a model. In many cases, you do not even know if there can be an intelligible model, and the machine can operate without one. The goal of algorithmic processing is not truth but predictive accuracy.[41] In machine learning you start from the assumption that you are dealing with "complex, mysterious and, at least, partly unknowable" models.[42] You do not want to understand them but to know how the future will look like with regard to some variables. Machine learning faces the future and tries to predict it as accurately as possible, independently of our knowledge of the world. As we can read in a web debate, "statistics emphasizes inference, whereas machine learning emphasizes prediction."[43]

As a consequence of their different attitudes, statistics and machine learning produce fundamentally different forms of prediction. Statistics uses samples based on a limited amount of specifically prepared and selected experimental data in order to deal with the statistical universe. Statistics produces findings about the *average of the elements or subjects involved*—that is, results that correspond to nothing specific and to no one in particular (nobody has 1.4 children); however, these results increase our general knowledge. Algorithmic procedures, instead, use all available observational data and work with very large data sets, but produce no general results. They indicate what can be expected *for a specific subject at a given time* on the basis of correlations found in the data.

This feature of algorithmic procedures is similar to ancient divination, which also did not respond to an abstract interest in explanation but to a specific individual's very practical questions: How should I (a particular individual) behave today to be in the most favorable condition tomorrow?[44] Where should the new city be founded? What is the best time to start a battle—or to sow wheat? Will my marriage be successful? The divinatory response produced punctual and individual predictions.[45] Likewise an algorithmic forecast is specific to the case before it. "Whereas forecasting estimates the total number of ice cream cones to be purchased next month in Nebraska, PA [predictive analysis] tells you which *individual* Nebraskans are most likely to be seen with a cone in hand."[46]

This is the main difference between the tradition of statistics and new developments in machine learning. Digital techniques abandon the statistical idea of averaging, in which all elements of a population represent more or less imperfect replicas of the average value.[47] The approach of big data claims to be more realistic because it rejects this abstraction and claims to process individual elements of the population with all their idiosyncrasies and incommensurability. The new frontier of customization will lie in the movement from the search for universals to the understanding of variability. According to the perspective of predictive analytics, "now in medical science we don't want to know . . . just how cancer works; we want to know how your cancer is different from my cancer. . . . Individualization trumps universals."[48] Society is calculated without categorizing individuals, but by considering the specificity of everyone. Calculations start from people's activities and do not try to infer features applicable to larger phenomena.[49]

Paradoxically, the focus on individual specificity is achieved through neglect of the individual perspective, and actually of any perspective.[50] Algorithms should be able to predict the singularity of subjects because they do not depend on what people think and want, nor on what they say they want. Algorithms base their calculations on what people actually do, often without saying so or even without knowing it.[51] What the algorithm treats as the perspective of the single individual is derived from digital "footprints" of people's activities: zip codes, credit reports, driving records, language patterns, friends and relationships, and many other elements that are compared with similar data of other individuals.[52]

But even if algorithms do not depend on a specific perspective, their personalized indications cannot be extended to other cases. They only apply to the available data set (with its implicit biases), to the targeted individual, and to the particular moment. That the results are local, specific and provisional, however, should be their strength. In the words of Andy Clark: "Context, it seems, is everything."[53] Learning algorithms are extremely effective and can achieve impressive results, but only referring to the specific context in which they have been trained. As software programmers know very well, trained machines can be "exquisitely well suited to their environment—and ill adapted to any other."[54] For example, an algorithm that has to answer a question about drapes in a picture does not look for windows but starts its search from the bottom and stops if it finds a bed (because in the data set used to train it, drapes are found on bedroom windows). The results can be very appropriate for that specific data set, yet do not rely on a knowledge of drapes that can be used in different contexts (e.g., in a classification of fabrics). In fact, the algorithm does not know drapes at all. If general results are needed, one has to reconstruct the group inductively, analyzing many different contexts and aggregating them a posteriori[55]—a procedure that is exactly the opposite of the one of classical statistical science.

MANUFACTURING THE PREDICTED FUTURE

According to the criteria of statistics and modern science, the approach of machine learning presents some fundamental liabilities. Like divinatory techniques, algorithmic procedures are contextual, individual, concrete, and basically obscure. These very aspects, however, are the grounds of their predictive effectiveness. Precisely because they address individual cases and specific contexts, algorithms are expected to predict the future. What is this claim about? And does the forecasting really work?

In machine learning, the predictive ability of algorithms depends on the same factors that make their procedures often incomprehensible to the human mind. Machine-learning algorithms are able to identify patterns in the data that cannot be grasped by reasoning because they are not based on meaning. For the same reason, they cannot be captured by standard statistical procedures that depend on models and data samples artificially selected for some reason. These patterns, however, are expected to disclose the structure of the future regardless of subjects' knowledge and intentions.[56] Algorithms should find patterns in the mass of unselected observation data, independent from a model.

The lack of a model should lead to a more direct relationship with reality. But what does reality mean when talking about data? The meaning of "real" is very peculiar and refers only to the lack of sampling, that is, to data independence from an interpretive model. This does not imply that algorithms work with "raw data" that come directly from the world. Setting aside philosophical discussions of interpreting reality and the possibility of knowing it, the idea of raw data is very criticizable and has been thoroughly criticized.[57] Even when the system processes all observational data, the data set on which algorithms work always depends on human intervention: the set includes only the data it includes, could be a different set if it were approached in another way, and has many data points that arise from the behavior and the decisions of people, including decisions about which data is worth collecting in the first place. The procedures of algorithms, moreover, are obviously the result of human design, whether or not the designers themselves know the details of how the machines work. In speaking of "real" data in reference to algorithms, then, you cannot speak of human neutrality or "rawness" of data due to a lack of human intervention.

That algorithms work with real data does not mean that their data faithfully correspond to the outside world in the sense of classical metaphysics.[58] Algorithms are not neutral observers who objectively know the world as it is. Algorithms do not know the world at all—"know" nothing. The point is rather that algorithms are themselves real and part of the world in which they operate—from within, not from the outside referring to a model. This changes the meaning of "prediction." When algorithms make predictions, they do not see in advance an independent external given, the future that is not yet there. This would be impossible. Algorithms "manufacture" with their operations the future they anticipate.[59] Algorithms predict the future shaped by their prediction.

Predictions are individual and contextual, and refer only to the specific item they address. The algorithms used in predictive shopping, for example, do not reveal how consumer buying trends will be in the next season or which products will have an increased or lowered market share. Instead, algorithms anticipate and suggest which specific products an individual consumer will be willing to buy, even before the individual chooses them, and possibly before someone become aware of a need.[60] The products can also be ones that the person does not know, but that the algorithm identifies as compatible with their features and with the past choices that they or other similar people accomplished, according to often inscrutable criteria. If the prediction of the algorithm is correct and the person buys the product, this is not because the algorithm saw the future in advance, in part because that future would not exist without this intervention.[61] The person would not have thought to buy that product and may not have even known of its existence. By suggesting the product to the future buyer, the algorithm produces the future and thereby confirms itself—or learns from experience if the suggestion is rejected.[62] Both errors and correct predictions are useful and help the algorithm to learn, confirming its structures or the need to modify them to take into account new data. In this way, the algorithm becomes increasingly effective in dealing with a world that remains unknown. The same should happen in other cases, such as crime prevention: the prediction should make it possible to act before an individual at risk begins a criminal career.[63]

The claim that the data processed by algorithms are "real" does not refer to an independent world to be described as accurately as possible, but to the result of a process of "active inference" in which prediction error is reduced "using the twin strategies of altering predictions to fit the world, and altering the world to fit the predictions."[64] The world changes as a consequence of algorithms, and algorithms learn from the world how to modify their predictions. Programmers state that "the goal is no longer truth, but performativity. . . . We do no longer (only) decide based on what we know; we know based on the decisions we have to make";[65] "expectations are simultaneously descriptive and prescriptive in nature."[66]

WHEN CORRECT PREDICTIONS ARE WRONG

Despite their limitations, then, algorithmic predictions should always be effective. Even when their anticipations are not realized, algorithms should offer the best possible predictions given the available data, and even the failure of prediction, when it happens, should contribute to learning and improving future performance. If no abstract and general forecasts (as in statistics) are required, for specific cases and in local contexts algorithms should provide accurate and reliable predictive scores, optimizing resource use and enabling humans to detect new possibilities. Tourists discover destinations they would never have thought about and manage to better organize their travels; law enforcement or security agency become more effective; sellers focus their promotions on the relevant portion of a population, avoiding waste and unnecessary annoyance; banks and credit card companies detect more reliable clients and focus their financing on them.

This is not always the case. Critics observe that in some cases the use of algorithms to predict the future may be damaging even when in some sense their predictions are accurate. Harcourt, for example, argues that the increased use of algorithmic tools in criminal law to identify who to search and punish, and how to administer penal sanctions, not only can be morally and politically criticized, but risks undermining the primary goal of law enforcement—namely reducing crime rather than merely increasing arrests.[67] Reliance on prediction can increase the overall amount of crime, not only because the increase in attention on specific targets leads to the discovery of "nuisance crimes" that would otherwise go unnoticed and unpursued, or because an initial bias in the data tends to be reproduced by the use of the model, but also because the target population reacts to the targeting effort.[68] Algorithms are "tools for behavioral modification" whose use must be tempered because they confirm their findings based on the reality they create.[69]

This is the dark side of the performativity of prediction, which reproduces a well-known circularity of divination procedures. If there was no specific intervention,[70] divinatory predictions tended to be self-fulfilling, As the case of Oedipus shows, everything he did to avoid the predicted outcome contributes to the announced conclusion: he will kill his father and sleep with his mother. In the ancient world the circularity of prediction was regarded as the confirmation of the existence of a higher cosmic order and the negation of chaos. In modern cultures referring to an open future, instead, this circularity results in feedback loops and a serious inability to learn. Algorithms see the reality that results from their intervention and do not learn from what they cannot see because it has been canceled by the consequences of their work. The use of algorithms produces a second-order blindness.[71]

The community of programmers is keenly aware of the problems produced by environments that can be changed by the use of algorithms.[72] The environment can even be actively adversarial, as in the use of algorithms for credit rating purposes that drive people to meet the criteria to which algorithms are oriented. In most of these cases, though, the problems are social rather than technical. Algorithms participate in communication, and this has consequences. According to Harcourt's argument, for example, if algorithmically profiled persons are less responsive to changes in police policies than others, concentrating crime prevention measures on profiled people can be counterproductive because profiled individuals often have little choice and commit crimes anyway.[73] Other areas of the population where surveillance and prevention could be effective instead remain uncovered, and overall crime increases. The algorithm is trained on the world as it was before the action of the algorithm, and thus finds out the most relevant cases: individuals at risk of crime, or products that the user is more likely to buy.[74] The algorithm then gets answers about these items, and learns if its predictions were correct or not. But it can happen that the products that the user actually decides to buy, or the individuals who actually commit crimes, continue to escape the prediction because they initially had a very low probability of being targeted, and become more relevant only as a result of the action of the algorithm.[75] Crime increases because surveillance has moved elsewhere, or niche products become more attractive as a reaction to personalized advertisements of mass products.[76]

The problem is not so much that the punctual prediction of algorithms can be wrong, but that how the future was prepared for is wrong. It is a social problem that must be faced by studying social structures—that is, the environment of prediction. Precise predictions activate reactions that can lead to self-fulfilling or self-defeating circularities, and also (at the same time) to *preemptive* policies, which limit future possibilities.[77] If decisions are taken today on security measures about individuals who are profiled as possible criminals, their behavior is constrained, but also the options of the decision-maker are limited. If then the crimes turn out to happen somewhere else, one will be watching the wrong people. Or, as in the case of recommendation systems, the use of self-learning algorithms may produce a biased and incomplete view of the future preferences of the users, because the system only sees the responses of users to the recommended items and not to other items, and still doesn't know how they would have reacted to the ignored ones. An algorithm doesn't get any information on users for whom no recommendation has been made, while at the same time targeting mostly clients who were already interested.[78] The problem in this case is not just the risk of a wrong prediction, but the reduction of future possibilities for all involved actors.

BLINDNESS AND OVERFITTING

The difficulties of algorithmic prediction are different from the ones of statistical forecasting.[79] The problems do not arise from sampling problems, data shortages, or from the use of misleading interpretive models. Algorithms do not have these worries. Their difficulties depend instead on specific problems of machine learning and in particular on the way algorithms address the relationship between the past and the future.

Algorithms are trained by maximizing their performance on some set of training data, which came from the past.[80] The predictive effectiveness of algorithms, however, depends on their ability to perform well on previously unseen data that will appear in the future. Training data and real data are as different as the past is different from the future, yet algorithms only know the training data, and the difference between the two sets gives rise to a number of difficulties,[81] which we often are not equipped to face.[82]

The first consequence is a recognized major problem in machine learning and practice: the problem of *generalization*.[83] In machine learning, to effectively generalize means to use what is known to make a prediction about something the algorithm hasn't seen before, as practical experience constantly requires us to do. Every communication, every sentence, every viewing of an object is different from any previous communication or viewing.[84] How can algorithms deal with the difference between the training data they know and an unknown variety of future data?

Again, the problem is well known to the machine-learning community and intensely debated. Learning algorithms must find a balance between two partially incompatible objectives. Training error must be minimized and the algorithm must learn to process successfully the examples on which it is trained. If not, the problem is *underfitting*: the algorithm has poor performances and is unable to solve complex problems. At the same time, test error should be minimized, increasing the effectiveness of dealing with examples never seen before. If the algorithm learns to work well on the examples given to it, but becomes rigid with respect to each variation, *predictive* error will increase: the algorithm has learned the training examples so well that it becomes blind to every new item. The problem in this case is *overfitting*, which has been called "the bugbear of machine learning."[85] Overfitting arises when the system builds its own rigid and somewhat autistic image of objects, losing the ability to capture the empirical variety of the world. The system is overly adapted to the examples it knows. For example, it learned so well to interact with the right-handed users it has been trained with that it does not recognize a left-handed person as a possible user. In technical terms, the system fails to effectively distinguish relevant information (a signal) from the irrelevant (noise). In sociological terms, the experience of the past risks undermining the openness of the future.

In conditions of high complexity and high uncertainty, the risk of overfitting increases because the noise component tends to increase more than the signal component—the future tends to become more and more different from the past. There are more elements of the past that should be neglected to effectively predict the future, otherwise the predictions of the system only reproduce the past and its idiosyncrasies. The problem is determining which elements to ignore, that is, to effectively forget. As argued in chapter 5, however, deciding to forget is always a tricky issue.[86] Overfitting is a risk for all learning systems, especially when learning is performed too long or training examples are rare (few items are observed and in too much detail); however, it is particularly a risk dealing with big data. In very large datasets, often the data are high dimensional and many elements are new.[87] Elements can be images, handwritten digits, or informal conversations that involve a large number of aspects, many of which are idiosyncratic and different each time. Diversity is so high that even with a lot of available data, the number of examples is still insufficient for the dimensions involved.[88] In practice it is as if training were always too long and the sample always too small. Learning this past data is not enough to predict the future that does not yet exist.

MEMORY AND FANTASY

About the future algorithms produce, they are and remain blind to it. How can this condition be addressed? In order to avoid the risks of overfitting and corresponding hallucinatory results, machine-learning programmers are often recommended to favor simpler systems, because complexity would tend to increase noise rather than prediction accuracy.[89] The problem is discussed in terms of the relationship between *bias* and *variance*,[90] wherein bias measures how accurate the model is, and variance, how different its predictions are from each other. From the sociological perspective bias corresponds to memory and variance to fantasy, with more complex systems tending to have high bias (that is, adherence to the past). That bias is not necessarily wrong (many stereotypes have a realistic basis), yet is unhelpful on another level because it narrows the focus and prevents models from seeing what does not match their preconceived ideas. Simpler systems would be less accurate but more open, and therefore, more capable of dealing with the unpredictability of the new.

The problem is related to the management of the relationship between the past and the future, which is traditionally the task of memory. An overfitted system practically memorizes the past and uses this skill to predict the future. Hindsight is more accurate than foresight, and the system risks having poor predictive performances and being prone to generalization errors. To deal with overfitting, then, data scientists propose to "drag down" the algorithm by imposing random errors that prevent learning from becoming too accurate.[91] Other solutions recommend forgetting the past altogether: memory is thus seen as a form of bias, and prediction jeopardizes the openness to novelty.[92]

Is this necessarily the best solution? To better face the future, should one remember worse? As Nietzsche claimed, the ability to forget is crucial to being able to deal with the world, to hope and to learn;[93] but on the other hand, without memories, you could not plan and would have to start anew every time.[94] The result is not better. Those who do not remember the past are not necessarily innovative, and often tend to unknowingly produce trivial and old forms.[95] The evolution of social memory shows that it is possible to simultaneously increase knowledge of the past and openness to the future.[96] In modern society the systematic study of the past led to development of the sense of history, but also to the ability to see the future as an open horizon.[97] The modern age has abandoned the idea that the future reproduces the past and has started to deal with and even value novelty and surprise. Modern society has developed a memory that is capable of forgetting more because it can remember enormously more.

CONCLUSION

The challenge of prediction in our digital society is to combine individual algorithmic forecasting with the openness of the future—a challenge that seems to take the form of the paradox of combining prediction with unpredictability. Can we know our future in advance and still be surprised? Can we proactively act on coming events without constraining future creativity and the possibility to innovate?

Algorithmic predictions, like ancient divinatory predictions, are contextual, individualized, and basically obscure. Despite the many analogies, however, algorithmic prediction is fundamentally different from divination. Our contemporary world is not the structured universe of divination, in which it was assumed that a global higher order coordinated all phenomena. Even when algorithmic prediction contributes to producing specific predicted events, digital forecast acts in an incomparably more complex, reactive, and unstable social environment than divination—and in a world that does not necessarily have a fundamental order. In divinatory semantics the idea of seeing in advance the structures of the future could be plausible. But in modern society, and even more so in the digitized society in which algorithms work, the intensity of communication is such that any prediction, even if correct, is anticipated, commented on, and reworked, producing new unpredictable complexity with no guarantee of a basic order. An adequate analysis of the effectiveness and the problems of predictive algorithms cannot only be technical, but requires considering the social and communicative conditions of their use.

CONCLUSION

Can a computer devise a theory of everything? This question is debated in 2020 in an article in the *New York Times* that presents the possibility that a machine equipped with the most sophisticated deep-learning technologies, capable of sifting data for patterns and autonomously discovering basic formulas of physics, could connect the findings into a unified theory of the universe.[1] It would seem a surprising outcome of the debate on the "end of theory" started by Chris Anderson in 2008 in *Wired*,[2] but in fact, the premise is the same: "The end might not be in sight for theoretical physics. But it might be in sight for theoretical physicists."[3] The theory would be produced by self-programming machines and would be incomprehensible to humans and independent of our forms of reasoning. To deny this possibility, according to Tegmark, would be to engage in a form of "carbon chauvinism."[4]

But is it really convenient to put it in these terms? What is the point of an incomprehensible theory, and do we need one? Within days of that *New York Times* article, the possibility of using the autonomous work of algorithms to deal with the classic "protein folding problem" was announced: machine learning was able to predict the three-dimensional shape of a protein given the string of amino acids that compose it, in a way completely different from human research.[5] This development could speed the discovery of new drugs and improve the treatment of viruses and diseases—but not because the algorithms had devised a theory, which in any case would be incomprehensible. Instead, they had learned to reliably predict the shape of proteins by analyzing thousands of known cases and their physical shapes. If the result of their prediction is reliable, is the basic issue really "to have machines that can think like a physicist," as Jesse Thaler wishes?[6] Or is it rather to find a way to communicate efficiently with these incomprehensible machines, in order to use their results and control possible errors or undesired effects?

As I have argued in the previous chapters, the latter is the challenge posed by the development of nontransparent algorithms, capable of learning and programming themselves. Communication is a complex and multifaceted process, and observing the working of algorithms in this perspective discloses a multiplicity of fascinating and difficult questions. Some problems dissolve, others take a different form, and still others arise.

For example, the controversial question at the basis of the Turing test *dissolves*: how do we know if our interlocutor is a human being or a machine? Seventy years after the publication of the article in which the test was proposed,[7] and after countless discussions and comments, the answer did not come from some elaborated version of the test, but simply from interaction with algorithms: in most cases the answer does not matter at all. If anything, it is the machines that have to make sure with some version of captcha,[8] that their interlocutors are people. Rather, what matters is that the communication works, that the partner participates in an interesting, informative, reliable, and even entertaining, way. Normally there is not the time and the motivation to question whether it is a machine or a human being.

Other issues, such as the thorny problem of bias, take another form. Bias has become one of the most discussed and difficult issues to deal with in all practical applications of artificial intelligence.[9] Algorithms are biased, as we know very well, and they produce biased results. Facial-recognition systems are more accurate in identifying white faces than those of other people,[10] programs used to predict crime disproportionately target certain ethnic groups and certain neighborhoods,[11] artificial intelligence chatbots on the web tend to post racist and offensive tweets.[12] In many fields, including insurance, advertising, education, and credit scoring, the use of algorithms and big data can lead to decisions that increase inequality and discrimination.[13] Yet do these outcomes depend on the kind of intelligence that is artificially produced in the algorithms?

Crawford, among many others, claims that "like all technologies before it, artificial intelligence will reflect the values of its creators."[14] Is this really the problem, when we are dealing with machines that program themselves? After all, it is not entirely clear that the designers of the algorithms are actually the creators of the procedures that are put in place. It seems to me that the problem in this case is not so much that the working of the machines reflects the biases of their creators, but on the contrary, that it is biased in large part because their workings do *not* reflect their creators' values. Algorithm designers inevitably have their own prejudices, conscious or not, and in the field of AI they are predominantly white and male.[15] It is very likely, then, that the algorithms themselves will be shaped accordingly. The most significant problem, however, is not that algorithms reflect the biases of their creators—who, granted, do tend to be white men. Rather, algorithmic bias is only one component of the problem. Deeper, and more difficult to manage is what is often labeled as "data bias," which does not depend on the values of the programmers.[16] Instead, it depends on the underlying source of the algorithms' efficiency: the access to the big data they find on the web, which frequently builds upon the uncoordinated input of billions of participants, sensors, and other digital sources. Machines participate in a communication that is neither neutral nor egalitarian, and they learn to work correspondingly, in ways that can be biased very differently from the preferences of their designers.[17] In pursuing the goal of algorithmic justice,[18] then, the most difficult problems are communicative, not cognitive.

Finally, other problems *arise* when the focus shifts to communication. Practical experience with the use of algorithms for specific tasks, now accumulated in many fields, has almost inadvertently led to the emergence of diverse, and extremely complex, issues related to their involvement in communication. In law, for example, "mechanical jurisprudence"[19] is already a reality: computational systems of legal reasoning are capable of exploring legal databases, discovering patterns, identifying the relevant rules, applying them, generating arguments—and even explaining their chain of reasoning to the users.[20] However, the problems that arise and animate the debate do not concern the fact that the author of the reasoning is a machine. As Canale and Tuzet claim, "Jurisdictional motivation does not consist in the psychological account of the process that led to the decision, but in the indication of the legal reasons that justify it."[21]

It is communication that must work, and it is not simple. How can the fundamental ambiguity of legal argumentation be reproduced in communication with algorithms?[22] To account for the inevitable variety of cases and contexts, legal arguments are "typically vague and ambiguous,"[23] and legal communication must be "susceptible of more than one reasonable interpretation."[24] The task of lawyers—as Garfinkel claims—is to make ambiguous the interpretations of facts and laws.[25] For algorithms, however, ambiguity is notoriously a challenge. Machines not only struggle with understanding the ambiguity of human communication, they struggle harder to *generate* ambiguous communication—that is, to use in competent ways the ambiguity required by legal arguments.

The debate about the difference between explanation and interpretation in law reflects this difficulty.[26] What machines do to make their decision transparent—as demanded by explainable AI—is to illustrate in detail the procedural steps through which their decisions were produced. This requires a "decision analysis in microscopic refinement," far beyond what is produced in communication between human beings.[27] For effective communication among humans, it is sufficient to regulate "the presentation, not the production of the decision."[28] Interpretation can and often must remain vague, because it is "not concerned with how we understand or produce texts, but with how we establish the acceptability of a specific reading thereof."[29] To explain their decisions, lawyers and judges must provide a convincing account, which does not necessarily imply that they reconstruct all passages of their reasoning—and their recipients interpret them as they choose. When coping with algorithms, instead, interpretation often coincides with explanation—without the required space for vagueness and without using ambiguity. Paradoxically, one could say that the problem of interpretation in legal argumentation— even and precisely when dealing with algorithms whose processes are hidden from human intelligence—is not that the machine does not explain enough, but that it explains too much, and too precisely. The problem is not how the machine works, but how it communicates.

Problems of this kind, which affect all sectors of society in specific forms, cannot be grasped, let alone dealt with, without an adequate theory of communication and a thorough knowledge of different social domains. The analysis of the most pressing problems related to the use of algorithms in our society is not only a technical issue, but first of all a communicative issue—an issue of artificial communication.

ACKNOWLEDGMENTS

This book benefited from the support and encouragement of many institutions and people, and I am grateful for the intellectual stimulations that shaped the project.

I have been fortunate to benefit from a high level of discussions with fellows at the Italian Academy at Columbia University, the Institute of Advanced Studies at the University of Warwick, MECS at Leuphana University Lüneburg, the Institute for Advanced Study at Zhejiang University, and recently the Wissenschaftskolleg in Berlin. Special thanks to Achille Varzi, Claus Pias, Martin Warnke, Celia Lury, Noortje Marres, Nicole Brisch, Dror Wahrmann, Holger Spamann, Cansu Cansa, Luca Giuliani, Barbara Stollberg-Rillinger, and Daniel Schönpflug. Thanks to Barbara Carnevali and Emanuele Coccia for great ideas and conversations during my stay at EHESS in Paris.

Research for this book was supported by an Advanced Research grant from the European Research Council for the PREDICT project no. 833749.

Starting with the Niklas Luhmann Visiting Chair that gave me the impetus to initiate this research, Bielefeld University provided me with the best working and research conditions. For this I will always be grateful to Rector Gerhard Sagerer. Silke Schwandt, Kirsten Kramer, Tobias Werron, Holger Dainat, and the participants in our seminars helped me to adjust the focus of my reflections and to clarify my questions. The kindness of Vito Gironda and Anita Adamczyk made many things easier and more enjoyable. James McNally and Jonas Mieke have collaborated with precision and intelligence in preparing and revising my texts.

David Weinberger transformed the revision and correction of texts into an exciting intellectual adventure, which also turned out to be fun. Working with him is a privilege. At the MIT Press I am grateful to have been in the care of Gita Devi Manaktala and Erika Barrios. I am honored that Alicja Kwade provided the image for the book's cover, and I especially appreciate how she engaged with the content of the volume in choosing the image.

Giancarlo Corsi and Alberto Cevolini joined me in years of collaboration and lively debate, of which my entire work bears the traces. My ideas have been developed in constant dialogue with David Stark, engaging with his acute critical sense and inexhaustible creativity and enthusiasm. I can't thank him enough for his generosity, wonderful sense of humor, and ever-amazing ability to surprise me.

Emma's curiosity and passion are a joy every day.

NOTES

INTRODUCTION

1. Seabrook, "Can a Machine Learn to Write?"

2. Mori, "The Uncanny Valley."

3. On the ability of algorithms of carrying out sophisticated conversations in a "natural" way, see Welch, "Google Just Gave a Stunning Demo."

4. Alan Turing proposed the Turing test in "Computing Machinery and Intelligence" to evaluate the ability of a machine to exhibit intelligent behavior. The machine passes the test if an observer cannot distinguish its contributions in a natural language conversation from those of its human partner.

5. See, e.g., Kurzweil, *The Singularity Is Near*; Bostrom, *Superintelligence*.

6. From Searle, "Minds, Brains and Programs" (1980), to Negarestani, *Intelligence and Spirit* (2018).

7. Eco, *Opera aperta*.

8. That they are controlled obviously does not mean that they are correct, neutral, or should be accepted without reservation or criticism. As the dynamics of feedback show, the presence of control does not exclude risks, manipulations, or negative results. On the other hand, human control, as is well known, is certainly not a guarantee of success, nor even of rationality.

9. Quoted in Seabrook, "Can a Machine Learn to Write for *The New Yorker*?"

CHAPTER 1

1. This chapter is a heavily revised version of "Artificial Communication? The Production of Contingency by Algorithms," *Zeitschrift für Soziologie* 46, no. 4 (2017): 249–265.

2. Ferrara et al., "The Rise of Social Bots"; Imperva, *The Imperva Global Bot Traffic Report 2019*.

3. According to Twitter itself, which provides users a tool, Twitteraudit, to calculate how many of their followers are "real" (meaning human beings).

4. In the first three-quarters of 2020, Facebook "disabled" 4.5 billion fake accounts. See Facebook's transparency report: https://transparency.facebook.com/community -standards-enforcement#fake-accounts.

5. Kloc, "Wikipedia Is Edited by Bots."

6. Kollanyi, Howard, and Woolley, "Bots and Automation over Twitter."

7. Gillespie, "Algorithms, Clickworkers, and the Befuddled Fury."

8. See Miklós, "Computer Respond to This Email."

9. Pierce, "Spotify's Latest Algorithmic Playlist."

10. See https://www.narrativescience.com.

11. See https://automatedinsights.com.

12. Podolny, "If an Algorithm Wrote This?"; Peiser, "The Rise of the Robot Reporter."

13. Youyou, Kosinski, and Stillwell, "Computer-Based Personality Judgments Are More Accurate."

14. Here the founding event is generally considered to be the Dartmouth Conference of 1956: see Moor, "The Dartmouth College Artificial Intelligence Conference."

15. For more on al-Khwarīzmī, see Chabert, *A History of Algorithms*.

16. Davis, *Computability and Unsolvability*, xv.

17. Esposito, "Algorithmische Kontingenz." Whereas in classical AI, an algorithm is the sequence of actions that must be performed to calculate a result, in machine learning, the term indicates the sequence of actions performed to make the machine learn the distinctions one wants to obtain. In the first case executing an algorithm means doing a calculation; in the second case it means "tuning" the system. I thank Stefano Borgo for this clarification.

18. "Do we want more effective machine learning models without clear theoretical explanations, or simpler, transparent models that are less effective in solving specific tasks?" asks Peng in "LeCun vs Rahimi?" It has even been claimed that in the field of machine learning a certain "inexplicability" can be a positive factor, because imprecision and errors make the working of algorithms more flexible, and are neutralized by the increase in data; see Mayer-Schönberger and Cukier, *Big Data*, 33.

19. Burrell, "How the Machine 'Thinks.'"

20. Borgo, "Ontological Challenges to Cohabitation with Self-Taught Robots."

21. For Hans Blumenberg's metaphor, see Blumenberg, "Nachahmung der Natur."

22. The idea of a progressive autonomy from human performance is not new: all media introduce a form of communication that in some respect becomes autonomous from a direct coordination with human processes: see Luhmann, *Die Gesellschaft der Gesellschaft*, 216–217. In written communication it is not necessary that

the partners are present, whereas press and mass media do not even require that they know anything about each other or that they have ever met. The readers produce their own communication, with a rhythm, a timing, and an order that can be quite different from those of the issuer. The information that the receiver gets is increasingly independent from what the issuer had in mind. With algorithms, however, apparently it is not even necessary that the issuer ever had any information in mind.

23. Goodfellow, Bengio, and Courville, *Deep Learning*, 15; and Wolchover, "AI Recognizes Cats the Same Way."

24. "In trying to build a thinking machine, scientists have so far succeeded only in reiterating the mystery of how our brain thinks." Seabrook, "Can a Machine Learn to ?"

25. Searle, "Mind, Brains and Programs."

26. Solon, "Weavrs: The Autonomous, Tweeting Blog-Bots."

27. Boellstorff, "Making Big Data, in Theory."

28. Hammond, *Practical Artificial Intelligence for Dummies*, 7.

29. Silver and Hassabis, "AlphaGo: Mastering the Ancient Game of Go." The programmers of Libratus, the poker AI that defeated the best human players in January 2017, say that "it develops a strategy completely independently from human play, and it can be very different from the way humans play the game"; see Metz, "Inside Libratus, the Poker AI That Out-Bluffed."

30. Grossman, "How Computers Know What We Want"; and Ktichin, "Big Data, New Epistemologies and Paradigm Shifts," 4.

31. Youyou, Kosinski, and Stillwell, "Computer-based personality judgments are more accurate," 1036.

32. Rogers, *Digital Methods*, 155; and Vis, "A Critical Reflection on Big Data."

33. The very distinction between social facts and personal opinions seems to be fading; see Latour, "Beware, Your Imagination Leaves Digital Traces."

34. Seaver, "Algorithmic Recommendations and Synaptic Functions."

35. Hayles, *How We Became Posthuman*; Braidotti, *The Posthuman*.

36. Shannon and Weaver's transmission model of communication is still the (revised and supplemented) basis of most sociological and semiotic approaches. Shannon and Weaver, *The Mathematical Theory of Communication*; Fiske, *Introduction to Communication Studies*; Eco, *Trattato di semiotica generale*, 65–69.

37. Data that exist as simply differences become informative when contextualized and interpreted. On the distinction between data and information, see Bateson, *Steps to an Ecology of Mind*, 582.

38. "We should take seriously the possibility that humans and robots act according to views of reality that are . . . largely incommunicable." Borgo, "Ontological Challenges to Cohabitation with Self-Taught Robots," 2.

39. In the sense of semiotics' "aberrant decoding": see Eco and Fabbri, "Progetto di ricerca sull'utilizzazione dell'informazione ambientale."

40. Luhmann, *Soziale Systeme*; *Die Gesellschaft der Gesellschaft*.

41. Luhmann, "Was ist Kommunikation?," 113.

42. Von Foerster, "Notes on an Epistemology for Living Things," 6.

43. Or writes, or indicates, or broadcasts—the concept is not bound to oral communication. See Luhmann, *Soziale Systeme*, 193–201.

44. Communication is technically defined as the unity of three selections: information, utterance (*Mitteilung*) and understanding; see Luhmann, *Soziale Systeme*, 196. To be precise, it should be specified that the understanding included in the definition of communication has a social and not a psychic reference: it does not coincide with what the receiver understands and thinks, but refers to the potential of meaning (*Sinn*) available to any possible participant in the communication; cf. Luhmann, "Wie ist Bewußtsein an Kommunikation beteiligt?" and Luhmann, *Die Gesellschaft der Gesellschaft*, 73.

45. On Luhmann's theory of society, see his *Die Gesellschaft der Gesellschaft*.

46. That communication is not made of thoughts, however, does not mean that communication can proceed without the participation of thinking people. If no one listens and no one participates, communication doesn't occur. Communication requires participants who think; nevertheless, is not made of their thoughts. One doesn't need to enter the mind of a partner to understand his or her communication, and a third party will always understand it in a different (but also legitimate) way. One just needs to make sense of what has been said.

47. Or possibly an animal when people claim to communicate with their dogs.

48. A test on WeChat (a popular messaging app in China) with the chatbot xiaoice (May 29, 2015) showed that people generally don't care that they are chatting with a machine; see Wang, "Your Next New Best Friend Might Be a Robot." In a few weeks, xiaoice had become the sixth-most-active celebrity on Weibo and had tens of billions of conversations with people, mostly about private matters. The experiment has been considered the largest Turing test in history.

49. In philosophy, and specifically in modal logic, "contingent" indicates something that is neither necessary nor impossible, that may exist but may also not exist or be otherwise. See, e.g., Hughes and Cresswell, *An Introduction to Modal Logic*.

50. Von Foerster, "Cibernetica ed epistemologia: storia e prospettive," 129.

51. See https://anki.com/en-us/cozmo for the company's website.

52. Pierce, "Meet the Smartest, Cutest AI-Powered Robot."

53. Esposito, "Risiko und Computer: Das Problem der Kontrolle," 93–108; on Weinberger's discussion of "Give up control" as a strategic principle of digital culture, see Weinberger, *Everything Is Miscellaneous*, 105.

54. See Turkle, *Alone Together*. It is not only children who do this, and it does not only happen in interactions with anthropomorphic devices, nor indeed zoomorphic

devices like robotic seals and dogs. Various experiments show that people, without realizing it, deal with computers as if they were real people; see Nass and Yan, *The Man Who Lied to His Laptop.*

55. Turkle, *Alone Together*, 26. This is also true in the case of refined robots like Cozmo. Pierce, in "Meet the Smartest, Cutest AI-Powered Robot," writes that "it's up to the humans playing with them to provide creativity." Dill, in "What Is Game AI?" 3–4, notes that in video game design, the basic issue is "creating the illusion of intelligence . . . rather than creating true intelligence."

56. Russell and Norvig, *Artificial Intelligence. A Modern Approach*, 763–764; Etzioni, "Deep Learning Isn't a Dangerous Magic Genie."

57. Hardy, "Artificial Intelligence Software Is Booming."

58. O'Reilly, "What Is Web 2.0: Design Patterns and Business Models"; Berners-Lee, Hendler, and Lassila, "The Semantic Web: A New Form of Web Content ."

59. More details on this follow in chapter 4.

60. Langville and Meyer, *Google's PageRank and Beyond*, 4–5.

61. Metz, "If Xerox Parc Invented the PC, Google Invented the Internet."

62. Page et al., *The PageRank Citation Ranking*. Interestingly, along with Larry Page, Sergey Brin, and Rajeev Motwani, the fourth author is Terry Winograd, who a decade earlier wrote with Fernando Flores one of the reference texts for a communication-oriented approach to artificial intelligence; see Winograd and Flores, *Understanding Computer and Cognition.*

63. Page et al., *PageRank Citation Ranking*, 3.

64. See Weinberger, *Taxonomies to Tags*, 8–9. Yahoo's Editor in Chief Srinija Srinivasan said to Weinberger: "Our job is to know the web, know what searchers want, and marry the two."

65. Grimmelmann, "The Google Dilemma," 941.

66. Gillespie, "The Relevance of Algorithms."

67. Granka, "The Politics of Search: A Decade Retrospective," 367.

68. See https://www.google.com/insidesearch/howsearchworks/ (accessed November 8, 2018).

69. Hamburger, "Building the Star Trek Computer."

70. According to cofounder Stewart Butterfield, search on tags at Flickr "is like page rank for pictures"—cited in Weinberger, *Taxonomies to Tags*, 23.

71. Rogers, *Digital Methods*, 83–94.

72. Vaidhyanathan, *The Googlization of Everything*, 51.

73. Luhmann, *Einführung in die Systemtheorie*, 143. The real innovation in communication with algorithms is that selection is no longer oriented to meaning. "The unity of utterance (*Mitteilung*) and understanding is abandoned"—even if both are still required in any communication: Luhmann, *Die Gesellschaft der Gesellschaft*, 309.

74. And obviously many communications involve manufactured entities: ANT's sociotechnical devices; see, e.g., Callon, "The Role of Hybrid Communities and Socio-Technical Arrangements." But they do not participate as communication partners.

75. All social objects are constructed, hence not natural; but this does not mean that in using them, one communicates. One does not communicate with the maker of a corkscrew by understanding how it works, or communicate with the corkscrew itself, see Eco, "Ci sono delle cose che non si possono dire," 22–25. One can communicate through objects, as in the case of works of art or design, and of course in the case of books—but then one communicates with the author. The object is artificial, not the communication.

76. Supervision or reinforcement are needed to direct the learning process toward useful results or to select the meaningful ones. The approach of machine learning is quite general: algorithms can be applied to solve a wide range of problems, from playing Go to controlling the parameters of a cooling system to improve fuel efficiency; see Taylor, "The Concept of 'Cat Face.'"

77. Quoted in Pierce, "Smartest, Cutest AI-Powered Robot."

78. Reinforcement can come from programmers, but algorithms that operate online recently began to regularly receive reinforcement directly from the web, taking as a reference the participation of users. In interactions with users a learning algorithm can gather a lot of reinforcement from the behavior of people—on how people are likely to react, and whether or not they accept an algorithm's proposals or continue searching. Once again one of the clearest examples can be found in Google, through the auto-correct function of its online spell check. The frequent question "did you mean . . . ?" that the algorithm addresses to users serves first of all to produce reinforcement.

79. Silver and Hassabis, "AlphaGo: Mastering the Ancient Game of Go ."

80. Schölkopf, "Learning to See and Act."; Mnih et al., "Human-Level Control."

81. Metz, "How Google's AI Viewed the Move." In this process of "self-supervised" learning, the algorithm becomes incomparably better than the players from which it learned, who would not be able to understand its moves; see Etzioni, Banko and Cafarella, "Machine Reading." The most recent version does not even need to have starting data from human players: AlphaGo Zero is trained solely by self-play reinforcement learning; see Silver et al., "Mastering the Game of Go."

82. Burrell, "How the Machine 'Thinks'"; Weinberger, "Machines Now Have Knowledge"; Gilpin et al., "Explaining Explanations: An Overview of Interpretability of Machine Learning."

83. Metz, "What the AI Behind AlphaGo."

84. Ke Jie, a Chinese grandmaster who met AphaGo in a match in May 2017, explicitly declared that the algorithm changed the way top masters play the game, making moves that are reminiscent of AlphaGo's own style. See Mozur, "Google's AlphaGo Defeats Chinese Go Master."

85. Metz, "In Two Moves, AlphaGo and Lee Sedol Redefined the Future"; Taylor, "The Concept of 'Cat Face.'"

86. AlphaGo actually also won the three-match series against Ke Jie in May 2017.

87. Etzioni, "Deep Learning Isn't a Dangerous Magic Genie."

88. "Because the methods we have used are general purpose, our hope is that one day they could be extended to help us address some of society's toughest and most pressing problems": Silver and Hassabis, "AlphaGo: Mastering the Ancient Game." The techniques developed in AlphaGo are presently used to deal with scientific issues, as for example the "protein folding problem," possibly leading to the development of new drugs or innovative ways to apply existing medications. John Jumper, a lead scientist on the DeepMind team developing these technologies, said: "We don't want to be a leader board company. We want to have real biological relevance." Quoted in Metz, "London A.I. Lab Claims Breakthrough That Could Accelerate Drug Discovery."

89. Pasquale, *The Black Box Society*.

90. Wachter, Mittelstadt, and Floridi, "Transparent, Explainable, and Accountable AI"; Doshi-Velez et al., "Accountability of AI Under the Law"; Miller, "Explanation in Artificial Intelligence"; Rohlfing et al., "Explanation as a Social Practice."

91. Weinberger, "Our Machines Now Have Knowledge."

92. On the distinction between transparency and post-hoc interpretability, see Lipton, "The Mythos of Model Interpretability."

93. See, e.g., Cimiano, Rudolph, and Hartfiel, "Computing Intentional Answers to Questions,"; Karim and Zhou, "X-TREPAN: An Extended Trepan for Comprehensibility and Classification Accuracy ." Suchman, in *Plans and Situated Actions* (1987), already explored the possibility of a collaboration between human beings and machines in producting intelligibility, relying on the exploitation of their differences in understanding.

94. Luhmann, *Gesellschaft der Gesellschaft*, 304.

95. Lévy, *L'Intelligence collective*.

CHAPTER 2

1. A previous version of this chapter appeared in *Zeitschrift für Literaturwissenschaft und Linguistik* 47, no. 3 (2017): 351–359.

2. Eco, *Vertigine della lista*, 290.

3. Poole, "Top Nine Things You Need to Know."

4. Oring, "Jokes on the Internet."

5. Poole, "Top Nine Things You Need to Know."

6. Espeland and Sauders, "Rankings and Reactivity"; Musselin, *La Grande Course des Universités*; Langohr and Langohr, *The Rating Agencies and Their Credit Ratings*; Levich, Majnoni, and Reinhard, *Ratings, Rating Agencies*; Scott and Orlikowski,

Most

"Reconfiguring Relations of Accountability"; Mennicken, "'Too Big to Fail and Too Big to Succeed'"; Mennicken, "Numbers and Lists: Ratings and Rankings in Healthcare"; Cooley and Snyder, *Ranking the World: Grading States as a Tool of Global Governance*; Esposito and Stark, "What's Observed in a Rating? Rankings as Orientation in the Face of Uncertainty."

7. Karpik, "La Guide rouge Michelin"; and Karpik, *L'économie des singularités*, 113.

8. Stuart, "Reputational Rankings: Background and Development."

9. Borges, "The Analytical Language of John Wilkins."

10. Von Contzen, "Die Affordanzen der Liste," 322; Weinberger, *Everything Is Miscellaneous*, 66.

11. Hunger and Archi, "Vicino Oriente"; Goody, *The Domestication of the Savage Mind*.

12. Luria, *Cognitive Development*, 12–19.

13. Ong, *Orality and Literacy*, 42–43, 48–56.

14. Goody, *Domestication of the Savage Mind*, 104.

15. Annus, "On the Beginnings and Continuities of Omen Sciences."

16. Weinberger, *Everything Is Miscellaneous*.

17. The often completely heterogeneous elements collected in a flat list are in a relationship of equivalence: see Schaffrick and Werber, "Die Liste, paradigmatisch," 307.

18. Bowker and Star describe list making as "one of the fundamental activities of advanced human society": Bowker and Star, *Sorting Things Out*, 137.

19. According to Mainberger, lists have the effect that what is near appears far away and what is far away near. Mainberger, "Exotisch—endotisch oder Georges Perec lernt von Sei Shonagon," 334.

20. "A list is our most basic way of ordering ideas. . . . If it got any simpler, it wouldn't be organized at all": Weinberger, *Everything Is Miscellaneous*, 65.

21. Doležalová, "Ad Hoc Lists of Bernard Itier (1163–1225)," 80.

22. Cf. Havelock, *Origins of Western Literacy*, chapter 3. With a certain approximation, one can say that in syllabic writing the same sign stands for the sounds "ka," "ke," "ki," "ko," and "ku."

23. For example, in my youth I was hosted as an au pair by a German family. I spoke very little German, which is a phonologically transparent language that is read as it is written. I could then read fairy-tale books out loud to the child I was looking after. Even if I did not understand anything about the content, apparently my reading was (sufficiently) satisfactory for my little listener.

24. De Mauro, *Linguistica elementare*, 187.

25. Havelock, *Preface to Plato*, ix-xi; Havelock, *The Greek Concept of Justice*, 4–14.

26. Eco, *Vertigine della lista*, 133.

27. Plato, *Meno*, part II, and *Hippias Major*, in *Complete Works*.

28. Aristotle, *Posterior Analytics*, book II, 13.

29. Visi, "A Science of List?" 14.

30. Homer, *Iliad*, book II, lines 494–759.

31. Von Contzen, "Die Affordanzen der Liste," 318. Lists also appear in modern literary texts, but have a different interpretation than those used in everyday life. Instead of being seen as supporting the ordering of information, they are perceived as foreign, disturbing factors, which the author can use for artistic or communicative purposes; see Mainberger, "Exotisch—endotisch."

32. Vandermeersch, "Dalla tartaruga all'achillea (Cina)" ; Bottéro, "Sintomi, segni, scritture nell'antica Mesopotamia."

33. Described in Porphyry, *Isagoge*.

34. See Eco, *Dall'albero al labirinto*; Weinberger, *Everything Is Miscellaneous*. This is also confirmed by Bowker and Star's description of an ideal classification system and its properties. Bowker and Star, *Sorting Things Out*, 10–11.

35. See Mainberger, "Exotisch—endotisch." As Mainberger shows, for this reason lists are a fundamental tool in ethnographic and ethnological studies, and in general in the investigation of foreign cultures—up to Montaigne and Frazer. The empty form of the list allows us to manage the unknown.

36. Davis, *Computability and Unsolvability*.

37. For more on this, see chapter 1.

38. Michura et al., "Slot Machines, Graphs, and Radar Screens," 168. The MONK (Metadata Offer New Knowledge) project for text analysis, for example, "uses lists in several different ways: layered lists, user-determined random or sequential lists, lists as graphs, user-defined lists, lists as history states, dashed lists, and search results as collapsible lists." Michura et al., 171.

39. Weinberger, *Everything Is Miscellaneous*, 8.

40. Weinberger, *Everything Is Miscellaneous*, 29.

41. Weinberger, *Taxonomies to Tags*, 30.

42. Taylor, "The Concept of 'Cat Face.'"

43. Observers typically try to make sense of algorithmic procedures when errors occur, as in the much-discussed case of software that distinguishes huskies from wolves by the presence or absence of snow in the background: cf. Ribeiro, Singh, and Guestrin, "'Why Should I Trust You?'"

44. Lepore, "The Cobweb"

45. Poole, "Top Nine Things You Need to Know."

46. On a single, typical day (March 7, 2019), besides bestseller lists, one could find on the *New York Times* online: "6 Black Chefs (and 1 Inventor) Who Changed the History of Food," "Three Stunning New Memoirs of Love and Loss," "5 Film Series to Catch in NYC This Weekend," "5 Places to Eat in the Dolomites," "The Top 25

Songs That Matter Right Now," "The 50 Best Movies on Netflix Right Now," and "5 Space Documentaries to Stream."

47. Jeremy W. Peters, Matt Flegenheimer, Elizabeth Dias, Susan Chira, Kate Zernike and Alexander Burns, "Midterm Election Results: 4 Key Takeaways," *New York Times*, Nov. 7, 2018, https://www.nytimes.com/2018/11/07/us/politics/election-news.html; Nicholas Confessore and Matthew Rosenberg, "Damage Control at Facebook: 6 Takeaways from the Times's Investigation," *New York Times*, Nov. 14, 2018, https://www.nytimes.com/2018/11/14/technology/facebook-crisis-mark-zuckerberg-sheryl -sandberg.html; Megan Specia, "Five Takeaways from Our New China Project," *New York Times*, Nov. 21, 2018, https://www.nytimes.com/2018/11/21/world/asia/china -rules-takeaways.html.

48. Lepore, "The Cobweb."

49. According to the "googlization" procedures described in chapter 1.

50. Von Soden, "Leistung und Grenze sumerischer und babylonischer Wissen-schaft."

CHAPTER 3

1. Jänicke et al., "On Close and Distant Reading in Digital Humanities."

2. Moretti and Sobchuk, "Hidden in Plain Sight," 86.

3. Katsma, "Loudness in the Novel,"; Moretti, "Style, Inc. Reflections on Seven Thousand Titles, (British Novels, 1740–1850)."

4. Morin and Acerbi, for example, use a visualization to "show a decrease in emo-tionality in English-speaking literature starting plausibly in the nineteenth century." Morin and Acerbi, "Birth of the Cool," 1664.

5. "Big data requires visualization to even start understanding its possible struc-tures." Schöch, "Big? Smart? Clean? Messy? Data in the Humanities," 19.

6. Gitelman and Jackson, introduction to *"Raw Data" Is an Oxymoron*, 12.

7. Moretti, *Maps, Graphs, Trees.*

8. Manovich, "How to Compare One Million Images?"

9. Card, Mackinlay, and Shneiderman, *Readings in Information Visualization, Using Vision to Think*, xiii. Jänicke emphasizes the overall increasing value of visualizations as a means of research for digital humanists since 2013—testified to by the fact that not only have surveys and state-of-the-art papers on text visualization techniques been produced, but even a Survey of Surveys (SoS) reviewing and classifying them. See Jänicke, "Valuable Research for Visualization"; Alharbi and Laramee, "SoS Text-Vis: A Survey of Surveys."

10. Münster and Terras, "The Visual Side of Digital Humanities."

11. "The concrete use of the new tools—the practice—preceded and overshadowed their theoretical justification." Moretti and Sobchuk, "Hidden in Plain Sight," 87.

12. A similar question—"Why might it be helpful to geovisualize literary texts?"—underlies the contributions collected in Cooper, Donaldson, and Murrieta-Flores, *Literary Mapping in the Digital Age*. In my analysis, however, visualization has a more abstract meaning than in the debate about the "Spatial Turn" in the digital humanities; cf. Presner and Shepard, "Mapping the Geospatial Turn."

13. Burrell, "How the Machine 'Thinks.'"

14. Luhmann, *Soziale Systeme*, 560–561.

15. Ware, *Information Visualization: Perception for Design*, 1–2.

16. In her reflections on operative imagery, Krämer points out the difference between oral language bound to temporal succession and two-dimensional visualization taking advantage of simultaneity. Krämer, "Operative Bildlichkeit."

17. We still do it in our widespread use of PowerPoint. See Stark and Paravel, "PowerPoint in Public."

18. Card, Mackinlay, and Shneiderman, *Readings in Information Visualization*, 1.

19. Jessop, "Digital Visualization as a Scholarly Activity," 282.

20. Keim and Ankerst, "Visual Data Mining Techniques," 816.

21. "We are experimenting with visualization as a tool to develop new arguments (and new questions) about historical processes and understandings of major historical events." Stanford Spatial History Project (Stanford University), https://web.stanford.edu/group/spatialhistory/cgi-bin/site/gallery.php.

22. Goody, *The Domestication of the Savage Mind*; Friendly, "A Brief History of Data Visualization." Cf. also the discussion on the use of lists and tables as heuristic tools in chapter 3.

23. Latour, "Visualisation and Cognition."

24. Card, Mackinlay, and Shneiderman, *Readings in Information Visualization*, 10; and Spence, *Information Visualization*, 12.

25. Manovich, "What Is Visualization?" 131.

26. In the sense of linguistics, in infovis the images have an arbitrary relationship with their signifier; see Saussure, *Cours de linguistique générale*, chapter 1. The word "dog," for example, does not resemble a real dog with legs and a tail. On the meaning of arbitrariness in visualization, see Ware, *Information Visualization*. "It's infovis [information visualization] when the spatial representation is chosen, and it's scivis [scientific visualization] when the spatial representation is given": Munzner, "Process and Pitfalls in Writing Information Visualization Research Papers," 149. For a technical comparison between scivis and infovis, see Telea, *Data Visualization*, 438–445.

27. Tufte, *The Visual Display of Quantitative Information*, 9.

28. Card, Mackinlay, and Shneiderman, *Readings in Information Visualization*, 6; Tufte, *Visual Explanations*, 9. Using Agostinho's expression, it is a "post-optical" use of images: they support not seeing but thinking. Agostinho, "The Optical Unconscious of Big Data."

29. Tufte, *Envisioning Information*, 9.

30. Ferreira de Oliveira and Levkowitz, "From Visual Data Exploration to Visual Data Mining."

31. Davis, "At Last, a Graph That Explains Scifi TV."

32. On December 2, 2019, the *New York Times* used a dynamic visualization to show in an immediately effective way the level of pollution of different cities around the world. These kinds of tools are increasingly frequent in the digital versions of mass media. See Popovich, Popovich et al., "See How the World's Most Polluted Air Compares with Your City's."

33. Telea, *Data Visualization. Principles and Practice*, 10.

34. Manovich, "What Is Visualization?"

35. Carusi, "Making the Visual Visible."

36. Telea, *Data Visualization*, 6.

37. Schwandt, "Digitale Objektivität in der Geschichtswissenschaft?" The process resembles the search procedure analyzed by Stark, where one does not know what one is looking for yet is able to recognize it when found. See Stark, *The Sense of Dissonance*.

38. A case of visualization triggering the formulation of new hypothesis is presented in Kanatova et al., "Broken Time, Continued Evolution." Kanatova and colleagues present a case of visualization triggering the formulation of a new hypothesis. In a study of the tendency towards using more anachronisms in movies over the last 40 years, the visualization of the data showed an unexpected "branching." The authors explain it in retrospect, hypothesizing a change in the function of anachronisms, which can be used to connect different time lines in the plot.

39. Clement, "The Story of One" ; Cecire, "Ways of Not Reading Gertrude Stein."

40. Algee-Hewitt et al., "Canon/Archive"; Algee-Hewitt, Heuser, and Moretti, "On Paragraphs," 1.

41. Miller, "Explanation in Artificial Intelligence"; Ribeiro, Singh, and Guestrin, "'Why Should I Trust You?'"

42. Knowledge graphs, for example, were popularized recently to provide both a human-interpretable representation and a formalized machine-readable basis for information retrieval tasks; see Haslhofer, Isaac, and Simon, "Knowledge Graphs in the Libraries and Digital Humanities Domain."

43. Sinclair and Rockwell, "Text Analysis and Visualization," 288.

44. Weinberger, *Everything Is Miscellaneous*, 189.

45. Ware, *Information Visualization: Perception for Design*, 4.

46. Wristley and Jänicke, *Visualizing Uncertainty*.

47. Elting et al. discuss an example of how the choice of visualization impacts the decision process. They discuss four presentations of the same data about the effectiveness of conventional and investigational treatments on a group of patients: a

simple table, pie charts, stacked bar charts, and a sequence of rectangles representing the patients. The decision about treatment varies significantly depending on the presentation of the data. Elting et al, "Influence of Data Display Formats on Decisions."

48. Tufte, *The Visual Display of Quantitative Information.*

49. Behrisch et al., "Quality Metrics for Information Visualization."

50. Bubblelines visualize the frequency and distribution of terms in a corpus providing a line for each document, populated by a series of bubbles of varying sizes representing the relative occurrence of words.

51. Behrisch et al., "Quality Metrics for Information Visualization."

52. Visualization can also be misleading and suggest intuitive connections that turn out to be fallacious; see Schwandt, "Digitale Objektivität in der Geschichtswissenschaft?"

53. See https://voyant-tools.org.

54. Galloway, "Are Some Things Unrepresentable?" 88. Obviously visualization is never neutral; see Amoore, "Algorithmic War." Because visualizations leave interpretation open, however, we often tend to consider them more objective and almost observer-independent; see Drucker, "Humanities Approaches to Graphical Display," and Drucker, "Graphical Approaches to the Digital Humanities." As Sinclair and Rockfell argue, it is always possible, and sometimes useful, to "get interested in the interpretation of these tools of interpretation, but this is another type of text analysis." Sinclair and Rockfell, "Making Meaning Count," 288.

55. Galloway, "Are Some Things Unrepresentable?" 89.

56. Card, Mackinlay, and Shneiderman, *Readings in Information Visualization,* 6–7.

57. Schwandt, "Digitale Methoden für die Historische Semantik," 16.

58. Jänicke, "Valuable Research for Visualization and Digital Humanities."

59. This changes with time and the conditions of communication. Until modernity, we didn't even have a verb to indicate our familiar practice of reading; see Chantraine, "Les verbes grecs signifiant 'lire'"; and Cevolini, "Der Leser im Gelesenen." The Latin verb *lego, -ere* meant "gather, put together," and referred to the activity of accumulating materials in collections such as a florilegium (anthology), without any reference to the unity of text or to the perspective of the author.

60. Liu, "From Reading to Social Computing"; Bode, *Reading by Numbers.*

61. Moretti, "Conjectures on World Literature," 57.

62. Hayles, "How We Read," 65. Cf. the discussion about not-reading as a kind of reading, in Kirschenbaum, "The Remaking of Reading."

63. The canon can get so narrow that the object of close reading is a single text, as in Derrida's reading of Joyce's *Ulysses* (Derrida, *Ulysse gramophone, Deux mots pour Joyce*).

64. Moretti, "Conjectures on World Literature," 57.

65. Moretti, "Style, Inc.: Reflections on Seven Thousand Titles."

66. Manovich, "How to Compare One Million Images?"

67. Jänicke et al., "On Close and Distant Reading in Digital Humanities."

68. Liu, "From Reading to Social Computing." The same goes for printed text. Before the printing press, reading texts was a very different activity from our familiar practice. In cultures that were still predominantly oral, written materials used to be memorized, and this required a different, extremely intensive form of reading; see Luhmann, *Gesellschaft der Gesellschaft*, 293f. Actually, authentic close reading could be identified with the medieval practice of repeatedly reading the same materials, with no distance from the content or from the formulations.

69. Moretti, "Patterns and Interpretation," 2.

70. Kirschenbaum, "The .txtual Condition."

71. Hayles, *How We Think*, 149.

72. Sneha, "Reading from a Distance—Data as Text."

73. Whitmore, "Text: A Massively Addressable Object."

74. As predicted by Luhmann; see *Einführung in die Systemtheorie*, 143.

75. Hayles, *My mother was a computer: digital subjects and literary texts*, 101.

76. Whitmore, "Text: A Massively Addressable Object."

77. Texts so understood are treated as things. The practices of distant reading could be seen as the heirs of the instruments introduced in early modern age after the spread of the printing press when, for the first time, text and interpretation were separated and the text was manipulated and elaborated as an object to be used in the most effective way. Indexes, summaries, front matter, page numbers, chapters, and paragraphs were introduced, and then the apparatus of filing and content organization. See Ong, *Orality and Literacy*; Cevolini, *De arte excerpendi*; Blair, "Annotating and Indexing Natural Philosophy"; and Cevolini, *Forgetting Machines*.

78. Whitmore, "Text: A Massively Addressable Object," 327.

79. Moretti, "Patterns and Interpretation," 2.

80. Hayles, *My Mother Was a Computer*.

81. Hayles, "How We Think. Transforming Power and Digital Technologies," 47.

82. Hayles, "How We Read: Close, Hyper, Machine," 73; and Moretti, *La letteratura vista da lontano*, 10.

83. Following Roland Barthes's exhortation: "Amputate literature from the individual" (quoted in Moretti, *La letteratura vista da lontano*, 12).

84. Bode, *Reading by Numbers*, 11; referring to Lacan, *Seminar XI: The Four Fundamental Concepts*, 71–73.

85. Hayles, *How We Think*, 201. Kath, Schaal, and Dumm, in "New Visual Hermeneutics," call for the development of a "second order hermeneutics" to deal with the interpretation of visualizations in the digital humanities.

86. Schwandt, "Digitale Objektivität in der Geschichtswissenschaft?"

87. Kirschenbaum, "The Remaking of Reading"; Moretti, "Style, Inc."

88. Hayles, "How We Read," 72.

89. Moretti, "Conjectures on World Literature," 57.

90. Moretti, "Patterns and Interpretation," 1.

91. Moretti, *Maps, Graphs, Trees.*

92. Manovich, "How to Compare One Million Images?"

93. Moretti, "Conjectures on World Literature," 57.

94. Hayles, "How We Read: Close, Hyper, Machine," 74.

95. Martin Mueller's idea of "scalable reading" goes in a similar direction: "a broad 'scale' of surrogates that can be put into operation as a continuum." Weitin, "Thinking Slowly," 10; see also Mueller's website about scalable reading, https://scalablereading.northwestern.edu/.

96. Liu, "The Meaning in the Digital Humanities," 414.

97. Hayles, "How We Read," 73.

98. Liu, "From Reading to Social Computing."

99. Distant reading has precedents that it dramatically extends and increases through the computational capacity of machines. It does not extend reading practices, but rather the complex "not-reading" practices that already existed for use in an extremely refined way of dealing with printed texts. They require training and can be even more informative than reading itself. Pierre Bayard describes sharply and wittily the forms and merits of not-reading books, namely the countless information that can be found about texts without reading them—looking at the cover and the publisher, referring to what people say about them, knowing the authors and their reputation through secondary sources. Only in refraining from reading books, he provocatively claims, does one gets "the necessary *distance* to speak about them accurately." Bayard, *How to Talk about Books You Haven't Read*, 113 (my italics).

100. Hayes, "How We Read," 73.

101. Moretti, "Patterns and Interpretation."

102. Clement, "The Story of One"; Cecire, "Ways of Not Reading Gertrude Stein."

103. According to Shannon and Weaver's standard model and its subsequent elaborations in various forms of semantic noise linked to disparity of codes: Shannon and Weaver, *The Mathematical Theory of Communication.* See also Eco and Fabbri, *Prima proposta per un modello di ricerca interdisciplinare sul rapporto televisione/pubblico*; for a recent survey, see Floridi, *Information: A Very Short Introduction.*

104. Moretti, "Patterns and Interpretation," 10.

105. McLuhan, *Understanding Media.*

106. On the ubiquity of patterns, see Hand, "Why Data Mining Is More Than Statistics."

107. Ramsay, *Reading Machines*, 78.

108. Tyler Vigen, at http://www.tylervigen.com/spurious-correlations, presents many examples of "spurious correlations" that algorithms identify in data: for example, that the age of Miss America correlates with murders by steam, hot vapours, and hot objects, or that the divorce rate in Maine correlates with per capita consumption of margarine.

109. Weinberger, *Everything Is Miscellaneous*, 168.

110. Jessop, "Digital Visualization as a Scholarly Activity," 284.

111. "We feel strongly that text analysis tools can represent a significant contributor to digital research, whether they were used to help confirm hunches or to lead the researcher into completely unanticipated realms." Sinclair and Rockwell, "Voyant Tools."

112. See, e.g., Poemage, a tool that supports the reading of a poem by visualizing its sonic topology: http://www.sci.utah.edu/~nmccurdy/Poemage/, accessed September 20, 2019. Sinclair and Rockwell describe their "agile interpretive style" as a combination of human and algorithmic activities: texts are explored with analytic tools and visualizations, which lead to reading the text differently. Sinclair and Rockwell, "Text Analysis and Visualization: Making Meaning Count," 277–278.

113. Etzioni, Banko, and Cafarella, "Machine Reading."

CHAPTER 4

1. See, e.g., Lury and Day, "Algorithmic Personalization as a Mode of Individuation"; Ruppert, "Population Objects: Interpassive Subjects"; Cheney-Lippold, "A New Algorithmic Identity"; Prey, "Nothing Personal: Algorithmic Individuation."

2. Brubaker, "Digital Hyperconnectivity and the Self."

3. The expression was introduced by DiNucci in 1999, and then popularized by O'Reilly and the "Web 2.0 Conference" in 2004. DiNucci, "Fragmented Future"; for the conference, see https://web.archive.org/web/20050312204307/http://www.web 2con.com/web2con/.

4. Carr, *The Big Switch*, and Benkler, *The Wealth of Networks*.

5. Neff and Stark, "Permanently Beta."

6. Wasik, *And Then There's This*, 9.

7. Abruzzese and Pireddu, "Facebook come Fakebook," 77; see also Kelly, "On Chris Anderson's the End of Theory."

8. Benkler, *Wealth of Networks*, 167–170; see also Beer, "Power through the Algorithm?"

9. Anderson, *The Long Tail*, 191.

10. Gillmor, *We the Media*.

11. Pine, Peppers, and Rogers, "Do You Want to Keep Your Customers Forever?," 103.

12. Esposito, "Interaktion, Interaktivität und die Personalisierung der Massenmedien."

13. Douglas, *The End of Books.*

14. Gerlitz and Helmond, "The Like Economy."

15. See, e.g., Cevolini and Bronner, eds., *What Is New in Fake News.*

16. Benway and Lane, "Banner Blindness"; and O'Donnell and Cramer, "People's Perceptions of Personalized Ads."

17. As in the episode "Bandersnatch" of *Black Mirror,* released in December 2018.

18. See McCombs and Shaw, "The Agenda-Setting Function of Mass Media." According to Luhmann, the function of broadcast media for society is to create a shared "second reality." Luhmann, *The Reality of the Mass Media.*

19. Quito, "The Next Design Trend."

20. See Duhigg, "How Companies Learn Our Secrets."

21. See, e.g., Kotras, "Mass Personalization."

22. See Hawalah and Fasli, "Utilizing Contextual Ontological User Profiles"; Xiao, Qibei, and Feipeng, "Mobile Personalized Recommendation Model Based on Privacy Concerns"; and Pichl, Zangerle, and Specht, "Towards a Context-Aware Music Recommendation Approach."

23. See, e.g., Al-Rfou et al., "Conversational Contextual Cues"; Miele, Quintarelli, and Tanca, "A Methodology for Preference-Based Personalization of Contextual Data"; and Pagano et al., "The Contextual Turn."

24. Ciaccia, Martinenghi, and Torlone, "Foundations of Context-Aware Preference Propagation."

25. Hawalah and Fasli, "Contextual Ontological User Profiles," 4778.

26. "People have more in common with other people in the same situation, or with the same goals, than they do with past versions of themselves." Pagano et al., "The Contextual Turn," 1.

27. See Xiao, Qibei, and Feipeng, "Mobile Personalized Recommendation Model Based on Privacy Concerns"; Al-Rfou et al., "Conversational Contextual Cues."

28. This new frame of reference is welcomed as a "shift in paradigm" by Hawalah and Fasli, "Contextual Ontological User Profiles," 4781.

29. As Lury and Day observe, on the web "personalization is not only personal: it is never about only one person, just me or just you, but always involves generalization." Lury and Day, "Algorithmic Personalization as a Mode of Individuation," 18.

30. Herrman, "How TikTok Is Rewriting the World."

31. In 2018, views on premium video grew by 27 percent in the US and 15 percent in Europe, continuing a multiyear trend.

32. Smith, "Why the Success of The New York Times May Be Bad News for Journalism."

33. See Lepore, "The Cobweb"; and Rusbridger, *Breaking News.*

34. See, e.g., Flipfeed, https://www.media.mit.edu/projects/flipfeed/overview/, accessed April 20, 2019.

35. Brubaker, "Digital Hyperconnectivity and the Self," 785.

36. Goffman, *The Presentation of Self in Everyday Life*.

37. Jurgenson, *The Social Photo*, 55.

38. Jurgenson, *The Social Photo*, 8.

39. I investigate the social use of digital photos further in chapter 6.

40. Frosh, "The Gestural Image," 1611.

41. Formilan and Stark, "Testing the Creative Identity."

42. Moeller, "On Second-Order Observation and Genuine Pretending."

43. See https://ra.co/dj/abayomi.

44. Formilan and Stark, "Testing the Creative Identity."

45. Al-Rfou et al., "Conversational Contextual Cues"; and Xiao, Qibei, and Feipeng, "Mobile Personalized Recommendation Model."

46. Mullin, "Why Content Personalization Is Not Web Personalization"; Cheney-Lippold, "A New Algorithmic Identity"; As Herrman puts it: "It is possible, today, to receive highly personalized and effectively infinite content recommendations in YouTube without ever following a single account, because Google already watches what you do, and makes guesses about who you are." Herrman, "How TikTok Is Rewriting the World."

47. Cheney-Lippold, "A New Algorithmic Identity"; Ruppert, "Population Objects: Interpassive Subjects"; and Brubaker, "Digital Hyperconnectivity and the Self."

48. Prey, "Nothing Personal."

49. Cheney-Lippold, "A New Algorithmic Identity," 165.

50. Ruppert, "Population Objects: Interpassive Subjects," 220.

51. Prey, "Nothing Personal," 1087.

52. Critical media studies have long warned of the risks to privacy and freedom of self-determination, the flipside of digital individualization. See, e.g., Carr, *The Big Switch*; Morozov, *The Net Delusion*; or recently, Zuboff, *The Age of Surveillance Capitalism*.

53. Pariser, *The Filter Bubble*, 14–18.

54. McGoey, "Strategic Unknowns."

55. The growing polarization of political communication and other "echo chamber" phenomena seem to confirm this approach. See Sunstein, *Republic.com*; Sunstein, *#Republic: Divided Democracy in the Age of Social Media*; Peruzzi et al., "From Confirmation Bias to Echo-Chambers."

56. See Joyce, "Five Examples of Creepy Marketing"; Sweeney, "75% of Consumers Find Many Forms of Marketing Personalization Creepy."

57. Scott, "Use of Ad-Blocking Software Rises by 30% Worldwide."

58. Wu, *The Attention Merchants*, 335–339.

59. Nichols, "Customization vs Personalization"; Davis, "What Is the Difference between Personalization and Customization?"

60. Hearn and Schoenhoff, "From Celebrity to Influencer"; Brubaker, "Digital Hyperconnectivity and the Self," 786.

61. Wasik, *And Then There's This*, 112.

62. Wasik, *And Then There's This*. Such planned actions had no meaning: for example, all participants had to go into the lobby of the Grand Hyatt in New York and look out of the balcony at 7:07 p.m., staring down in silence for 5 minutes, then applaud for 15 seconds, and finally disperse and disappear.

63. Bresnick, *Intensified Play*; Assante, "Tutti pazzi per TikTok, il social che dà 15 secondi di celebrità."

64. Herrman, "How TikTok Is Rewriting the World."

65. Wasik, *And Then There's This*, 136.

66. Modern fiction is perceived as realistic because we "forget" that it is someone's invention, just as the central perspective of modern painting (Leon Battista Alberti's "window on the world") is perceived as realistic because we "forget" that the painting refers to the specific point of view of the painter (the vanishing point of the perspective)—while it would appear distorted by any other angle (see Baltrušaitis, *Anamorphoses ou Thaumaturgus opticus*).

67. Luhmann, *The Reality of the Mass Media*, 55–62.

68. Bissell, *Extra Lives*; Bissell, "The Grammar of Fun."

69. The virtual space of the game, in fact, requires you to go beyond the experiential space of fiction based on the tradition of linear perspective, which excludes the observer from the observed space; see Taylor, "When Seams Fall Apart." Videogames that offer players the possibility to intervene in the story "can both reproduce and challenge everyday rules of social interaction, while also generating interesting and creative innovations." Wright, Boria, and Breidenbach, "Creative Player Actions in FPS Online Video Games."

70. A second-person POV is also possible, but less common—it is the condition in which the user is directly addressed with "you," as often happens in children books. Jeffrey Eugenides's novel *The Virgin Suicides* is written from the unusual perspective of "we," in the first-person plural.

71. Waggoner, *My Avatar, My Self.*, 41; and Sabbagh, "The Important Differences Between First-Person."

72. If the avatar looks at himself in the mirror, the experience is unsettling for the player and risks jeopardizing the entire game experience. This is the case of the *X-Files* game described in Taylor, "When Seams Fall Apart": if the character Craig Wilmore looks at himself in the mirror, the player who identifies with him doesn't see "myself seeing myself" (cf. Lacan, *Ècrits*, 80), but sees Willmore.

73. Waggoner, *My Avatar, My Self*, 42.

74. Pariser, *The Filter Bubble*, 47–76.

CHAPTER 5

1. This chapter is a slightly revised version of an article published under the same title in *Big Data & Society* 4, no. 1 (2017).

2. See http://curia.europa.eu/juris/document/document.jsf?docid=152065.

3. Solove, "Speech, Privacy, and Reputation on the Internet," 18.

4. "Zu allem Handeln gehört Vergessen . . . ; es ist möglich fast ohne Erinnerung zu leben, ja glücklich zu leben, wie das Tier zeigt; es ist aber ganz und gar unmöglich, ohne Vergessen überhaupt zu leben."—"All action requires forgetting . . . ; it is possible to live almost without remembering, it is even possible to live happily, as animals show. But it is absolutely impossible to live without forgetting." Nietzsche, *Unzeitgemässe Betrachtungen: Zweites Stück*, 116 (my translation).

5. Toobin, "The Solace of Oblivion"; Nabi, "~~Resistance~~ Censorship Is Futile."

6. Nissenbaum, "Privacy as Contextual integrity"; Solove, "'I've Got Nothing to Hide'"; Solove, "Speech, Privacy, and Reputation on the Internet."

7. On the distinction between responsibility and accountability, see Simon, "Epistemic Responsibility in Entangled Socio-Technical Systems." According to Simon, responsibility would require intentionality, which cannot be attributed to technical artifacts. Algorithms may be accountable, but should not be made responsible—which of course leaves the issue of responsibility open.

8. Google not only has the task of suppressing the links, but also of deciding whether to accept the requests of "being forgotten," balancing those with the public right to information. This raises an important question of legitimacy; see Ambrose, "Forgetting Made (Too) Easy." What right allows a private entity to make decisions of public importance, without having being elected or appointed with a transparent procedure, and even without specification of the criteria to be followed in the decision (if and how long data can be considered of public interest, who are the private individuals to protect, when should the right to privacy of the individual prevail over public access)? Citizens still have the possibility of appealing to the judicial authority (§82), but this is a secondary step.

9. The extensive debate on cultural memory is focused on the definition of social memory referring to this question, starting with Halbwachs's classic text, *Les cadres sociaux de la mémoire*. See also Assmann and Hölscher, *Kultur und Gedächtnis*; Assmann, *Das kulturelle Gedächtnis*; and Esposito, *Soziales Vergessen*.

10. Google tried to get directives and guidelines in a series of meetings and discussions organized in 2014 in a tour of European capitals. As likely should have been expected, the results involved media attention more than content—but this does not make the move less meaningful from the point of view of the company and of the management of its decision-making responsibility.

11. The legislation on the right to be forgotten includes a "media exception" for the processing of personal data "carried out solely for journalistic purposes" (§9) (Rosen, "The Right to Be Forgotten"). But also archives and catalogs are protected: there is a further exception for processing data for historical, statistical, and scientific research

purposes (§7) (van Hoboken, "The Proposed Right to be Forgotten," 20). Intermediaries, on the other hand, are not held responsible if they do not know the information to which they provide access (van Hoboken, 26)—as stated in the Euopean Union directive on electronic commerce that establishes a "safe harbor" for internet service providers that operate as a "mere conduit."

12. Toobin, "The Solace of Oblivion."

13. Hildebrandt, *Smart Technologies and the End(s) of Law*.

14. Bateson, *Steps to an Ecology of Mind*, 459.

15. Agrawal, "Rakesh Agrawal Speaks Out"; and Hammond, *Practical Artificial Intelligence for Dummies*.

16. Hildebrandt, *Smart Technologies and the End(s) of Law*, 46.

17. This is one of the points emphasized by Mayer-Schönberger in his book with the evocative title *Delete: The Virtue of Forgetting in the Digital Age*.

18. It even remembers the future, working as an "anticipation machine" that also answers questions not yet asked. On the predictive power of algorithms, see chapter 7.

19. Blanchette and Johnson, "Data Retention and the Panoptic Society."

20. As many observers remark, however, the web also forgets a lot, but again in different ways than our familiar memory. Web content is ephemeral on many dimensions, most of them new; see Ambrose, "You Are What Google Says You Are"; Chun, *Programmed Visions: Software and Memory*; Barone, Zeitlyn, and Mayer-Schönberger, "Learning from Failure"; and Lepore, "The Cobweb." Besides the classic problems of physical rot (from natural causes such as fire or flood), there are technical problems like hardware, software or network failures, viruses, accidental file deletion, changes of media and protocols. Moreover, there are all the difficulties of reference rot and link rot, resulting from content that becomes impossible to access, with clicking on a link producing the infamous "404: Page Not Found" error message; or pages may still exist but have a different URL; see Davis, "Moving Targets." The average life span of web pages is less than 100 days, and in many cases, is more accurately measured in hours rather than days (http://blogs.loc.gov/digitalpreservation/2011/11/the-aver age-lifespan-of-a-webpage/). Reacting to these problems, specialized tools for web preservation have been developed, such as permalinks (https://perma.cc); another is the Wayback Machine (https://archive.org/web /) and another is Google's cache.

21. The two aspects of forgetting are obviously different, as highlighted by Rouvroy, who distinguishes the interest to forget from the interest (or even the right) to be forgotten; see Rouvroy, "Réinventer l'art d'oublier et de se faire oublier dans la société de l'information?" The first aspect concerns the possibility of projecting an open future; the second, the desire not to be bound by the past (or by certain portions of it) in one's social identity. In the debate on the European ruling, however, the two issues overlap so that in this context I do not consider the differences. Nobody, however, wants to forget or be forgotten altogether, and in this sense the expression "right to be forgotten" is somehow misleading.

22. Ricoeur, *Memory, History, Forgetting*, 412.

23. Cicero, de Oratore 2.74.299; Weinrich, *Gibt es eine Kunst des Vergessens?*

24. Esposito, *Soziales Vergessen.*

25. Anderson, "Rethinking Interference Theory"; Hulbert and Anderson, "The Role of Inhibition in Learning."

26. One must be able to distinguish the present moment from an eternal presence of the past. Forgetting then is also needed to be able to remember in a proper sense, building an internal horizon of references and recursions to face the present. The act of remembering produces and requires a parallel forgetting. See Hulbert and Anderson, "The Role of Inhibition in Learning," 8.

27. Lepore, "The Cobweb."

28. Luria, *The Mind of a Mnemonist.* The phenomenon is narratively reproduced in Borges's famous short story, "Funes el memorioso."

29. Parker, Cahill, and McGaugh, "A Case of Unusual Autobiographical Remembering"; Erdelyi, *The Recovery of Unconscious Memories.*

30. As described in chapter 2, there is an intrinsic affinity between the working of algorithms and the form of the list.

31. And if relevant users link to it—while users are relevant if they themselves are linked to by others. See Page et al., *The PageRank Citation Ranking.*

32. And somehow the algorithm learns because machine-learning techniques use selections also to orient the subsequent behavior.

33. The situation is actually more complex, since storage and accessibility are, in fact, two separate issues requiring different tools and different decisions. Digital memory remembers a lot but also forgets a lot, in new and articulated ways. Information can be lost because it is not stored, because its support is damaged, or because it cannot be accessed with the available tools.

34. See Yates, *The Art of Memory.*

35. Lachmann, "Die Unlöschbarkeit der Zeichen: Das semiotische Unglück des Memoristen," 11; Weinrich, *Lethe. Kunst und Kritik des Vergessens*, 7–8; and Eco, *Dall'albero al labirinto: studi storici sul segno e l'interpretazione*, 79–80.

36. See Eco, "An Ars Oblivionalis? Forget It!"

37. Woodruff, "Necessary, Unpleasant, and Disempowering."

38. An "index of the de-indexed"; see Binns, "How to Be Open about Being Closed."

39. Weinrich, *Gibt es eine Kunst des Vergessens?*

40. Brunton and Nissenbaum, *Obfuscation: A User's Guide for Privacy and Protest.*

41. With a similar attitude, FaceCloak generates fictitious information to oppose the excess of individual transparency on Facebook by creating, parallel to sensitive data, a series of completely irrelevant invented information. There are also procedures that, whenever you do a query on Google, generate a series of parallel ghost queries that make it difficult for companies to identify your pattern of preferences.

42. The most complex aspect of reputation management is repair; see Woodruff, "Necessary, Unpleasant, and Disempowering." Ausloos observes that the right to be forgotten only provides *ex post* solutions to privacy issues. Ausloos, "The 'Right to be Forgotten'—Worth Remembering?"

43. Ronson, *So You've Been Publicly Shamed*, 214–217.

44. http://reputationdefender.com.

45. Bolzoni, *La stanza della memoria*.

46. Foer, *Moonwalking with Einstein*.

47. Woodruff, "Necessary, Unpleasant, and Disempowering," 157; Ronson, *So You've Been Publicly Shamed*, 266–268.

48. Reding, *The EU Data Protection Reform 2012*.

49. "Most of the Digital Universe Are Unstructured Data": Gantz and Reinsel, *The Digital Universe Decade*.

50. Mayer-Schönberger and Cukier, *Big Data*, 6; see also Koops, "Forgetting Footprints, Shunning Shadows."

51. Adkins and Lury, *Measure and Value*, 6.

52. Amoore and Piotuck, "Life Beyond big Data," 355. The same problems arise in the debate about digital privacy, which in its most refined forms also concerns the problem of preserving the self-determination of individuals as a possibility of reinvention; see Solove's *The Future of Reputation*, "'I've Got Nothing to Hide,'" and "Speech, Privacy, and Reputation on the Internet." Here the advocates of privacy like Nissenbaum claim the protection of "Privacy as Contextual Integrity": one should not allow the use of data in contexts that are inappropriate to the original one. The difficulty, however, is that in many cases the workings of algorithms completely disregard context.

53. Custers, "Click Here to consent forever."

CHAPTER 6

1. Peter Szendy, Emmanuel Alloa, and Marta Ponsa, *The Supermarket of Images*, Exhibition organized by the Jeu de Paume, 2020, accessed April 5, 2020, http://www.jeudepaume.org/index.php?page=article&idArt=3349.

2. See, e.g., Williams, "24 Hours in Photos"; or Kelly, "Erik Kessels, Photographer, Prints Out 24 Hours Worth of Flickr Photos."

3. Szendy, Alloa, and Ponsa, *Supermarket of Images*.

4. Sontag, *On Photography*, 1.

5. See, e.g., Hand, *Ubiquitous Photography*; Kember, "Ubiquitous Photography."

6. Beck, *Risk Society*.

7. Van Dijck, "Digital Photography"; van House, "Personal Photography, Digital Technologies and the Uses of the Visual"; Sarvas and Frohlich, *From Snapshots to Social Media*; and Hand, *Ubiquitous Photography*.

8. Sontag, *On Photography*, 5.

9. Panofsky, "Die Perspektive als 'symbolische Form.'"

10. Sontag, *On Photography*, 15.

11. Yates, *The Art of Memory*.

12. Mayer-Schönberger, *The Virtue of Forgetting in the Digital Age*.

13. Weinberger, *Taxonomies to Tags*.

14. This enormously expands the possibility, already existing with analog pictures, of using photography to "refuse" or "ignore" experience. Sontag, *On Photography*, 6, 8.

15. Sontag, *On Photography*, 120.

16. Luhmann, *Soziologie des Risikos*; Beck, *Risk Society: Towards a New Modernity*.

17. Jurgenson, *The Social Photo. On Photography*, 48.

18. O'Doherty, *Inside the White Cube*, 55.

19. Already in the 1980s O'Doherty observed: "We can no longer experience anything if we don't first alienate it. . . . The vernacular example is the snapshot. You can only see what a good time you had from the summer snapshots. . . . These Kodachrome icons are used to convince friends you did have a good time: if they believe it, you believe it." O'Doherty, *Inside the White Cube*, 52.

20. Jurgenson, *The Social Photo*, 8.

21. Moeller, "On Second-Order Observation and Genuine Pretending"; Formilan and Stark, "Testing the Creative Identity."

22. Wasik, *And Then There's This*, 212.

23. O'Doherty, *Inside the White Cube*.

24. See https://holtsmithsonfoundation.org/spiral-jetty.

25. Obrist, *Ways of Curating*, 139–145. See, e.g., Douglas Gordon's experiments with time in the 1999 exhibition *Retrace Your Steps, Remember Tomorrow* and his 1993 installation *From the Moment You Read These Words, Until You Meet Someone with Blue Eyes*.

26. See *Il Tempo del Postino* or the forty volumes of his "Infinite Conversations"; Obrist, *Ways of Curating*, 55–59. A lengthy interview in the *New Yorker* informs us that "the Internet is always on Obrist's mind"—he is an "avid user of Instagram" with a keen interest in Snapchat. Max, "The Art of Conversation."

27. https://www.tate.org.uk/whats-on/tate-modern/exhibition/christian-marclay -clock.

28. The Tate, "Five Ways Christian Marclay's *The Clock* Does More Than Just Tell the Time," https://www.tate.org.uk/art/lists/five-ways-christian-marclays-clock-does -more-just-tell-time (accessed July 8, 2021).

29. Luhmann, *Die Wissenschaft der Gesellschaft*, 73–75.

30. Jurgenson, *The Social Photo*, 78, 85.

CHAPTER 7

1. Strictly speaking, the only purpose of machine-learning procedures is to extract patterns from data. These patterns can be used to test systems and improve on them by learning from mistakes. The approach of predictive analytics, however, claims to go further and to use these techniques to "defy the law of nature" that you cannot see the future because it isn't here yet. Learning algorithms would make it possible to build a system "that peers right through the previously impenetrable barrier between today and tomorrow." Siegel, "Predictive Analytics," 30.

2. O'Neil, *Weapons of Math Destruction*; Amoore, "Data Derivatives"; Anderson, "Preemption, Precaution, Preparedness"; De Goede and Randalls, "Precaution, Preemption."

3. Hacking, *The Emergence of Probability*; Porter, *The Rise of Statistical Thinking 1820–1900*.

4. Daston, *Classical Probability in the Enlightenment*, 49–111.

5. This does not mean, of course, that the programming of algorithms is reviving the superstitious and anti-scientific aspects that are often associated with divination. Algorithms offer a different form of prediction connected with the technical features of their work. But precisely because research on machine learning is perfectly integrated into contemporary scientific activity, the similarities with divination can be enlightening to investigate current developments.

6. Fahad Manjoo, "Where No Search Engine Has Gone Before."

7. Kitchin, "Big Data, New Epistemologies and Paradigm Shifts," 4.

8. "At its core, big data is about prediction," claim Mayer-Schönberger and Cukier in *Big Data*, 11. With almost the same words, Domingos argues that "at its core, machine learning is about prediction." Domingos, *The Master Algorithm*, xv. The research area of predictive analytics, which is rapidly spreading across all fields, from marketing to healthcare to government and financial services, is explicitly devoted to this: mining data to discover the structures of the future; cf. Siegel, *Predictive Analytics*.

9. Hofman, Sharma, and Watts, "Prediction and Explanation in Social systems."

10. Shmueli, "To Explain or to Predict?" The classic reference is Hempel's explanation/prediction symmetry thesis in "Aspects of Scientific Explanation," claiming that explanation and prediction have the same logical structure and differ only in the time of occurrence. A prediction is basically an explanation referring to a time later than that at which the argument is offered; see Hempel, "The Theoretician's Dilemma," 37–38.

11. "With enough data, the numbers speak for themselves," claims Anderson in "The End of Theory," In the digital world there is no need to know "why" it comes to a given result, only "what" it is; see Mayer-Schönberger and Cukier, *Big Data*, 7. If relationships can be identified without causality, explanation is not needed: "correlation supersedes causation" (Anderson, "End of Theory").

12. Daston, *Classical Probability in the Enlightenment*, chapter 5.

13. Called *observational* or *found* data. McFarland and McFarland, "Big Data."

14. Shalev-Shwartz and Ben-David, *Understanding Machine Learning: From Theory to Algorithms*, 25.

15. Wachter, Mittelstadt, and Floridi, "Transparent, Explainable, and Accountable AI."

16. Breiman, "Statistical Modeling: The Two Cultures," 208.

17. This obviously does not mean that understanding becomes irrelevant but separates the problem of transparency from the problem of interpretability; see Lipton, "The Mythos of Model Interpretability." When the way algorithms work is not comprehensible to the human mind, problems can arise in the use of algorithms. Even when the model is right, it is not always right to use it, and a decision is required; see Doshi-Velez et al., "Accountability of AI Under the Law." One can then request post-hoc interpretability: an explanation of the decisions of the algorithms that does not necessarily require describing the mechanisms involved. Often, however, it will imply producing a model to generate explanations separate from the model to generate predictions. Chapter 1 deals more thoroughly with the consequences of this condition.

18. See, e.g., the debate around Ali Rahimi's claim in his presentation at the Conference on Neural Information Processing Systems (NIPS) 2017: "Machine Learning Has Become Alchemy," https://www.youtube.com/watch?v=ORHFOnaEzPc.

19. Vernant, "Parole e segni muti"; Maul, *Die Wahrsagekunst im alten Orient*; Rochberg, *The Heavenly Writing*.

20. Brisson, "Del buon uso della sregolatezza (Grecia)."

21. Rochberg, "The History of Science and Ancient Mesopotamia," 55; Rochberg, "Reasoning, Representing, and Modeling in Babylonian Astronomy."

22. Koch, "Three Strikes and You're Out!"

23. Nissinen, "Prophecy and Omen Divination."

24. Vandermeersch, "Dalla tartaruga all'achillea (Cina)."

25. Vernant, "Parole e segni muti," 14.

26. Annus, "On the Beginnings and Continuities of Omen Sciences"; Koch-Westenholz, *Mesopotamian Astrology*, 18.

27. Maul, "Divination Culture and the Handling of the Future," 363.

28. Rochberg, "Reasoning, Representing, and Modeling in Babylonian Astronomy," 9.

29. Rochberg, *The Heavenly Writing*, 203.

30. Anzulewicz, "Aeternitas—aevum—tempus"; Luhmann, *Soziologie des Risikos*, 42.

31. See the debate on contingent futures in Aristotle, *De Interpretatione 9*: Assertions on the outcome of a future naval battle are true or false already today, but we are not yet able to choose between the two values.

32. Maul, "Divination Culture and the Handling of the Future," 363.

33. Nevertheless, divination did not necessarily correspond to a fatalistic or deterministic attitude. In Mesopotamia divinatory omens expressed a sort of warning of was what to come, providing the necessary knowledge to intervene and revise it, bending the future to one's own advantage; see Maul, "How the Babylonians Protected Themselves against Calamities." Even if the divinatory worldview did not allow for chance or hazard and everything followed a divine order, the revealed future was not irrevocable.

34. Luhmann, "Temporalisierung von Komplexität: Zur Semantik neuzeitlicher Zeitbegriffe"; Koselleck, *Vergangene Zukunft*.

35. Esposito, *Die Fiktion der wahrscheinlichen Realität*.

36. See Alessandro Vespignani, *L'algoritmo e l'oracolo: Come la scienza predice il futuro e ci aiuta a cambiarlo* [The algorithm and the oracle: How science predicts the future and helps us change it].

37. Domingos expects that the different approaches used in algorithmic programming will eventually be unified to compose an "ultimate Master Algorithm" that "can derive all knowledge in the world—past, present and future—from data." Like divinity in ancient divinatory culture, there would be one entity to whom all knowledge is accessible, for whom the difference between time horizons is irrelevant: "If you believe in an *omnipotent God*, then you can model the universe as a vast naïve Bayes distribution where everything that happens is independent given God's will. The catch is that *we can't read God's mind*" (emphasis added). Domingos, *The Master Algorithm* xviii, 152.

38. Goodfellow, Bengio, and Courville, *Deep Learning*, 98.

39. Breiman, "Statistical Modeling: The Two Cultures."

40. Amoore and Piotukh, "Life Beyond Big Data."

41. Sober, *Ockham's Razors: A User's Manual*, 134.

42. Breiman, "Statistical Modeling," 205.

43. "The Two Cultures: Statistics vs. Machine Learning?" http://stats.stackexchange .com/questions/6/the-two-cultures-statistics-vs-machine-learning (accessed February 15, 2017).

44. Assmann, *Das kulturelle Gedächtnis*, 17; Koch, "Three Strikes and You're Out!"

45. Maul, "Divination Culture and the Handling of the Future," 369.

46. Siegel, *Predictive Analytics*, 12.

47. Desrósieres, "Mapping the Social World"; Lee and Martin, "Surfeit and Surface."

48. Siegel, *Predictive Analytics*, 23.

49. Rieder, "Scrutinizing an Algorithmic Technique," 12.

50. See the discussion of algorithmic individualization in chapter 4.

51. Cardon, *À quoi rêvent les algorithmes?* 27.

52. Golder and Macy, "Digital Footprints."

53. Clark, *Surfing Uncertainty: Prediction, Action*, 163.

54. Bornstein, "Is Artificial Intelligence Permanently Inscrutable?"

55. Lee and Martin, "Surfeit and Surface"; MacKenzie, "The Production of Prediction," 440.

56. A growing number of colleges and universities in the US, for instance, use predictive analytics to spot students who are unknowingly in danger of dropping out: cf. Treaster, "Will You Graduate?"

57. See, e.g., Gitelman,*"Raw Data" Is an Oxymoron*; boyd and Crawford, "Critical Questions for Big Data"; Gillespie, "The Relevance of Algorithms"; Mittelstadt et al., "The Ethics of Algorithms."

58. The concept of reality is far away from ideas of truth as correspondence (Aristotle, *Metaphysics*, 1011b26), and rather close to a Popperian approach, assuming that the reference to reality can conclusively refute wrong hypotheses rather than confirm correct ones; see Popper, *Conjectures and Refutations*. It is an implicitly constructivist concept of reality: reality is the result of the intervention of the systems that intend to know it. See Watzlawick, *Die erfundene Wirklichkeit*; von Foerster, *Observing Systems*.

59. Cardon, *À quoi rêvent les algorithmes*, 22; Kotras, "Mass Personalization and the reshaping of consumer knowledge."

60. Sharma, "How Predictive AI Will Change Shopping."

61. MacKenzie, "The Production of Prediction," 436.

62. Sinha, Foscht, and Fung, "How Analytics and AI Are Driving the Subscription E-commerce Phenomenon."

63. Jouvenal, "Police Are Using Software to Predict Crime."

64. Clark, *Surfing Uncertainty*, 123.

65. Rieder, "Scrutinizing an Algorithmic Technique," 11, 12. Regarding the research about performative effects of models, focused on the field of economics, see MacKenzie, *An Engine, Not a Camera*; MacKenzie, Muniesa and Siu, *Do Economists Make Markets?: On the Performativity of Economics*; and Esposito, "The Structures of Uncertainty."

66. Clark, *Surfing Uncertainty*, 286.

67. Harcourt, *Against Prediction*. Apparently gun violence in Chicago has surged since 2015, even if the city has been using an algorithmically produced Strategic Subject List that tries to predict who is most likely to be involved in a shooting; see Asher and Arthur, "Inside the Algorithm That Tries to Predict Gun Violence in Chicago." On the evaluation of predictive policing experiments, see Hunt, Sauders, and Hollywood, *Evaluation of the Shreveport Predictive Policing Experiment*.

68. Unlike seismic events that are the reference of predictive policing software such as PredPol (http://www.predpol.com/); see Shapiro, "Reform Predictive Policing"; O'Neil, *Weapons of Math Destruction*, 87; Lum and Issac, "To Predict and Serve?"

69. O'Neil, *Weapons of Math Destruction*, 9.

70. According to apotropaic rituals intended to turn away harm or evil influences: see Annus, "On the Beginnings and Continuities of Omen Sciences," 2; Maul, "How the Babylonians Protected Themselves against Calamities," 124–126.

71. Kotras, "Mass Personalization." Cf. the highly debated case of Google Flu Trends, which, after initial success, proved ineffective in predicting the spread of influenza: see Vespignani *L'algoritmo e l'oracolo.*, 61–62, 110–112. The failure has also been attributed to internal changes to Google's recommendation systems, which reacted to the increase in searches about flu and began suggesting flu-related queries to people who did not have flu: Lazer et al., "The Parable of Google Flu."

72. Lipton, "The Mythos of Model Interpretability."

73. See Harcourt, *Against Prediction.*

74. The forecast is based on the very doubtful assumption that the future reproduces the past. See Cardon, *À quoi rêvent les algorithmes,* 58; Amoore and Piotukh, "Life Beyond Big Data," 359; Rona-Tas, "Predicting the Future."

75. Goodfellow, Benjo, and Courville, *Deep Learning,* 481.

76. According to Sober one of the basic limitations of Bayesian conditionalization, inherited by machine learning procedures, is the inability to consider new objects. The system only learns (better and better) what it previously identified as its object. Models do not consider what they do not count. Sober, *Ockham's Razors: A User's Manual,* 78; O'Neil, *Weapons of Math Destruction,* 59.

77. Kerr and Earle, "Prediction, Preemption, Presumption," 67–68; Amoore, "Algorithmic War," 53–55.

78. Kotras describes the resulting "paradoxes of ultra-personalization." Kotras, "Mass Personalization."

79. Huff, *How to Lie with Statistics.*

80. Backtesting procedures used to verify algorithms are a form of predicting the past; see Siegel, *Predictive Analytics,* 88.

81. And to practical limitations: algorithms lack, for example, the creativity to make noncircular predictions—not just predicting what posts on Facebook people will like, but writing new posts that people will like; see Mullainathan, "Why Computers Won't Be Replacing You."

82. Rona-Tas, "Predicting the Future."

83. Goodfellow, Benjo, and Courville, *Deep Learning,* 110; MacKenzie, "The Production of Prediction," 439. Generalization in machine learning has a different meaning than in statistics, where generalization involves extending to the population the findings about a sample; see Hacking, *The Emergence of Probability,* chapter 19. But algorithms work with the entire population and do not need to generalize in this sense.

84. The reference to singularities is a further difference from the mainstream approach of statistics. While frequentist probability refers to repeatable events and

calculates their rate of occurrence, Bayesian probability and machine learning deal with unrepeatable events; see Goodfellow, Benjo, and Courville, *Deep Learning*, 55.

85. Domingos, "A Few Useful Things to Know about Machine Learning."

86. Eco, "An Ars Oblivionalis? Forget It!"

87. Goodfellow, Benjo, and Courville, *Deep Learning*, 155–156.

88. Barber, *Bayesian Reasoning and Machine Learning*, chapter 15.

89. Barber, *Bayesian Reasoning and Machine Learning*, chapter 13.3. The preference for simpler systems is presented as a variant of Occam's razor, which advised scholastic philosophers not to get lost in irrelevant complications, but to prefer the simplest explanation: Domingos, "The Role of Occam's Razor in Knowledge Discovery."

90. Goodfellow, Benjo, and Courville, *Deep Learning*, 130.

91. Kotras, "Mass Personalization," 7.

92. Harcourt, *Against Prediction*, 237–239.

93. Nietzsche, *Unzeitgemässe Betrachtungen*, 116. See also "Remembering to Forget" in chapter 5 above.

94. Bias reduction is paid for with futility: Mitchell, *Machine Learning*, 43. In learning algorithms, high bias translates into a tendency to consistently learn the same things, but low bias leads to learning random things irrespective of the real signal—i.e., to learn very little or to learn irrelevant things.

95. In machine learning, the issue is discussed in terms of the relationship between *exploitation* and *exploration* (initially proposed in March, "Exploration and Exploitation in Organization Learning"), where exploitation refers to the use of experience to deal with an already known world, whereas exploration refers to the pursuit of unknown facts and surprises (which can be illuminating but also risky—or futile).

96. Esposito, *Soziales Vergessen*.

97. Koselleck, *Vergangene Zukunft*, 38–66.

CONCLUSION

1. Overbye, "Can a Computer Devise a Theory of Everything?"

2. Anderson, "The End of Theory."

3. Overbye, "Can a Computer Devise a Theory of Everything?"

4. Tegmark, *Life 3.0: Being Human in the Age of Artificial Intelligence*.

5. Metz, "London A.I. Lab Claims Breakthrough."

6. Jess Thaler, director of the Institute for Artificial Intelligence and Fundamental Interactions (https://iaifi.org/), as quoted in Overbye, "Can a Computer Devise a Theory of Everything?"

7. Turing, "Computing Machinery and Intelligence."

8. "Captcha" stands for "Completely Automated Public Turing Test to Tell Computers and Humans Apart": http://www.captcha.net/.

9. "Bias is the original sin of AI," as Howard puts it in *Sex, Race, and Robots*.

10. Buolamwini and Gebru, "Intersectional Accuracy Disparities in Commercial Gender Classification."

11. Angwin et al., "Machine Bias"; Lum and Isaac, "To Predict and Serve?"

12. Reese, "Why Microsoft's 'Tay' Bot Went Wrong."

13. O'Neil, *Weapons of Math Destruction*.

14. Crawford, "Artificial Intelligence's White Guy Problem."

15. Berreby, "Can We Make Our Robots Less Biased Than We Are?"

16. On the difference between algorithmic bias and data bias, see Mehrabi et al., "A Survey on Bias and Fairness in Machine Learning."

17. The Microsoft staff who programmed Tay apparently were horrified upon reading the racist and sexually charged messages released by the chatbot, which was quickly suspended (Mason 2016). The machine's actions evidently did not reflect their values and preferences.

18. See the Algorithmic Justice League's website: https://www.ajl.org/.

19. See Walton, Macagno, and Sartor, *Statutory Interpretation*.

20. Ashley, *Artificial Intelligence and Legal Analytics*.

21. Canale and Tuzet, *La giustificazione della decisione*, IX; Or with Luhmann, *Das Recht der Gesellschaft*, 362: "The argument does not reflect what the reader has in mind."

22. Lettieri, "Law, Rights, and the Fallacy of Computation."

23. Walton, Macagno, and Sartor, *Statutory Interpretation*, 4.

24. Solan, "Pernicious Ambiguity in Contracts and Statutes," 862.

25. Garfinkel, *Studies in Ethnomethodology*, 111.

26. Vanderstichele, "Interpretable AI, Explainable AI and the Sui Generis Method"; Durt, "Why Explainability Is Not Interpretability."

27. Luhmann, *Recht und Automation in der öffentlichen Verwaltung*, 49.

28. Luhmann, *Recht und Automation in der öffentlichen Verwaltung*, 106.

29. Walton, Macagno, and Sartor, *Statutory Interpretation. Pragmatics and Argumentation*, 9.

BIBLIOGRAPHY

Abruzzese, Alberto, and Mario Pireddu. "Facebook come Fakebook." In *Facebook come: Le nuove relazioni virtuali*, edited by Renata Borgato, Ferruccio Capelli, and Mauro Ferraresi, 76–82. Milan: Franco Angeli, 2009.

Adkins, Lisa, and Celia Lury, eds. *Measure and Value*. Malden, MA: Wiley, 2012.

Agostinho, Daniela. "The Optical Unconscious of Big Data: Datafication of Vision and Care for Unknown Futures." *Big Data & Society* 6, no. 1 (January 2019).

Agrawal, Rakesh. "Rakesh Agrawal Speaks Out." Interview by Marianne Winslett, 2003. http://sigmod.org/publications/interviews/pdf/D15.rakesh-final-final.pdf.

Agrawal, Rakesh, Tomasz Imielinski, and Arun Swami. "Mining Association Rules Between Sets of Items in Large Databases." *SIGMOD Record* 22, no. 2 (June 1993): 207–216. https://doi.org/10.1145/170036.170072.

Algee-Hewitt, Mark, Sarah Allison, Marissa Gemma, Ryan Heuser, Franco Moretti, and Hannah Walser. "Canon/Archive: Large-Scale Dynamics in the Literary Field." *Literary Lab Pamphlet* 11 (January 2016). https://litlab.stanford.edu/LiteraryLabPamphlet11.pdf.

Algee-Hewitt, Mark, Ryan Heuser, and Franco Moretti. "On Paragraphs: Scale, Themes, and Narrative Form." *Literary Lab Pamphlet* 10 (October 2015). https://litlab.stanford.edu/LiteraryLabPamphlet10.pdf.

Alharbi, Mohammad, and Robert S. Laramee. "SoS TextVis: A Survey of Surveys on Text Visualization." *Computer Graphics & Visual Computing* (2018): 143–152.

Al-Rfou, Rami, Marc Pickett, Javier Snaider, Yun-hsuan Sung, Brian Strope, and Ray Kurzweil. "Conversational Contextual Cues: The Case of Personalization and

History for Response Ranking." arXiv.org, submitted on June 1, 2016. https://arxiv.org/abs/1606.00372v1.

Amoore, Louise. "Algorithmic War: Everyday Geographies of the War on Terror." *Antipode: A Radical Journal of Geography* 41 (2009): 49–69.

Amoore, Louise. "Data Derivatives: On the Emergence of a Security Risk Calculus for Our Times." *Theory, Culture & Society* 28, no. 6 (2011): 24–43.

Amoore, Louise, and Volha Piotukh. "Life Beyond Big Data: Governing with Little Analytics." *Economy and Society* 44, no. 3 (2015): 341–366.

Anderson, Ben. "Preemption, Precaution, Preparedness: Anticipatory Action and Future Geographies." *Progress in Human Geography* 34, no. 6 (2010): 777–798.

Anderson, Chris. "The End of Theory: The Data Deluge Makes the Scientific Method Obsolete." *Wired* 16 (2008). https://www.wired.com/2008/06/pb-theory/.

Anderson, Chris. *The Long Tail: Why the Future of Business Is Selling Less of More.* New York: Hyperion, 2006.

Anderson, Michael C. "Rethinking Interference Theory: Executive Control and the Mechanisms of Forgetting." *Journal of Memory and Language* 49 (2003): 415–445.

Angwin, Julia, Jeff Larson, Surya Mattu, and Lauren Kirchner. "Machine Bias: There's Software Used across the Country to Predict Future Criminals. And It's Biased against Blacks." *ProPublica*, May 23, 2016. https://www.propublica.org/article/machine-bias-risk-assessments-in-criminal-sentencing.

Annus, Amar. "On the Beginnings and Continuities of Omen Sciences in the Ancient World." In *Divination and Interpretation of Signs in the Ancient World*, edited by Amar Annus, 1–18. Chicago: The Oriental Institute of the University of Chicago, 2010.

Anzulewicz, Henryk. "Aeternitas—Aevum—Tempus: The Concept of Time in the System of Albert the Great." In *The Medieval Concept of Time: Studies on the Scholastic Debate and Its Reception in Early Modern Philosophy*, edited by Pasquale Porro, 83–129. Leiden: Brill, 2001.

Aristotle. *Posterior Analytics.* Translated by Jonathan Barnes. Oxford: Clarendon Press, 1993.

Asher, Jeff, and Rob Arthur. "Inside the Algorithm That Tries to Predict Gun Violence in Chicago." *New York Times*, June 13, 2017.

Ashley, Kevin D. *Artificial Intelligence and Legal Analytics: New Tools for Law Practice in the Digital Age.* Cambridge: Cambridge University Press, 2017.

Assante, Ernesto. "Tutti pazzi per TikTok, il social che dà 15 secondi di celebrità." *La Repubblica*, March 2, 2020.

Assmann, Jan. *Das kulturelle Gedächtnis. Schrift, Erinnerung und politische Identität in frühen Hochkulturen.* Munich: Beck, 1992.

Assmann, Jan, and Tonio Hölscher, eds. *Kultur und Gedächtnis*. Frankfurt am Main: Suhrkamp, 1988.

Auerbach, David. "A.I. Has Grown Up and Left Home: It Matters Only That We Think, Not How We Think." *Nautilus*, December 19, 2013. http://nautil.us/issue/8 /home/ai-has-grown-up-and-left-home.

Ausloos, Jef. "The 'Right to be Forgotten'—Worth Remembering?" *Computer Law & Security Report* 28, no. 2 (2012): 143–152.

Baltrušaitis, Jurgis. *Anamorphoses ou Thaumaturgus opticus*. Paris: Flammarion, 1984.

Barabas, Chelsea, Karthik Dinakar, Joichi Ito, Madars Virza, and Jonathan Zittrain. "Interventions over Predictions: Reframing the Ethical Debate for Actuarial Risk Assessment." *Proceedings of Machine Learning Research* 81 (2018): 1–15.

Barber, David. *Bayesian Reasoning and Machine Learning*. Cambridge: Cambridge University Press, 2012. http://web4.cs.ucl.ac.uk/staff/D.Barber/textbook/171216.pdf.

Barone, Francine, David Zeitlyn, and Viktor Mayer-Schönberger. "Learning from Failure: The Case of the Disappearing Web Site." *First Monday* 20, no. 5 (2015). https://doi.org/10.5210/fm.v20i5.5852.

Bateson, Gregory. *Steps to an Ecology of Mind*. San Francisco: Chandler, 1972.

Bayard, Pierre. *How to Talk about Books You Haven't Read*. New York: Bloomsbury, 2007.

Beck, Ulrich. *Risk Society: Towards a New Modernity*. London: Sage, 1992.

Beer, David. "Power through the Algorithm? Participatory Web Cultures and the Technological Unconscious." *New Media & Society* 11, no. 6 (2009): 985–1002.

Behrisch, M., M. Blumenschein, N. W. Kim, L. Shao, M. El-Assady, J. Fuchs, D. Seebacher, A. Diehl, U. Brandes, H. Pfister, T. Schreck, D. Weiskopf, and D.A. Keim. "Quality Metrics for Information Visualization." *Computer Graphics Forum* 37 (2018): 625–662. https://doi.org/10.1111/cgf.13446.

Benkler, Yochai. *The Wealth of Networks: How Social Production Transforms Markets and Freedom*. New Haven, CT: Yale University Press, 2006.

Benway, Jan Panero, and David M. Lane. "Banner Blindness: Web Searchers Often Miss 'Obvious' Links." *Itg Newsletter* 1, no. 3 (1998): 1–22. Retrieved March 13, 2019.

Berners-Lee, Tim, James Hendler, and Ora Lassila. "The Semantic Web: A New Form of Web Content That Is Meaningful to Computers Will Unleash a Revolution of New Possibilities." *Scientific American* 284 (May 2001): 1–5.

Berreby, David. "Can We Make Our Robots Less Biased Than We Are?" *New York Times*, November 22, 2020.

Binns, Reuben. "How to Be Open about Being Closed." *Limn* 6 (March 2016) https://limn.it/articles/how-to-be-open-about-being-closed/.

Bissell, Tom. *Extra Lives: Why Video Games Matter*. New York: Random House, 2010.

Bissell, Tom. "The Grammar of Fun: CliffyB and the World of the Video Game." *New Yorker*, October 27, 2008.

Blair, Ann. "Annotating and Indexing Natural Philosophy." In *Books and the Sciences in History*, edited by Marina Frasca-Spada, and Nick Jardine, 69–89. Cambridge: Cambridge University Press, 2000.

Blanchette, Jean-François, and Deborah G. Johnson. "Data Retention and the Panoptic Society: The Social Benefits of Forgetfulness." *Information Society* 18 (2002): 33–45.

Blumenberg, Hans. "Nachahmung der Natur: Zur Vorgeschichte der Idee des schöpferischen Menschen." *Studium Generale* 10 (1957): 266–283.

Bode, Katherine. *Reading by Numbers: Recalibrating the Literary Field*. London: Anthem Press, 2012.

Boellstorff, Tom. "Making Big Data, in Theory." *First Monday* 18, no. 10 (2013).

Bolzoni, Lina. *La stanza della memoria: Modelli letterari e iconografici nell'età della stampa*. Torino: Einaudi, 1995.

Borges, Jorge Luis. "The Analytical Language of John Wilkins." In *Other Inquisitions 1937–1952*, translated by Ruth L. C. Simms, 101–105. Austin: University of Texas Press, 1993.

Borges, Jorge Luis. "Funes el memorioso." In *Ficciones*. Buenos Aires: Editorial Sur, 1944.

Borgo, Stefano. "Ontological Challenges to Cohabitation with Self-Taught Robots." *Semantic Web* 11, no. 3 (2020): 161–167.

Bornstein, Aaron M. "Is Artificial Intelligence Permanently Inscrutable? Despite New Biology-Like Tools, Some Insist Interpretation Is Impossible." *Nautilus*, September 1, 2016. http://nautil.us/issue/40/learning/is-artificial-intelligence-permanently-inscrutable.

Bostrom, Nick. *Superintelligence: Paths, Dangers, Strategies*. Oxford: Oxford University Press, 2014.

Bottéro, Jean. "Sintomi, segni, scritture nell'antica Mesopotamia." In *Divination et Rationalité*, edited by J. P. Vernant, L. Vandermeersch, J. Gernet, J. Bottéro, R. Crahay, L. Brisson, J. Carlier, D. Grodzynski, and A. Retel-Laurentin, 73–214. Paris: Seuil, 1974.

Bowker Geoffrey C., Susan Leigh Star. *Sorting Things Out. Classification and Its Consequences*. Cambridge, MA: MIT Press, 1999.

boyd, danah, and Kate Crawford. "Critical Questions for Big Data." *Information, Communication and Society* 15, no. 5 (2012): 662–679. https://doi.org/10.1080/1369 118x.2012.678878.

Braidotti, Rosi. *The Posthuman.* Cambridge: Polity, 2013.

Breiman, Leo. "Statistical Modeling: The Two Cultures." *Statistical Science* 16, no. 3 (2001): 199–231.

Bresnick, Ethan. *Intensified Play: Cinematic Study of TikTok Mobile App.* University of Southern California, 2019. Accessed March 2, 2020. https://www.academia.edu /40213511/Intensified_Play_Cinematic_study_of_TikTok_mobile_app .

Brisson, Luc. "Del buon uso della sregolatezza (Grecia)." In *Divination et Rationalité*, edited by J. P. Vernant, L. Vandermeersch, J. Gernet, J. Bottéro, R. Crahay, L. Brisson, J. Carlier, D. Grodzynski, and A. Retel-Laurentin, 239–272. Paris: Seuil, 1974.

Brubaker, Rogers. "Digital Hyperconnectivity and the Self." *Theory and Society* 49 (2020): 771–801.

Brunton, Finn, and Helen Nissenbaum. *Obfuscation: A User's Guide for Privacy and Protest.* Cambridge, MA: MIT Press, 2015.

Buolamwini, Joy, and Timnit Gebru. "Intersectional Accuracy Disparities in Commercial Gender Classification." *Proceedings of Machine Learning Research* 81 (2018): 1–15.

Burrell, Jenna. "How the Machine 'Thinks': Understanding Opacity in Machine Learning Algorithms." *Big Data & Society* 1 (2016): 1–12.

Callon, Michel, ed. *The Laws of the Markets.* Oxford, Blackwell, 1998.

Callon, Michel. "The Role of Hybrid Communities and Socio-Technical Arrangements in the Participatory Design." *Journal of the Centre for Information Studies* 5, no. 3 (2004): 3–10.

Canale, D. and G. Tuzet *La giustificazione della decisione giudiziale.* Torino: Giappichelli, 2020.

Card, Stuart K., Jock D. Mackinlay, and Ben Shneiderman. *Readings in Information Visualization, Using Vision to Think.* San Francisco: Morgan Kaufmann, 1999.

Cardon, Dominique. *À quoi rêvent les algorithms.* Paris: Seuil, 2015.

Carr, Nicholas. *The Big Switch: Rewiring the World, From Edison To Google.* New York: Norton, 2008.

Carusi, Annamaria. "Making the Visual Visible in Philosophy of Science." *Spontaneous Generations* 6, no. 1 (2012): 106–114.

Cecire, Natalia. "Ways of Not Reading Gertrude Stein." *ELH: English Literary History* 82, no. 1 (2015): 281–312.

Cevolini, Alberto. *De arte excerpendi: Imparare a dimenticare nella modernità*. Firenze: Olschki, 2006.

Cevolini, Alberto. "Der Leser im Gelesenen: Beobachtung dritter Ordnung im Umgang mit Gelehrtenmaschinen." Paper presented at the conference Die Veränderung der Realitätswahrnehmung durch die digitalen Medien, Universität der Bundeswehr München, September 1–2, 2016.

Cevolini, Alberto, ed. *Forgetting Machines: Knowledge Management Evolution in Early Modern Europe*. Leiden: Brill, 2016.

Cevolini, Alberto, and Gérald Bronner, eds. "What Is New in Fake News? Public Opinion and Second-Order Observation in a Hyperconnected Society." Special issue of *Sociologia e Politiche Sociali* 21, no. 3 (2018).

Chabert, Jean-Luc, ed. *A History of Algorithms. From the Pebble to the Microchip*. Berlin-Heidelberg: Springer, 1999.

Chantraine, P. "Les verbes grecs signifiant 'lire.'" In *Mélanges Henri Grégoire, Annuaires de l'Institute de Philologie et d'Histoire Orientales et Slaves 2*, 115–126. Bruxelles: Secrètariat des Editions de l'Institut, 1950.

Chen, Brian X. "Are Targeted Ads Stalking You? Here's How to Make Them Stop." *New York Times*, Aug 15, 2018.

Cheney-Lippold, John. "A New Algorithmic Identity: Soft Biopolitics and the Modulation of Control." *Theory, Culture & Society* 28, no. 6 (2011): 164–181.

Chun, Wendy Hui Kyong. *Programmed Visions: Software and Memory*. Cambridge, MA: MIT Press, 2011.

Ciaccia Paolo, Davide Martinenghi, and Riccardo Torlone. "Foundations of Context-Aware Preference Propagation." *Journal of the ACM* 67, no. 1 (January 2020): 1–43.

Cimiano, Philipp, Sebastian Rudolph, and Helena Hartfiel. "Computing Intensional Answers to Questions—An Inductive Logic Programming Approach." *Data & Knowledge Engineering* 69, no. 3 (2010): 261–278.

Clark, Andy. *Surfing Uncertainty: Prediction, Action, and the Embodied Mind*. New York: Oxford University Press, 2016.

Clement, Tanya. "The Story of One: Narrative and Composition in Gertrude Stein's *The Making of Americans*." *Texas Studies in Literature and Language* 54, no. 3 (2012): 426–448.

Collins, Harry. *Artificial Experts: Social Knowledge and Intelligent Machines*. Cambridge, MA: MIT Press, 1990.

Contzen, Eva von. "Die Affordanzen der Liste." [The affordances of the list.] *Zeitschrift für Literaturwissenschaft und Linguistik* 3 (2017): 317–326.

Cooley, Alexander, and Jack Snyder, eds. *Ranking the World: Grading States as a Tool of Global Governance*. Cambridge: Cambridge University Press, 2016.

Cooper, David, Christopher Donaldson, and Patricia Murrieta-Flores. *Literary Mapping in the Digital Age*. Abingdon: Routledge, 2016.

Cowls, Josh, and Ralph Schroeder. "Causation, Correlation, and Big Data in Social Science Research." *Policy & Internet* 7 (2015): 447–472.

Crawford, Kate. "Artificial Intelligence's White Guy Problem." *New York Times*, June 25, 2016.

Crawford, Kate, Kate Miltner, and Mary L. Gray. "Critiquing Big Data: Politics, Ethics, Epistemology." *International Journal of Communication* 8 (2014): 1663–1672.

Custers, Bart. "Click Here to Consent Forever: Expiry Dates for Informed Consent." *Big Data & Society* 2 (2016): 1–6.

Daston, Lorraine. *Classical Probability in the Enlightenment*. Princeton: Princeton University Press, 1988.

Davis, Lauren. "At Last, a Graph That Explains Scifi TV after Star Trek." *Gizmodo*, August 28, 2009. https://io9.gizmodo.com/at-last-a-graph-that-explains-scifi-tv-after -star-trek-5347631.

Davis, Martin. *Computability and Unsolvability*. New York: McGraw-Hill, 1958.

Davis, Phil. "What Is the Difference between Personalization and Customization?" Towerdata. Accessed June 19, 2019. https://www.towerdata.com/blog/what-is-the -difference-between-personalization-and-customization.

Davis, Richard. "Moving Targets: Web Preservation and Reference Management." Presentation at Innovations in Reference Management workshop, January 2010. http://www.ariadne.ac.uk/issue/62/davis/.

De Goede, Marie, and Samuel Randalls. "Precaution, Preemption: Arts and Technologies of the Actionable Future." *Environment and Planning D: Society and Space* 27 (2009): 859–878.

De Mauro, Tullio. *Linguistica elementare*. Rome: Laterza, 1998.

Derrida, Jacques. *Ulysse gramophone, Deux mots pour Joyce*. Paris: Galilée, 1987.

Desrosières, Alain. "Mapping the Social World: From Aggregates to Individuals." *Limn* 2 (2012). https://limn.it/articles/mapping-the-social-world-from-aggregates-to -individuals/.

Diakopoulos, Nicholas. "Algorithmic Accountability." *Digital Journalism* 3, no. 3 (2014): 398–415. https://doi.org/10.1080/21670811.2014.976411.

Dill, Kevin. "What Is Game AI?" In *Game AI Pro: Collected Wisdom of Game AI Professionals*, edited by Steve Rabin, 3–9. Boca Raton: CRC Press, 2013.

DiNucci, Darcy. "Fragmented Future." *Print.* 53, no. 4 (1999): 221–222.

Doležalová, Lucie. "Ad Hoc Lists of Bernard Itier (1163–1225), Librarian of St. Martial de Limoges." In *The Charm of a List: From the Sumerians to Computerised Data Processing,* edited by Lucie Doležalová, 80–99. Newcastle upon Tyne: Cambridge Scholars Publishing, 2009.

Domingos, Pedro. "A Few Useful Things to Know about Machine Learning." *Communications of the ACM* 55, no. 10 (2012): 78–87.

Domingos, Pedro. *The Master Algorithm: How the Quest for the Ultimate Learning Machine Will Remake Our World.* New York: Basic Books, 2015.

Domingos, Pedro. "The Role of Occam's Razor in Knowledge Discovery." *Data Mining and Knowledge Discovery* 3, no. 4 (1999): 409–425. https://doi.org/10.1023 /A:1009868929893.

Doshi-Velez, Finale, Mason Kortz, Ryan Budish, Chris Bavitz, Sam Gershman, David O'Brien, Kate Scott, Stuart Schieber, James Waldo, David Weinberger, and Alexandra Wood. "Accountability of AI Under the Law: The Role of Explanation." arXiv.org. Submitted November 3, 2017. arXiv:1711.01134. https://arxiv.org/abs/1711.01134.

Douglas, J. Yellowlees. *The End of Books—Or Books without End?* Ann Arbor: University of Michigan Press, 2001.

Dreyfus, Hubert. *What Computers Can't Do.* Cambridge, MA: MIT Press, 1972.

Drucker, Johanna. *Graphesis: Visual Forms of Knowledge Production.* Cambridge, MA: Harvard University Press, 2014.

Drucker, Johanna. "Humanities Approaches to Graphical Display." *Digital Humanities Quarterly* 5, no. 1 (2011).

Drucker, Johanna. "Graphical Approaches to the Digital Humanities." In *A New Companion to Digital Humanities,* ed. Susan Schreibman, Raymond George Siemens, and John Unsworth, 238–250. Chichester: Wiley, 2016.

Duhigg, Charles. "How Companies Learn Our Secrets." *New York Times Magazine,* February 19, 2012.

Durt, Christoph. "Why Explainability Is Not Interpretability: Machine Learning and Its Relation to the World." Unpublished manuscript, 2020.

Eco, Umberto. "An Ars Oblivionalis? Forget it!" *Kos* 30 (1987): 40–53.

Eco, Umberto. "Ci sono delle cose che non si possono dire: Di un realismo negativo." *Alfabeta 2,* no. 17 (2012): 22–25.

Eco, Umberto. *Dall'albero al labirinto: Studi storici sul segno e l'interpretazione.* Milan: Bompiani, 2007.

Eco, Umberto. *I limiti dell'interpretazione.* Milan: Bompiani, 1990.

Eco, Umberto. *The Open Work*. Translated by Anna Cancogni. Cambridge, MA: Harvard University Press, 1989.

Eco, Umberto. *Opera aperta*. Milan: Bompiani, 1962.

Eco, Umberto. *Trattato di semiotica generale*. Milan: Bompiani, 1975.

Eco, Umberto. *Vertigine della lista*. Milan: Bompiani, 2009.

Eco, Umberto, and Paolo Fabbri. *Prima proposta per un modello di ricerca interdisciplinare sul rapporto televisione/pubblico*. Mimeo: Perugia, 1965.

Eco, Umberto, and Paolo Fabbri. "Progetto di ricerca sull'utilizzazione dell'informazione ambientale." *Problemi dell'informazione* 4 (1978): 555–597.

Elting, Linda S., James M. Walker, Charles G. Martin, Scott B. Cantor, and Edward B. Rubenstein. "Influence of Data Display Formats on Decisions to Stop Clinical Trials." *British Medical Journal* 318 (1999): 1527–1531.

Erdelyi, Matthew Hugh. *The Recovery of Unconscious Memories: Hypermnesia and Reminiscence*. Chicago: University of Chicago Press, 1996.

Espeland, Wendy Nelson, and Michael Sauders. "Rankings and Reactivity. How Public Measures Recreate Social Worlds." *American Journal of Sociology* 113, no. 1 (July 2007): 1–40.

Esposito, Elena. "Algorithmische Kontingenz: Der Umgang mit Unsicherheit im Web." In *Die Ordnung des Kontingenten: Beiträge zur zahlenmäßigen Selbstbeschreibung der modernen Gesellschaft*, edited by Alberto Cevolini, 233–249. Wiesbaden: Springer VS, 2014.

Esposito, Elena. "Artificial Communication? The Production of Contingency by Algorithms." *Zeitschrift für Soziologie* 46, no. 4 (2017): 249–265.

Esposito, Elena. *Die Fiktion der wahrscheinlichen Realität*. Frankfurt am Main: Suhrkamp, 2007.

Esposito, Elena. "Digital Prophecies and Web Intelligence." In *Privacy, Due Process and the Computional Turn: The Philosophy of Law Meets the Philosophy of Technology*, edited by Mireille Hildebrandt and Katja De Vries, 121–142. New York: Routledge, 2013.

Esposito, Elena. "Illusion und Virtualität: Kommunikative Veränderung der Fiktion." In *Soziologie und künstliche Intelligenz*, ed. Werner Rammert, 187–216. Frankfurt am Main: Campus, 1995.

Esposito, Elena. "Interaktion, Interaktivität und die Personalisierung der Massenmedien." *Soziale Systeme* 1, no. 2 (1995): 225–260.

Esposito, Elena. "Kontingenzerfahrung und Kontingenzbewusstsein in systemtheoretischer Perspektive." In *Politik und Kontingenz*, edited by Katrin Toens and Ulrich Willems, 39–48. Wiesbaden: VS Springer, 2012.

Esposito, Elena. "Limits of Interpretation, Closure of Communication: Umberto Eco and Niklas Luhmann Observing Texts." In *Luhmann Observed: Radical Theoretical Encounters*, edited by Anders la Cour and Andreas Philippopoloulos-Mihalopoulos, 171–184. London: Palgrave Macmillan, 2013.

Esposito, Elena. "Risiko und Computer: Das Problem der Kontrolle des Mangels der Kontrolle." In *Riskante Strategien: Beiträge zur Soziologie des Risikos*, edited by Toru Hijikata and Armin Nassehi, 93–108. Opladen: Westdeutscher Verlag, 1997.

Esposito, Elena. *Soziales Vergessen: Formen und Medien des Gedächtnisses der Gesellschaft*. Frankfurt am Main: Suhrkamp, 2002.

Esposito, Elena. "The Structures Of Uncertainty: Performativity and Unpredictability in Economic Operations." *Economy and Society* 42 (2013): 102–129.

Esposito, Elena, and David Stark. "Debate on Observation Theory." *Sociologica* 2 (2013). https://doi.org/10.2383/74855.

Esposito, Elena, and David Stark. "What's Observed in a Rating? Rankings as Orientation in the Face of Uncertainty." *Theory, Culture & Society* 36, no. 4 (2019): 3–26. https://doi.org/10.1177/0263276419826276.

Etzioni, Oren. "Deep Learning Isn't a Dangerous Magic Genie: It's Just Math." *Wired*, June 15, 2016.

Etzioni, Oren, Michele Banko, and Michael J. Cafarella. "Machine Reading." *American Association for Artificial Intelligence*, 2006.https://www.aaai.org/Papers/AAAI /2006/AAAI06-239.pdf.

Eugenides, Jeffrey. *The Virgin Suicides*. New York: Farrar, Straus and Giroux, 1993.

Facebook, "Community Standards Enforcement Report." Accessed January 22, 2021. https://transparency.facebook.com/community-standards-enforcement#fake-accounts.

Ferrara, Emilio, Onur Varol, Clayton Davis, Filippo Menczer, and Alessandro Flammini. "The Rise of Social Bots." *Communications of the ACM* 59, no. 7 (2016): 96–104.

Ferreira de Oliveira, Maria Christina, and Haim Levkowitz. "From Visual Data Exploration to Visual Data Mining: A Survey." *IEEE Transactions on Visualization and Computer Graphics* 9, no. 3 (2003): 378–394. https://doi.org/ieeecomputersociety.org /10.1109/TVCG.2003.1207445.

Fiske, John. *Introduction to Communication Studies*. London: Routledge, 1990.

Floridi, Luciano. *Information: A Very Short Introduction*. Oxford: Oxford University Press, 2010.

Floridi, Luciano. "L'ultima legge della robotica." *La Repubblica Robinson*, February 12 (2017): 5–7.

Floridi, Luciano, and Jeff W. Sanders. "On the Morality of Artificial Agents." *Minds and Machines* 14 (2004): 349–379.

Foer, Joshua. *Moonwalking with Einstein*. London: Penguin, 2011.

Formilan, Giovanni, and David Stark. "Testing the Creative Identity: Personas as Probes in Underground Electronic Music." Warwick: Unpublished manuscript, 2018.

Foucault, Michel. *Les mots et les choses*. Paris: Gallimard, 1966.

Friendly, Michael. "A Brief History of Data Visualization." In *Handbook of Computational Statistics: Data Visualization*, edited by Chun-houh Chen, Wolfgang Karl Härdle, and Antony Unwin, 15–56. Heidelberg: Springer, 2006.

Frosh, Paul. "The Gestural Image: The Selfie, Photography Theory, and Kinesthetic Sociability." *International Journal of Communication* 9 (2015): 1607–1628.

Fuchs, Peter. "Adressabilität als Grundbegriff der soziologischen Systemtheorie." *Soziale Systeme* 3, no. 1 (1997): 57–79.

Galloway, Alexander. "Are Some Things Unrepresentable?" *Theory, Culture & Society* 28, no. 7–8 (2011): 85–102.

Gantz, John, and Reinsel, David. "The Digital Universe Decade—Are You Ready?" IDC Analyze the Future, May 2010. https://ifap.ru/pr/2010/n100507a.pdf.

Garfinkel, Harold. *Studies in Ethnomethodology*. Englewood Cliffs, NJ: Prentice Hall, 1967.

Gerlitz, Carolin, and Anne Helmond. "The Like Economy: Social Buttons and the Data-Intensive Web." *New Media & Society* 15, no. 8 (2013): 1348–1365.

Gillespie, Tarleton. "Algorithms, Clickworkers, and the Befuddled Fury around Facebook Trends." NiemanLab.org, May 19, 2016. https://www.niemanlab.org/2016/05/algorithms-clickworkers-and-the-befuddled-fury-around-facebook-trends/.

Gillespie, Tarleton. "The Relevance of Algorithms." In *Media Technologies*, edited by Tarleton Gillespie, Pablo J. Boczkowski, and Kirsten A. Foot, 167–194. Cambridge, MA: MIT Press, 2014.

Gillmor, Dan. *We the Media: Grassroots Journalism by the People, for the People*. Sebastopol: O'Reilly, 2004.

Gilpin, Leilani H., David Bau, Ben Z. Yuan, Ayesha Bajwa, Michael Specter, and Lalana Kagal. "Explaining Explanations: An Overview of Interpretability of Machine Learning." arXiv.org, submitted May 31, 2018. https://arxiv.org/abs/1806.00069.

Ginsberg, Jeremy, Matthew H. Mohebbi, Rajan S. Patel, Lynnette Brammer, Mark S. Smolinski, and Larry Brilliant. "Detecting Influenza Epidemics Using Search Engine Query Data." *Nature* 457 (2009): 1012–1014. http://dx.doi.org/10.1038/nature07634.

Gitelman, Lisa, ed. *"Raw Data" Is an Oxymoron*. Cambridge, MA: MIT Press, 2013.

Gitelman, Lisa, and Virginia Jackson. Introduction to *"Raw Data" Is an Oxymoron*, edited by Lisa Gitelman. Cambridge, MA: MIT Press, 2013.

Goffman, Erving. *The Presentation of Self in Everyday Life*. New York: Doubleday, 1959.

Golder, Scott. A., and Michael W. Macy. "Digital Footprints: Opportunities and Challenges for Online Social Research." *Annual Review of Sociology* 40 (2014):129–52.

Goodfellow, Ian, Yoshua Bengio, and Aaron Courville. *Deep Learning*. Cambridge, MA: MIT Press, 2016.

Goody, Jack. *The Domestication of the Savage Mind*. Cambridge: Cambridge University Press, 1977.

Granka, Laura A. "The Politics of Search: A Decade Retrospective." *Information Society* 26 (2010): 364–374.

Grimmelmann, James. "The Google Dilemma." *New York Law School Law Review* 53 (2009): 939–950.

Grossman, Lev. "How Computers Know What We Want—Before We Do." *Time*, May 27, 2010.

Gumbrecht, Hans Ulrich, and K. Ludwig Pfeiffer, eds. *Materialität der Kommunikation*. Frankfurt am Main: Suhrkamp, 1988.

Habermas, Jürgen. *Strukturwandel der Öffentlichkeit*. Neuwied: Luchterhand, 1962.

Hacking, Ian. *The Emergence of Probability*. Cambridge: Cambridge University Press, 1975.

Halbwachs, Maurice. *Les cadres sociaux de la mémoire*. Paris: Presses Universitaires de France, 1952.

Halevy, Aalon, Peter Norvig, and Fernando Pereira. "The Unreasonable Effectiveness of Data." *IEEE Intelligent Systems* 24, no. 2 (2009): 8–12.

Hamburger, Ellis. "Building the Star Trek Computer: How Google's Knowledge Graph Is Changing Search." *The Verge*, June 8, 2012. https://www.theverge.com/2012/6/8/3071190/google-knowledge-graph-star-trek-computer-john-giannandrea-interview.

Hammond, Kristian. *Practical Artificial Intelligence for Dummies*. Hoboken, NJ: Wiley, 2015.

Hand David J. "Data Mining: Statistics and More?" *American Statistician* 52, (1998): 112–118.

Hand David J. "Why Data Mining Is More Than Statistics Writ Large." *Bulletin of the International Statistical Institute, 52nd Session* 1 (1999): 433–436.

Hand, Martin. *Ubiquitous Photography*. Cambridge: Polity, 2012.

Harcourt, Bernard E. *Against Prediction. Profiling, Policing, and Punishing in an Actuarial Age*. Chicago: University of Chicago Press, 2007.

Hardy, Quentin. "Artificial Intelligence Software Is Booming: But Why Now?" *New York Times*, September 19, 2016.

Haslhofer, Bernhard, Antoine Isaac, Rainer Simon. "Knowledge Graphs in the Libraries and Digital Humanities Domain." In *Encyclopedia of Big Data Technologies*, edited by S. Sakr and A. Zomaya. Cham: Springer, 2018.

Havelock, Eric Alfred. *The Greek Concept of Justice*. Cambridge, MA: Harvard University Press, 1978.

Havelock, Eric Alfred. *The Muse Learns to Write: Reflections on Orality and Literacy from Antiquity to the Present*. New Haven, CT: Yale University Press, 1986.

Havelock, Eric Alfred. *Origins of Western Literacy*. Toronto: Ontario Institute for Studies in Education, 1976.

Havelock, Eric Alfred. *Preface to Plato*. Cambridge, MA: Harvard University Press, 1963.

Hawalah, Ahmed, and Maria Fasli. "Utilizing Contextual Ontological User Profiles for Personalized Recommendations." *Expert Systems with Applications* 41, no. 10 (2014): 4777–4797.

Hayles, N. Katherine. *How We Became Posthuman: Virtual Bodies in Cybernetics, Literature, and Informatics*. Chicago: University of Chicago Press, 1999.

Hayles, N. Katherine. "How We Read: Close, Hyper, Machine." *ADE Bulletin* 150 (2010): 62–79.

Hayles, N. Katherine. *How We Think. Digital Media and Contemporary Technogenesis*. Chicago: University of Chicago Press, 2012.

Hayles, N. Katherine. "How We Think: Transforming Power and Digital Technologies." In *Understanding Digital Humanities*, edited by David M. Berry, 42–66. London: Palgrave Macmillan, 2012.

Hayles, N. Katherine. *My Mother Was a Computer: Digital Subjects and Literary Texts*. Chicago: University of Chicago Press, 2005.

Hearn, Alison, and Stephanie Schoenhoff. "From Celebrity to Influencer." In *A Companion to Celebrity*, edited by P. David Marshall and Sean Redmond, 194–212. Chichester: John Wiley & Sons, 2016.

Hempel, Carl G. "The Theoretician's Dilemma." In *Concepts, Theories, and the Mind-Body Problem*, edited by Herbert Feigl, Michael Scriven, and Grover Maxwell, 37–98. Minneapolis: University of Minnesota Press, 1958.

Hempel, Carl G., "Aspects of Scientific Explanation." In Carl G. Hempel, *Aspects of Scientific Explanation and the Others Essays in the Philosophy of Science*, 331–496. New York: Free Press, 1965.

Herrman, John. "How TikTok Is Rewriting the World." *New York Times*, March 10, 2019.

Hey, T., S. Tansley, and Kritin Tolle, eds. *The Fourth Paradigm: Data-Intensive Scientific Discovery*. Redmond: Microsoft Research, 2009.

Hildebrandt, Mireille. *Smart Technologies and the End(s) of Law*. Cheltenham: Elgar, 2015.

Hitchcock, Christopher, and Elliott Sober. "Prediction versus Accommodation and the Risk of Overfitting." *British Journal for the Philosophy of Science* 55, no. 1 (2004): 1–34.

Hofman, Jake M., Amit Sharma, and Dunkin J. Watts, D. J. "Prediction and Explanation in Social Systems." *Science* 355, no. 6324 (2017): 486–488. https://doi.org.10.1126/science.aal3856.

Hofstadter, Douglas R. *Gödel, Escher, Bach: An Eternal Golden Braid*. New York: Basic Books, 1979.

Höller, Jan, Vlasios Tsiatis, Catherine Mulligan, Stamatis Karnouskos, Stefan Avesand, and David Boyle. *From Machine-to-Machine to the Internet of Things: Introduction to a New Age of Intelligence*. Amsterdam: Elsevier, 2014.

Hornby, Nick. *High Fidelity*. London: Indigo, 1995.

Howard, Ayanna. *Sex, Race, and Robots: How to Be Human in the Age of AI*. Audible Originals, 2019.

Huff, Darrell. *How to Lie with Statistics*. New York: Norton, 1954.

Hughes, George Edward, and Maxwell John Cresswell. *An Introduction to Modal Logic*. London: Methuen, 1968.

Hulbert, Justin Conor, and Michael C. Anderson. "The Role of Inhibition in Learning." In *Human Learning*, edited by Aaron S. Benjamin, J. Steven de Belle, Bruce Etnyre, and Thad A. Polk, 7–20. New York: Elsevier, 2008.

Hunger, Hermann, and Alfonso Archi. "Vicino Oriente: Liste lessicali e tassonomie." Entry in *Enciclopedia Treccani*. Rome, 2001. http://www.treccani.it/enciclopedia/vicino-oriente-antico-liste-lessicali-e-tassonomie_%28Storia-della-Scienza%29/.

Hunt, Priscillia, Jessica Saunders, and John S. Hollywood. *Evaluation of the Shreveport Predictive Policing Experiment*. Santa Monica, CA: Rand, 2014. https://www.rand.org/pubs/research_reports/RR531.html.

Hutchins, Edward. *Cognition in the Wild*. Cambridge, MA: MIT Press, 1995.

Imperva. *The Imperva Global Bot Traffic Report*. 2019. https://www.imperva.com/resources/resource-library/reports/the-imperva-global-bot-traffic-report/.

Jänicke, Stefan. "Valuable Research for Visualization and Digital Humanities: A Balancing Act." Paper presented at the workshop Visualization for the Digital

Humanities, IEEE VIS. Baltimore, Maryland October 23–28, 2016. https://www.infor matik.uni-leipzig.de/~stjaenicke/balancing.pdf.

Jänicke, Stefan, Greta Franzini, Muhammad Faisal Cheema, and Gerik Scheuermann. "On Close and Distant Reading in Digital Humanities: A Survey and Future Challenges." In *Eurographics Conference on Visualization—State of the Art Report* (EuroVis), edited by R. Borgo and F. Ganovelli. Aire-la-Ville: Eurographics Association, 2015.

Jessop, Martyn. "Digital Visualization as a Scholarly Activity." *Literary and Linguistic Computing* 23, no. 3 (2008): 281–293.

Jones, Meg Leta. "Forgetting Made (Too) Easy." *Communications of the ACM* 34 (June 2015).

Jones, Meg Leta. "You Are What Google Says You Are: The Right to Be Forgotten and Information Stewardship." *International Review of Information Ethics* 17, no. 7 (2012): 21–30.

Jouvenal, Justin. "Police Are Using Software to Predict Crime. Is It a 'Holy Grail' or Biased against Minorities?" *Washington Post*, November 17, 2016.

Joyce, Gemma. "Five Examples of Creepy Marketing: When Personalization Goes Too Far." *Brandwatch Online Trends*, January 5, 2017. https://www.brandwatch.com /blog/react-creepy-marketing-personalisation-goes-far/.

Jurgenson, Nathan. *The Social Photo. On Photography and Social Media*. London: Verso, 2019.

Kanatova, Maria, Alexandra Milyakina, Tatyana Pilipovec, Artjom Shelya, Oleg Sobchuk, and Peeter Tinits. "Broken Time, Continued Evolution: Anachronies in Contemporary Films." *Literary Lab Pamphlet* 14 (2017). https://litlab.stanford.edu /LiteraryLabPamphlet14.pdf .

Karim, Awudu, Zhou Shangbo. "X-TREPAN: An Extended Trepan for Comprehensibility and Classification Accuracy in Artificial Neural Networks." *International Journal of Artificial Intelligence & Applications* 6, no. 5 (2015): 69–86.

Karpik, Lucien. "La Guide rouge Michelin." *Sociologie du Travail* 42, no. 3 (2000): 369–389.

Karpik, Lucien. *L'économie des singularités*. Paris: Gallimard, 2007.

Kath, Roxana, Gary S. Schaal, and Sebastian Dumm. "New Visual Hermeneutics." *Zeitschrift für Germanistische Linguistik* 43, no. 1 (2015): 27–51.

Katsma, Holst. "Loudness in the Novel." *Literary Lab Pamphlet* 7 (2014). Accessed February 12, 2020. https://litlab.stanford.edu/LiteraryLabPamphlet7.pdf.

Keightley, Emily, and Michael Pickering. "Technologies of Memory: Practices of Remembering in Analogue and Digital Photography." *New Media & Society* 16, no. 4 (2014): 576–593.

Keim, Daniel A., and Mihael Ankerst. "Visual Data-Mining Techniques." In *The Visualization Handbook*, edited by Charles D. Hansen and Chris R. Johnson, 813–826. Cambridge, MA: Academic Press, 2004.

Kelly, Kevin. "On Chris Anderson's the End of Theory." *Edge*, 2008. http://edge.org /discourse/the_end_of_theory.html.

Kelly, Tara. "Erik Kessels, Photographer, Prints Out 24 Hours Worth of Flickr Photos." *Huffington Post*, November 14, 2011. https://www.huffpost.com/entry/erik -kessels-photographer_n_1092989.

Kember, Sarah. "Ubiquitous Photography." *Philosophy of Photography* 3, no. 2 (2012): 331–348.

Kerr, Ian, and Jessica Earle. "Prediction, Preemption, Presumption. How Big Data Threatens Big Picture Privacy." *Stanford Law Review* 66, no. 65 (2013): 65–72. https:// review.law.stanford.edu/wp-content/uploads/sites/3/2016/08/66_StanLRevOnline _65_KerrEarle.pdf.

Kirschenbaum, Matthew. "The Remaking of Reading: Data Mining and Digital Humanities." *NGDM* '07, National Science Foundation, Baltimore, October 12, 2007. http://www.csee.umbc.edu/~hillol/NGDM07/abstracts/talks/MKirschenbaum.pdf.

Kirschenbaum, Matthew. "The .txtual Condition: Digital Humanities, Born-Digital Archives, and the Future Literary." *Digital Humanities Quarterly* 7, no. 1 (2013). http://www.digitalhumanities.org/dhq/vol/7/1/000151/000151.html.

Kitchin, Rob. "Big Data, New Epistemologies and Paradigm Shifts." *Big Data & Society* (April 2014).

Kloc, Joe. "Wikipedia Is Edited by Bots. That's a Good Thing." *Newsweek*, February 25, 2014.

Koch, Ulla. "Three Strikes and You're Out! A View on Cognitive Theory and the First–Millennium Extispicy Ritual." In *Divination and Interpretation of Signs in the Ancient World*, edited by Amar Annus, 43–60. Chicago: The Oriental Institute of the University of Chicago, 2010.

Koch-Westenholz, Ulla. *Mesopotamian Astrology: An Introduction to Babylonian and Assyrian Celestial Divination*. Copenhagen: Museum Tusculanum Press, 1995.

Kollanyi, Bence, Philip N. Howard, and Samuel C. Woolley. "Bots and Automation over Twitter during the U.S. Election." Data Memo 2016.4. Oxford: Project on Computational Propaganda, 2016. https://demtech.oii.ox.ac.uk/wp-content/uploads/sites /89/2016/11/Data-Memo-US-Election.pdf.

Koops, Bert-Jaap. "Forgetting Footprints, Shunning Shadows: A Critical Analysis of the Right to Be Forgotten in Big Data Practice." *Scripted* 8, no. 3 (2011): 229–256.

Koops Bert-Japp, Mireille Hildebrandt, and David-Oliver Jaquet-Chiffelle. "Bridging the Accountability Gap: Rights for New Entities in the Information Society?" *Minnesota Journal of Law, Science & Technology* 11, no. 2 (2010): 497–561.

Koselleck, Reinhart. *Vergangene Zukunft: Zur Semantik geschichtlicher Zeiten.* Frankfurt am Main: Suhrkamp, 1979.

Kotras, Baptiste. "Mass Personalization: Predictive Marketing Algorithms and the Reshaping of Consumer Knowledge." *Big Data & Society* 7, no. 2 (July–December 2020).

Krämer, Sybille. "Operative Bildlichkeit: Von der 'Grammatologie' zu einer 'Diagrammatologie'? Reflexionen über erkennendes 'Sehen.'" In *Logik des Bildlichen: Zur Kritik der ikonischen Vernunft,* edited by Martina Heßler and Dieter Mersch, 94–123. Bielefeld: Transcript, 2009.

Kurzweil, Ray. *The Singularity Is Near.* New York: Viking Books, 2005.

Lacan, Jacques. *Ècrits: A Selection.* New York: Norton, 1981.

Lacan, Jacques. *Seminar XI: The Four Fundamental Concepts of Psychoanalysis.* New York: Penguin, 1977.

Lachmann, Renate. "Die Unlöschbarkeit der Zeichen: Das semiotische Unglück des Memoristen." In *Gedächtniskunst: Raum-Bild-Schrift,* edited by Anselm Haverkamp and Renate Lachmann, 111–141. Frankfurt am Main: Suhrkamp, 1991.

Langohr, Herwig, and Patricia Langohr. *The Rating Agencies and Their Credit Ratings: What They Are, How They Work and Why They Are Relevant.* Chichester: Wiley, 2009.

Langville, Amy N., and Carl D. Meyer. *Google's PageRank and Beyond: The Science of Search Engine Rankings.* Princeton: Princeton University Press, 2006.

Latour, Bruno. "Beware, Your Imagination Leaves Digital Traces." *Times Higher Education Literary Supplement,* April 6, 2007.

Latour, Bruno. "Visualization and Cognition: Drawing Things Together." In *Knowledge and Society: Studies in the Sociology of Culture Past and Present,* ed. H. Kuklick, 1–40. Greenwich, CT: Jai Press, 1986.

Latour, Bruno. *We Have Never Been Modern.* Cambridge, MA: Harvard University Press, 1993.

Lazaro, Christophe. "Le pouvoir 'divinatoire' des algorithmes: De la prédiction à la préemption du futur." *Anthropologie et Sociétés* 42, no. 2–3 (2018): 127–150. https://doi.org/10.7202/1052640ar.

Lazer, David, Ryan Kennedy, Gary King, and Alessandro Vespignani. "The Parable of Google Flu: Traps in Big Data Analysis." *Science* 343, no. 6176 (2014): 1203–1205.

Lee, Monica, and John Levi Martin. "Surfeit and Surface." *Big Data and Society* 2, no. 2 (2015).

Lepore, Jill. "The Cobweb: Can the Internet Be Archived?" *New Yorker,* January 19, 2015.

Lerman, Jonas. "Big Data and Its Exclusions." *Stanford Law Review* 66, no. 65 (2013): 55–63.

Lettieri, Nicola. "Law, Rights, and the Fallacy of Computation: On the Hidden Pitfalls of Predictive Analytic." *Jura Gentium* 17, no. 2 (2020): 46–61.

Levich, Richard M., Giovanni Majnoni, and Carmen Reinhart. *Ratings, Rating Agencies and the Global Financial System.* New York: Springer US, 2002. https://doi .org/10.1007/978-1-4615-0999-8.

Lévy, Pierre. *L'Intelligence Collective: Pour une Anthropologie du Cyberspace.* Paris: La Découverte, 1994.

Lipton, Zachary C. "The Mythos of Model Interpretability." *ACM Queue* 16, no. 3 (2018): 1–27.

Liu, Alan. "From Reading to Social Computing." In *Literary Studies in the Digital Age: An Evolving Anthology*, edited by Kenneth M. Price and Ray Siemens. Modern Language Association of America, 2013. https://dlsanthology.mla.hcommons.org/.

Liu, Alan. "The Meaning in the Digital Humanities." *PMLA* 128, no. 2 (2013): 409–423.

Luhmann, Niklas. *Das Recht der Gesellschaft.* Frankfurt am Main: Suhrkamp, 1993.

Luhmann, Niklas. "Die Autopoiesis des Bewußtseins." *Soziale Welt* 36 (1985): 402–446.

Luhmann, Niklas. *Die Gesellschaft der Gesellschaft.* Frankfurt am Main: Suhrkamp, 1997.

Luhmann, Niklas. *Die Wissenschaft der Gesellschaft.* Frankfurt am Main: Suhrkamp, 1990.

Luhmann, Niklas. *Einführung in die Systemtheorie.* Heidelberg: Carl-Auer-Systeme, 2002.

Luhmann, Niklas. *Einführung in die Theorie der Gesellschaft.* Heidelberg: Carl-Auer-Systeme, 2005.

Luhmann, Niklas. "Ich sehe das, was Du nicht siehst." In Niklas Luhmann, *Soziologische Aufklärung*, vol. 5, 228–234. Opladen: Westdeutscher Verlag, 1990.

Luhmann, Niklas. "Individuum, Individualität, Individualismus." In *Gesellschaftsstruktur und Semantik. Studien zur Wissenssoziologie der modernen Gesellschaft* 3, 149–258. Frankfurt am Main: Suhrkamp, 1989.

Luhmann, Niklas. "Kommunikation mit Zettelkästen: Ein Erfahrungsbericht." In *Öffentliche Meinung und sozialer Wandel: Für Elisabeth Noelle-Neumann*, edited by Horst Baier, Hans Mathias Kepplinger, and Kurt Reumann, 222–228. Opladen: Westdeutscher Verlag, 1981.

Luhmann, Niklas. *Recht und Automation in der öffentlichen Verwaltung*. Berlin: Duncker & Humblot, 1966.

Luhmann, Niklas. *Soziale Systeme. Grundriß einer alllgemeinen Theorie*. Frankfurt am Maine: Suhrkamp, 1984.

Luhmann, Niklas. *Soziologie des Risikos*. Berlin and New York: de Gruyter, 1991.

Luhmann, Niklas. "Temporalisierung von Komplexität: Zur Semantik neuzeitlicher Zeitbegriffe." In *Gesellschaftsstruktur und Semantik. Studien zur Wissenssoziologie der modernen Gesellschaft* 1, 235–300. Frankfurt am Main: Suhrkamp, 1980.

Luhmann, Niklas. *The Reality of the Mass Media*. Stanford: Stanford University Press, 1996.

Luhmann, Niklas. "Was ist Kommunikation?" In Niklas Luhmann, *Soziologische Aufklärung*, vol. 6, 109–120. Opladen: Westdeutscher Verlag, 1995.

Luhmann, Niklas. "Wie ist Bewußtsein an Kommunikation beteiligt?" In *Materialität der Kommunikation*, edited by Hans Ulrich Gumbrecht and K. Ludwig Pfeiffer, 884–905. Frankfurt am Main: Suhrkamp, 1988.

Lum, Kristian, and William Isaac. "To Predict and Serve?" significancemagazine. com, October 7, 2016: 14–19.

Luria, Alexander Romanovich. *Cognitive Development: Its Cultural and Social Foundations*. Cambridge, MA: Harvard University Press, 1976.

Luria, Alexander Romanovich. *The Mind of a Mnemonist: A Little Book about a Vast Memory*. Cambridge, MA: Harvard University Press, 1986.

Lury, Celia, and Sophie Day. "Algorithmic Personalization as a Mode of Individuation." *Theory, Culture & Society* 36, no. 2 (2019): 17–37.

MacKenzie, Adrian. "The Production of Prediction: What Does Machine Learning Want?" *European Journal of Cultural Studies* 18, nos. 4–5 (2015): 429–445.

MacKenzie, Donald. *An Engine, Not a Camera. How Financial Models Shape Markets*. Cambridge, MA: MIT Press, 2006.

MacKenzie, Donald, Fabian Muniesa, and Lucia Siu. *Do Economists Make Markets? On the Performativity of Economics*. Princeton: Princeton University Press, 2008.

Mainberger, Sabine. "Exotisch—endotisch oder Georges Perec lernt von Sei Shonagon: Überlegungen zu Listen, Literatur und Ethnologie." *LiLi: Zeitschrift für Literatur und Linguistik* 48, no. 3 (2017), 327–350. https://doi.org/10.1007/s41244-017-0063-5.

Manjoo, Farhad. "Where No Search Engine Has Gone Before." *Slate*, April 11, 2013. https://slate.com/technology/2013/04/google-has-a-single-towering-obsession-it -wants-to-build-the-star-trek-computer.html.

Manovich, Lev. "How to Compare One Million Images?" In *Understanding Digital Humanities*, edited by David M. Berry, 249–278. London: Palgrave Macmillan, 2012.

Manovich, Lev. *The Language of New Media*. Cambridge, MA: MIT Press, 2001.

Manovich, Lev. "What Is Visualization?" In *DIGAREC Keynote-Lectures 2009/10*, edited by Stephan Günzel, Michael Liebe, and Dieter Mersch, 116–156. Potsdam: University Press, 2011.

March, James G. "Exploration and Exploitation in Organization Learning." *Organization Science* 2 (1991): 71–87.

Marcuse, Herbert. *One-Dimensional Man. Studies in the Ideology of Advanced Industrial Society*. Boston: Beacon Press, 1964.

Marres, Noortje, and Carolin Gerlitz. "Social Media as Experiments in Sociality." In *Inventing the Social*, edited by Noortje Marres, Michael Guggenheim and Alex Wilkie, 253–283. Manchester: Mattering Press, 2018.

Mason, Paul. "The Racist Hijacking of Microsoft's Chatbot Shows How the Internet Teems with Hate." *Guardian*, March 29, 2016.

Maul, Stefan M. *Die Wahrsagekunst im alten Orient*. Munich: Beck, 2013.

Maul, Stefan M. "Divination Culture and the Handling of the Future." In *The Babylonian World*, edited by G. Leick, 361–372. New York: Routledge, 2007.

Maul, Stefan M. "How the Babylonians Protected Themselves against Calamities Announced by Omens." In *Mesopotamian Magic: Textual, Historical, and Interpretative Perspectives: Ancient Magic and Divination I*, edited by Tzvi Abusch and Karel van der Toorn, 123–129. Groningen: Styx Publication, 1999.

Max, D. T. "The Art of Conversation. The Curator Who Talked His Way to the Top." *New Yorker*, December 1, 2014.

Mayer-Schönberger, Viktor. *Delete: The Virtue of Forgetting in the Digital Age*. Princeton: Princeton Univerity Press, 2009.

Mayer-Schönberger, Viktor, and Kenneth Cukier. *Big Data. A Revolution That Will Transform How We Live, Work, and Think*. London: Murray, 2013.

McCombs, Maxwell E., and Donald L. Shaw. "The Agenda-Setting Function of Mass Media." *Public Opinion Quarterly* 36, no. 2 (1972): 176–187.

McFarland, Daniel A., and H. Richard McFarland. "Big Data and the Danger of Being Precisely Inaccurate." *Big Data & Society* 2, no. 2 (December 2015). https://doi.org/10.1177/2053951715602495

McGoey, Linsey. "Strategic Unknowns: Towards a Sociology of Ignorance." *Economy and Society* 41, no. 1 (2012): 1–16.

McLuhan, Marshall. *Understanding Media*. New York: McGraw Hill, 1964.

Mead, George Herbert. *Mind, Self and Society*. Chicago (Ill.): The University of Chicago Press, 1943.

Mehrabi, Ninareh, Fred Morstatter, Nripsuta Saxena, Kristina Lerman, and Aram Galstyan. "A Survey on Bias and Fairness in Machine Learning." arXiv.org, submitted on August 23, 2019. arXiv:1908.09635.

Mennicken, Andrea. "Numbers and Lists: Ratings and Rankings in Healthcare and the Correctional Services." Unpublished manuscript, 2016.

Mennicken, Andrea. "'Too Big to Fail and Too Big to Succeed': Accounting and Privatisation in the Prison Service of England and Wales." *Financial Accountability & Management* 29, no. 2 (2013): 206–226.

Metz, Cade. "Google Made a Chatbot that Debates the Meaning of Life." *Wired*, June 26, 2015. https://www.wired.com/2015/06/google-made-chatbot-debates-meaning-life/.

Metz, Cade. "How Google's AI Viewed the Move No Human Could Understand." *Wired*, March 14, 2016. https://www.wired.com/2016/03/googles-ai-viewed-move-no -human-understand/.

Metz, Cade. "If Xerox Parc Invented the PC, Google Invented the Internet." *Wired*, August 8, 2012. https://www.wired.com/2012/08/google-as-xerox-parc/.

Metz, Cade. "Inside Libratus, the Poker AI That Out-Bluffed the Best Humans." *Wired*, February 2, 2017. https://www.wired.com/2017/02/libratus/.

Metz, Cade. "In Two Moves, AlphaGo and Lee Sedol Redefined the Future." *Wired*, March 16, 2016. https://www.wired.com/2016/03/two-moves-alphago-lee-sedol-rede fined-future/.

Metz, Cade. "London A.I. Lab Claims Breakthrough That Could Accelerate Drug Discovery." *New York Times*, November 30, 2020.

Metz, Cade. "What the AI behind AlphaGo Can Teach Us about Being Human." *Wired*, May 19, 2016. https://www.wired.com/2016/05/google-alpha-go-ai/.

Mialki, Stephanie. "How to Use Content Personalization with All Digital Marketing Campaigns," 2019. Updated (Feb. 2020): "4 Strategies of Content Personalization & How to Use Them in Digital Marketing Campaigns." https://instapage.com/blog /content-personalization.

Michura, Piotr, Stan Ruecker, Milena Radzikowska, Carlos Fiorentino, Tanya Clement, and Stéfan Sinclair. "Slot Machines, Graphs, and Radar Screens: Prototyping List-Based Literary Research Tools." In *The Charm of a List: From the Sumerians to Computerised Data Processing*, edited by Lucie Doležalová, 167–177. Newcastle upon Tyne: Cambridge Scholars Publishing, 2009.

Miele, Antonio, Elisa Quintarelli, and Letizia Tanca. "A Methodology for Preference-Based Personalization of Contextual Data." In *Proceedings of the 12th International Conference on Extending Database Technology: Advances in Database Technology*, 287–298. New York: Association for Computing Machinery, 2009.

Miklós, Bálint. "Computer Respond to This Email: Introducing Smart Reply in Inbox by Gmail." Google (blog). Nov. 3, 2015. https://gmail.googleblog.com/2015/1 1/computer-respond-to-this-email.html.

Miller, Tim. "Explanation in Artificial Intelligence: Insights from the Social Sciences." arXiv.org. Submitted August 15, 2018. https://arxiv.org/pdf/1706.07269.pdf.

Mitchell, Tom M. *Machine Learning*. Boston: McGraw Hill, 1997.

Mittelstadt, Brent Daniel, Patrick Allo, Mariarosaria Taddeo, Sandra Wachter, and Luciano Floridi. "The Ethics of Algorithms: Mapping the Debate." *Big Data and Society* 3, no. 2 (2016): 1–21.

Mnih, Volodymyr, Koray Kavukcuoglu, David Silver, Andrei A. Rusu, Joel Veness, Marc G. Bellemare, Alex Graves, Martin Riedmiller, et al. "Human-Level Control through Deep Reinforcement Learning." *Nature* 518 (2015): 529–533.

Moeller, Hans-Georg. "On Second-Order Observation and Genuine Pretending: Coming to Terms with Society." *Thesis Eleven* 143, no. 1 (2017): 28–43.

Moor, James. "The Dartmouth College Artificial Intelligence Conference: The Next Fifty Years." *AI Magazine* 27, no. 4 (2016): 87–91.

Moretti, Franco. "Conjectures on World Literature." *New Left Review* 1 (2000): 54–68.

Moretti, Franco. "Evolution, World-Systems, Weltliteratur." In *Studying Transcultural Literary History*, edited by Gunilla Lindberg-Wada, 113–121. Berlin: Walter de Gruyter, 2006.

Moretti, Franco. *La letteratura vista da lontano*. Torino: Einaudi, 2005.

Moretti, Franco. "Literature, Measured." *Literary Lab Pamphlet* 12 (April 2016). https://litlab.stanford.edu/LiteraryLabPamphlet12.pdf.

Moretti, Franco. *Maps, Graphs, Trees*. London and New York: Verso, 2005.

Moretti, Franco. "More Conjectures." *New Left Review* 20 (2003): 73–81.

Moretti, Franco. "Patterns and Interpretation." *Literary Lab Pamphlet* 15 (September 2017). https://litlab.stanford.edu/LiteraryLabPamphlet15.pdf.

Moretti, Franco. "Style, Inc. Reflections on Seven Thousand Titles (British Novels, 1740–1850)." *Critical Inquiry* 36, no. 1 (2009): 134–158.

Moretti, Franco, and Oleg Sobchuk. "Hidden in Plain Sight. Data Visualization in the Humanities." *New Left Review* 118 (2019): 86–115.

Mori, Masahiro. "The Uncanny Valley." Translated by Karl F. MacDorman, and Norri Kageki. *IEEE Robotics and Automation* 19, no. 2 (2012): 98–100. https://doi.org /10.1109/MRA.2012.2192811.

Morin, Oliver, and Alberto Acerbi. "Birth of the Cool: a Two-Centuries Decline in Emotional Expression in Anglophone Fiction." *Cognition and Emotion* 31, no. 8 (2017): 1663–1675.

Morozov, Evgeny. *The Net Delusion: The Dark Side of Internet Freedom*. New York: PublicAffairs, 2011.

Mozur, Paul. "Google's AlphaGo Defeats Chinese Go Master in Win for A.I." *New York Times*, May 23, 2017.

Mullainathan, Sendhil. "Why Computers Won't Be Replacing You Just Yet." *New York Times*, July 1, 2014.

Mullin, Shenelle. "Why Content Personalization Is Not Web Personalization (and What to Do About It)." CXL, September 4, 2019. https://cxl.com/blog/web -personalization/.

Münster, Sander, and Melissa Terras. "The Visual Side of Digital Humanities: a Survey on Topics, Researchers, and Epistemic Cultures." *Digital Scholarship in the Humanities* 35, no. 2 (2019): 366–389. https://doi.org/10.1093/llc/fqz022.

Munzner, Tamara. "Process and Pitfalls in Writing Information Visualization Research Papers." In *Information Visualization: Human-Centered Issues and Perspectives*, edited by Andreas Kerren, John T. Stasko, Jean-Daniel Fekete, and Chris North, 134–153. Heidelberg: Springer, 2008.

Musselin, Christine. *La Grande Course des Universités*. Paris: Presses de Sciences Po, 2017.

Nabi, Zubair. "~~Resistance~~ Censorship Is Futile." *First Monday* 19, no. 11 (November 2014), https://firstmonday.org/ojs/index.php/fm/article/view/5525.

Nass, Clifford, and Corina Yan. *The Man Who Lied to His Laptop: What We Can Learn About Ourselves from Our Machines*. London: Penguin, 2010.

Neff, Gina, and David Stark. "Permanently Beta: Responsive Organization in the Internet Era." In *The Internet and American Life*, edited by Philip N. Howard and Steve Jones, 173–188. Thousand Oaks, CA: SAGE, 2004.

Negarestani, Reza. *Intelligence and Spirit*. Cambridge, MA: Urbanomic/Sequence Press, 2018.

Nichols, Robin. "Customization vs Personalization." AB Tasty Blog, March 9, 2018. https://www.abtasty.com/blog/customization-vs-personalization/.

Nietzsche, Friedrich. *Unzeitgemässe Betrachtungen. Zweites Stück: Vom Nutzen und Nachteil der Historie für das Leben*. Berlin and New York: de Gruyter, 1972. (Originally published 1874.)

Nilsson, Nils J. *The Quest for Artificial Intelligence. A History of Ideas and Achievements*. New York: Cambridge University Press, 2010.

Nissenbaum, Helen. "Privacy as Contextual integrity." *Washington Law Review* 79, no. 1 (2004): 79–119.

Nissinen, Martti Heikki. "Prophecy and Omen Divination: Two Sides of the Same Coin." In *Divination and Interpretation of Signs in the Ancient World*, edited by Annus Amar, 341–350. Chicago: The Oriental Institute of the University of Chicago, 2010.

Obrist, Hans Ulrich. *Ways of Curating*. London: Allen Lane, 2014.

O'Doherty, Brian. *Inside the White Cube: The Ideology of the Gallery Space*. Santa Monica: Lapis Press, 1986.

O'Donnell, Katie, Henriette Cramer. "People's Perceptions of Personalized Ads." In *Proceedings of the 24th International Conference on World Wide Web*, 1293–1298. New York: ACM Press, 2015. https://doi.org/10.1145/2740908.2742003.

O'Neil, Cathy. *Weapons of Math Destruction*. New York: Crown, 2016.

Ong, Walter J. *Orality and Literacy. The Technologizing of the Word*. New York: Methuen, 1982.

O'Reilly, Tim. "What is Web 2.0: Design Patterns and Business Models for the Next Generation of Software." *Communications & Strategies* 1 (2007): 17–37. https://ssrn.com/abstract=1008839

Oring, Elliott. "Jokes on the Internet: Listing toward Lists." In *Folk Culture in the Digital Age: The Emergent Dynamics of Human Interaction*, edited by Trevor J. Blank, 98–118. Boulder, CO: Utah State University Press, 2012.

Overbye, Dennis, "Can a Computer Devise a Theory of Everything?" *New York Times*, November 23, 2020. https://www.nytimes.com/2020/11/23/science/artificial-intelligence-ai-physics-theory.html.

Pagano, Roberto, Paolo Cremonesi, Martha Larson, Balázs Hidasi, Domonkos Tikk, Alexandros Karatzoglou, and Massimo Quadrana. "The Contextual Turn: from Context-Aware to Context-Driven Recommender Systems."In *Proceedings of the 10th ACM Conference on Recommender Systems (RecSys '16)*, 249–252. New York: Association for Computing Machinery, 2016.https://doi.org/10.1145/2959100.2959136.

Page, Lawrence, Sergey Brin, Rajeev Motwani, and Terry Winograd. "The PageRank Citation Ranking: Bringing Order to the Web." Technical Report, Stanford Infolab, 1999. http://ilpubs.stanford.edu:8090/422/.

Panofsky, Erwin. "Die Perspektive als 'symbolische Form.'" In *Vorträge der Bibliothek Warburg 1924–1925*, 258–330. Leipzig: Teubner, 1927.

Pariser, Eli. *The Filter Bubble. What the Internet Is Hiding from You*. London: Viking, 2011.

Parker, Elizabeth S., Larry Cahill, and James L. McGaugh. "A Case of Unusual Autobiographical Remembering." *Neurocase* 12, no. 1 (2006): 35–49. https://doi.org/10.1080/13554790500473680.

Parsons, Talcott. "Interaction: Social Interaction." *International Encyclopedia of the Social Sciences* 7 (1968): 429–441.

Parsons, Talcott, and Edward A. Shils, eds. *Toward a General Theory of Action*. Cambridge, MA.: Harvard University Press, 1951.

Pasquale, Frank. *The Black Box Society. The Secret Algorithms That Control Money and Information*. Cambridge, MA: Harvard University Press, 2015.

Peng, Tony. "LeCun vs Rahimi: Has Machine Learning Become Alchemy?" *Synced*, December 12, 2017. https://syncedreview.com/2017/12/12/lecun-vs-rahimi-has-ma chine-learning-become-alchemy/.

Peruzzi, Antonio, Fabiana Zollo, Ana Lucía Schmidt, and Walter Quattrociocchi. "From Confirmation Bias to Echo-Chambers: A Data-Driven Approach." In *What Is New in Fake News? Public Opinion and Second-Order Observation in a Hyperconnected Society*, edited by Alberto Cevolini and Gérald Bronner. Special issue of *Sociologia e Politiche Sociali* 21, no. 3 (2018): 47–74.

Pichel, Martin, Eva Zangerle, and Gunther Specht. "Towards a Context-Aware Music Recommendation Approach: What is Hidden in the Playlist Name?" *Conference: 2015 IEEE International Conference on Data Mining Workshop*. https://doi.org/10.1109 /ICDMW.2015.145.

Pierce, David. "Meet the Smartest, Cutest AI-Powered Robot You've Ever Seen." *Wired*, June 27, 2016. https://www.wired.com/2016/06/anki-cozmo-ai-robot-toy/.

Pierce, David. "Spotify's Latest Algorithmic Playlist Is Full of Your Favorite New Music." *Wired*, August 5, 2016. http://wired.com/2016/08/spotifys-latest-algorith mic-playlist-full-favorite-new-music/.

Peiser, Jaclyn. "The Rise of the Robot Reporter." *New York Times*. February 5, 2019. https://www.nytimes.com/2019/02/05/business/media/artificial-intelligence-jour nalism-robots.html.

Pine, B. Joseph II, Don Peppers, and Martha Rogers. "Do You Want to Keep Your Customers Forever?" *Harvard Business Review* (March-April 1995): 103 114.

Plato. *Complete Works*. Indianapolis: Hackett, 1997.

Podolny, Shelley. "If an Algorithm Wrote This, How Would You Even Know?" *New York Times*, March 7, 2015.

Poole, Steven. "Top Nine Things You Need to Know about Listicles." *Guardian*, November 12, 2013.

Popovich, Nadja, Blacki Migliozzi, Karthik Patanjali, Anja Singhvi, and Jon Huang. "See How the World's Most Polluted Air Compares With Your City's." *New York Times*, December 2, 2019. https://www.nytimes.com/interactive/2019/12/02/climate /air-pollution-compare-ar-ul.html.

Popper, Karl. *Conjectures and Refutations. The Growth of Scientific Knowledge*. New York: Basic Books, 1962.

Porphyry (the Phoenician). *Isagoge*. Translated by Edward W. Warren. Toronto: Pontifical Institute of Mediaeval Studies, 1975.

Porter, Theodore M. *The Rise of Statistical Thinking 1820–1900*. Princeton: Princeton University Press, 1986.

Presner, Todd and David Shepard. "Mapping the Geospatial Turn." In *A New Companion to Digital Humanities*, edited by Susan Schreibman, Ray Siemens, and John Unsworth, 201–212. Chichester: Wiley, 2016.

Prey, Robert. "Nothing Personal: Algorithmic Individuation on Music Streaming Platforms." *Media, Culture & Society* 40, no. 7 (2018): 1086–1100. https://doi.org/10.1177/0163443717745147

Quito, Anne. "The Next Design Trend Is One That Eliminates All Choices." *Quartz*, June 18, 2015. https://qz.com/429929/the-next-design-trend-is-one-that-eliminates-all-choices.

Ramsay, Stephen. *Reading Machines: Toward an Algorithmic Criticism*. Champaign: University of Illinois Press, 2011.

Reding, Viviane. *The EU Data Protection Reform 2012: Making Europe the Standard Setter for Modern Data Protection Rules in the Digital Age 5* January 22, 2012. http://europa.eu/rapid/pressReleasesAction.do?reference=SPEECH/12/26&format=PDF.

Reese, Hope. "Why Microsoft's 'Tay' AI Bot Went Wrong." *Tech Republic*, March 24, 2016. https://www.techrepublic.com/article/why-microsofts-tay-ai-bot-went-wrong/.

Ribeiro, Marco Tulio, Sameer Singh, and Carlos Guestrin. "'Why Should I Trust You?' Explaining the Predictions of Any Classifier." arXiv.org. Submitted on August 9, 2016. https://arxiv.org/pdf/1602.04938.pdf.

Ricoeur, Paul. *Memory, History, Forgetting*. Chicago: University of Chicago Press, 2004.

Rieder, Bernhard. "Scrutinizing an Algorithmic Technique: The Bayes classifier as Interested Reading of Reality." *Information, Communication and Society* 20, no 1 (2017). http://dx.doi.org/10.1080/1369118X.2016.1181195.

Rochberg, Francesca. *The Heavenly Writing: Divination, Horoscopy, and Astronomy in Mesopotamian Culture*. Cambridge University Press, 2016.

Rochberg, Francesca. "The History of Science and Ancient Mesopotamia." *Journal of Ancient Near Eastern History* 1, no. 1 (2014): 37–60.

Rochberg, Francesca. "Reasoning, Representing, and Modeling in Babylonian Astronomy." *Journal of Ancient Near Eastern History* 5, no. 1–2 (2018). https://doi.org/10.1515/janeh-2018-0009

Rogers, Richard. *Digital Methods*. Cambridge, MA: MIT Press, 2013.

Rohlfing, Katharina J., Cimiano, Philipp, Scharlau, Ingrid, Matzner, Tobias, Buhl, Heike M.;,Buschmeier, Hendrik; Esposito, Elena; (2020): Explanation as a social practice: Towards a conceptual framework to foster social design of AI systems. IEEE Transactions on Cognitive and Developmental Systems (2020). https://doi .org/10.1109/TCDS.2020.3044366.

Rona-Tas, Akos. "Predicting the Future: Art and Algorithms." *Socio-Economic Review* 18, no. 3 (October 2020): 893–911.

Ronson, Jon. *So You've Been Publicly Shamed.* New York: Riverhead, 2015.

Rosen, Jeffrey. "The Right to Be Forgotten." *Stanford Law Review Online* 64 (2012): 88–92.

Rouvroy, Antoinette. "Réinventer l'art d'oublier et de se faire oublier dans la société de l'information?" In *La sécurité de l'individu numérisé. Réflexions prospectives et internationals*, edited by Stephanie Lacour, 249–278. Paris: L'Harmattan, 2008.

Ruppert, Evelyn. "Population Objects: Interpassive Subjects." *Sociology* 45, no. 2 (2011): 218–233.

Rusbridger, Alan. *Breaking News: The Remaking of Journalism and Why It Matters Now.* New York: Farrar, Straus and Giroux, 2018.

Russell, Stuart J., and Peter Norvig. *Artificial Intelligence. A Modern Approach.* 2nd ed. Upper Saddle River, NJ: Pearson Education, 2003.

Sabbagh, Michel. "The Important Differences between First-Person and Third-Person Games." *Gamasutra*, August 27, 2015. https://www.gamasutra.com/blogs/Michel Sabbagh/20150827/252341/The_important_differences_between_firstperson_and _thirdperson_games.php.

Sarvas, Risto, and David M. Frohlich. *From Snapshots to Social Media—The Changing Picture of Domestic Photography.* London: Springer. 2011.

Saussure, Ferdinand de. *Cours de linguistique générale.* Paris: Payot, 1922.

Schaffrick, Matthias, and Niels Werber. "Die Liste, paradigmatisch." *Zeitschrift für Literaturwissenschaft und Linguistik* 47 (2017): 303–317.

Schleiermacher, Friedrich. *Hermeneutik. Nach den Handschriften neu herausgegeben.* Heidelberg: Winter, 1959.

Schmidt, Johannes. "Niklas Luhmann's Card Index: Thinking Tool, Communication Partner, Publication Machine." In *Forgetting Machines. Knowledge Management Evolution in Early Modern Europe*, edited by Alberto Cevolini, 289–311. Leiden: Brill, 2016.

Schöch, Christof. "Big? Smart? Clean? Messy? Data in the Humanities." *Journal of Digital Humanities* 2, no. 3 (2013).

Schölkopf, Bernhard. "Learning to See and Act." *Nature* 518 (2015): 486–487.

Schulz, Kathryn. "What Is Distant Reading?" *New York Times*, June 24, 2011.

Schwandt, Silke. "Digitale Methoden für die Historische Semantik—Auf den Spuren von Begriffen in digitalen Korpora." *Geschichte und Gesellschaft* 44, no. 1 (2018): 107–134.

Schwandt, Silke. "Digitale Objektivität in der Geschichtswissenschaft? Oder: Kann man finden, was man nicht sucht?" *Rechtsgeschichte* 24 (2016): 337–338.

Schwandt, Silke. "Virtus as a Political Concept in the Middle Ages." *Contributions to the History of Concepts* 10 (2015): 71–90.

Schwartz, Oscar. "Digital ads are starting to feel psychic." *The Outline*, July 13, 2018. https://theoutline.com/post/5380/targeted-ad-creepy-surveillance-facebook-insta gram-google-listening-not-alone?zd=1&zi=t5zvwdzn.

Scott, Mark. "Use of Ad-Blocking Software Rises by 30% Worldwide." *New York Times*, January 31, 2017.

Scott, Susan V., and Wanda J. Orlikowski. "Reconfiguring Relations of Accountability: Materialization of Social Media in the Travel Sector." *Accounting, Organizations and Society* 37, no. 1 (2012): 26–40.

Seabrook, John. "Can a Machine Learn to Write for the *New Yorker*?" *New Yorker*, October 14, 2019. https://www.newyorker.com/magazine/2019/10/14/can-a-machine -learn-to-write-for-the-new-yorker.

Searle, John R. "Mind, Brains and Programs." *Behavioral and Brain Sciences* 3, no. 3 (1980): 417–457.

Seaver, Nick. "Algorithmic Recommendations and Synaptic Functions." *Limn* 2 (2012). http://limn.it/algorithmic-recommendations-and-synaptic-functions/.

Shalev-Shwartz, Shai, and Shai Ben-David. *Understanding Machine Learning: From Theory to Algorithms*. Cambridge: Cambridge University Press, 2014.

Shannon, Claude E., and Warren Weaver. *The Mathematical Theory of Communication*. Urbana: University of Illinois Press, 1949.

Shapiro, Aaron. "Reform Predictive Policing." *Nature* 541 (2017): 458–460.

Sharma, Amit. "How Predictive AI Will Change Shopping." *Harvard Business Review*, November 18, 2016. https://hbr.org/2016/11/how-predictive-ai-will-change -shopping.

Sharon, Tamar, and Dorien Zandbergen. "From Data Feticism to Quantifying Selves: SelfTtracking Practices and the Other Values of Data." *New Media & Society* 19, no. 11 (2016): 1695–1709. https://doi.org/10.1177/1461444816636090.

Shmueli, Galit. "To Explain or to Predict?" *Statistical Science* 25, no. 3 (2010): 289–310.

Siegel, Eric. *Predictive Analytics: The Power to Predict Who will Click, Buy, Lie or Die*. Hoboken, NJ: Wiley, 2016.

Silver, David, and Demis Hassabis. "AlphaGo: Mastering the Ancient Game of Go with Machine Learning." Google AI Blog, January 27, 2016. https://research.google blog.com/2016/01/alphago-mastering-ancient-game-of-go.html.

Silver, David, Julian Schrittwieser, Karen Simonyan, Ioannis Antanoglou, Aja Huang, Arthur Guez, Thomas Hubert, et al. "Mastering the Game of Go without Human Knowledge." *Nature* 550 (2017): 354–359.

Silver, Nate. *The Signal and the Noise: Why Most Predictions Fail—but Some Don't.* New York: Penguin, 2012.

Simon, Judith. "Epistemic Responsibility in Entangled Socio-Technical Systems." In *Social Computing, Social Cognition, Social Networks and Multiagent Systems. Social Turn—SNAMAS 2012*, edited by Gordana Dodig-Crnkovic, Antonio Rotolo, Giovanni Sartor, Judith Simon, and Clara Smith. Birmingham: The Society for the Study of Artificial Intelligence and Simulation of Behaviour, 2012.

Sinclair, Stéfan, and Geoffrey Rockwell. "Text Analysis and Visualization: Making Meaning Count." In *A New Companion to Digital Humanities*, edited by Susan Schreibman, Raymond Siemens, and John Unsworth, 274–290. Chichester: Wiley, 2016.

Sinclair, Stéfan, and Geoffrey Rockwell. "Voyant Tools." Accessed March 1, 2018. https://voyant-tools.org/docs/#!/guide/about.

Sinha, Jay I., Thomas Foscht, and Thomas T. Fung. "How Analytics and AI Are Driving the Subscription E-commerce Phenomenon." *MIT Sloan Management Review* (blog), December 6, 2016. https://sloanreview.mit.edu/article/using-analytics-and-ai-subscription-e-commerce-has-personalized-marketing-all-boxed-up/.

Smith, Ben. "Why the Success of the *New York Times* May Be Bad News for Journalism." *New York Times*, March 2, 2020.

Sneha, P. P. "Reading from a Distance—Data as Text." The Centre for Internet & Society, July 23, 2014. http://cis-india.org/raw/digital-humanities/reading-from-a-distance.

Sober, Elliott. *Ockham's Razors: A User's Manual.* Cambridge: Cambridge University Press, 2016.

Solan, Lawrence M. "Pernicious Ambiguity in Contracts and Statutes." *Chicago-Kent Law Review* 79 (2004): 859–888.

Solon, Olivia. "Weavrs. The Autonomous, Tweeting Blog-Bots That Feed on Social Content." Wired.co.uk, March 28, 2012. https://www.wired.co.uk/article/weavrs-spambots-or-discoverability-agents.

Solove, Daniel J. *The Future of Reputation: Gossip, Rumor and Privacy on the Internet.* New Haven: Yale University Press, 2007.

Solove, Daniel J. " 'I've Got Nothing to Hide' and other Misunderstandings of Privacy." *San Diego Law Review* 44 (2007): 745–772.

Solove, Daniel J. "Speech, Privacy, and Reputation on the Internet." In *The Offensive Internet: Speech, Privacy, and Reputation*, edited by Saul Levmore and Martha C. Nussbaum, 15–30. Cambridge MA: Harvard University Press, 2011.

Sontag, Susan. *On Photography*. London: Penguin, 1977.

Spence, Robert. *Information Visualization: Design for Interaction*. Harlow: Pearson, 2007.

Stark, David. *The Sense of Dissonance: Accounts of Worth in Economic Life*. Princeton: Princeton University Press, 2009.

Stark, David, and Verena Paravel. "PowerPoint in Public. Digital Technologies and the New Morphology of Demonstration." *Theory, Culture & Society* 25, no. 5 (2008): 30–55.

Stuart, Debra L. "Reputational Rankings: Background and Development." *New Directions for Institutional Research* 88 (1995): 13–20.

Suchman, Lucy A. *Plans and Situated Actions: The Problem of Human-Machine Communication*. Cambridge: Cambridge University Press, 1987.

Sunstein, Cass. *Republic.com*. Princeton: Princeton University Press, 2001.

Sunstein, Cass. *#Republic: Divided Democracy in the Age of Social Media*. Princeton: Princeton University Press, 2017.

Sweeney, Erica. "75% of Consumers Find Many Forms of Marketing Personalization Creepy, New Study Says." *MarketingDive*, February 21, 2018. https://www.market ingdive.com/news/75-of-consumers-find-many-forms-of-marketing-personalization -creepy-new-s/517488/.

Talbott, William. "Bayesian Epistemology." *Stanford Encyclopedia of Philosophy*, edited by Zalta, Edward N. Stanford: Center for the Study of Language and Information (CSLI), 2008. https://plato.stanford.edu/entries/epistemology-bayesian/.

Taylor, Laurie. "When Seams Fall Apart: Video Game Space and the Player." Game Studies 3, no. 2 (2003).

Taylor, Paul. "The Concept of 'Cat Face.'" *London Review of Books* 38, no. 16 (2016): 30–32.

Tegmark, Max. Life 3.0: *Being Human in the Age of Artificial Intelligence*. New York: Knopf, 2017.

Telea, Alexandru C. *Data Visualization: Principles and Practice*. Boca Raton: CRC, 2015.

Teubner, Gunther. "Elektronische Agenten und große Menschenaffen: Zur Ausweitung des Akteurstatus." *Recht und Politik. Zeitschrift für Rechtssoziologie* 27, no. 1 (2006): 5–30.

Thiedeke, Udo. "Wir Kosmopoliten. Einführung in eine Soziologie des Cyberspace." In *Soziologie des Cyberspace: Medien, Strukturen und Semantiken*, edited by Udo Thiedeke, 15–47. Wiesbaden: Springer VS, 2013.

Thrun, Sebastian, and Lorien Pratt, eds. *Learning to Learn*. Dordrecht: Kluwer, 1998.

Toobin, Jeffrey. "The Solace of Oblivion. In Europe, the Right to Be Forgotten Trumps the Internet." *New Yorker*, September 29, 2014.

Treaster, Joseph B. "Will You Graduate? Ask Big Data." *New York Times*, February 2, 2017.

Tufte, Edward R. *Envisioning Information*. Cheshire: Graphic Press, 1990.

Tufte, Edward R. *The Visual Display of Quantitative Information*. Cheshire: Graphic Press, 1983.

Tufte, Edward R. *Visual Explanations: Images and Quantities, Evidence and Narrative*. Cheshire: Graphic Press, 1997.

Turing, Alan M. "Computing Machinery and Intelligence." *Mind* 59, no. 236 (1950): 433–460.

Turkle, Sherry. *Alone Together. Why We Expect More from Technology and Less from Each Other*. New York: Basic Books, 2011.

Vaidhyanathan, Siva. *The Googlization of Everything (And Why We Should Worry)*. Berkley/Los Angeles: University of California Press, 2011.

Vandermeersch, Leon. "Dalla tartaruga all'achillea (Cina)." In *Divination et Rationalité*, edited by J.P. Vernant, L. Vandermeersch, J. Gernet, J. Bottéro, R. Crahay, L. Brisson, J. Carlier, D. Grodzynski, and A. Retel-Laurentin, 27–52. Paris: Seuil, 1974.

Vanderstichele, Geneviève. "Interpretable AI, Explainable AI and the Sui Generis Method in Adjudication." Unpublished manuscript, 2020.

van Dijck, José. "Digital Photography: Communication, Identity, Memory." *Visual Communication* 7 (2008): 57–76.

van Hoboken, Joris. "The Proposed Right to be Forgotten Seen from the Perspective of Our Right to Remember, Freedom of Expression Safeguards in a Converging Information Environment." Unpublished manuscript, 2013.

van Hoboken, Joris. "Search Engine Freedom: On the Implications of the Right to Freedom of Expression for the Legal Governance of Web Search Engines." *Information Law Series* 27. Alphen aan den Rijn: Kluwer Law International, 2012.

Van House, Nancy A. "Personal Photography, Digital Technologies and the Uses of the Visual." *Visual Studies* 26, no. 2 (2011): 125–134.

Vernant, Jean-Pierre. "Parole e segni muti." In *Divination et Rationalité*, edited by J. P. Vernant, L. Vandermeersch, J. Gernet, J. Bottéro, R. Crahay, L. Brisson, J. Carlier, D. Grodzynski, and A. Retel-Laurentin, 5–24. Paris: Seuil, 1974.

Vespignani, Alessandro. *L'algoritmo e l'oracolo: Come la scienza predice il futuro e ci aiuta a cambiarlo*. Milan: Il Saggiatore, 2019.

Vis, Farida. "A Critical Reflection on Big Data: Considering APIs, Researchers and Tools as Data Makers." *First Monday* 18, no. 10 (2013). https://doi.org/10.5210/fm.v18i10.4878.

Visi, Tamás. "A Science of List? Medieval Jewish Philosophers as List Makers." In *The Charm of a List: From the Sumerians to Computerised Data Processing*, edited by Lucie Doležalová, 12–33. Newcastle upon Tyne: Cambridge Scholars Publishing, 2009.

von Foerster, Heinz. "Cibernetica ed epistemologia: Storia e prospettive." In *La sfida della complessità*, edited by G. Bocchi and M. Ceruti, 112–140. Milan: Feltrinelli, 1985.

von Foerster, Heinz. *Observing Systems*. Seaside,CA: Intersystems Publications, 1981.

von Foerster, Heinz. "Notes on an Epistemology for Living Things." BCL Report No.9.3. Biological Computer Laboratory, University of Illinois, 1972.

von Glasersfeld, Ernst. "Einführung in den radikalen Konstruktivismus." In *Die erfundene Wirklichkeit*, edited by Paul Watzlawick, 16–38. Munich: Piper, 1981.

von Soden, Wolfram. "Leistung und Grenze sumerischer und babylonischer Wissenschaft. Die Welt als Geschichte." In *Die Eigenbegrifflichkeit der babylonischen Welt. Leistung und Grenze sumerischer und babylonischer Wissenschaft*, edited by Benno Landsberger, 21–133. Darmstadt: Wissenschaftliche Buchgesellschaft, 1975.

Wachter, Sandra, Brent Mittelstadt, and Luciano Floridi. "Transparent, Explainable, and Accountable AI for Robotics." Science Robotics 2, no. 6 (2017). https://doi.org/10.1126/scirobotics.aan6080.

Waggoner, Zach. *My Avatar, My Self: Identity in Video Role-Playing Games*. Jefferson: McFarland, 2009.

Wagner-Pacifici, Robin, John W. Mohr, and Ronald L. Breiger. "Ontologies, Methodologies and New Uses of Big Data in the Social and Cultural Sciences." *Big Data & Society* 2, no. 2 (2015): 1–11.

Walton, Douglas, Fabrizio Macagno, and Giovanni Sartor. *Statutory Interpretation: Pragmatics and Argumentation*. Cambridge: Cambridge University Press, 2021.

Wang, Yongdong. "Your Next New Best Friend Might Be a Robot: Meet Xiaoice. She's Empathic, Caring, and Always Available—Just Not Human." *Nautilus*, February 4, 2016. http://nautil.us/issue/33/attraction/your-next-new-best-friend-might-be-a-robot.

Ward, Matthew, Georges Grinstein, and Daniel Keim. *Interactive Data Visualization: Foundations, Techniques, and Applications*. Boca Raton: CRC, 2015.

Ware, Colin. *Information Visualization: Perception for Design*. San Diego: Academic Press, 2000.

Wasik, Bill. *And Then There's This: How Stories Live and Die in Viral Culture*. London/ New York: Viking, 2009.

Watzlawick, Paul. *Die erfundene Wirklichkeit*. Munich: Piper, 1981.

Watzlawick, Paul, Janet Beavin Bavelas, and Don D. Jackson. *Pragmatics of Human Communication: A Study of Interactional Patterns, Pathologies, and Paradoxes*. New York: Norton, 1962.

Weinberger, David. *Everything Is Miscellaneous: The Power of the New Digital Disorder*. New York: Henry Holt, 2007.

Weinberger, David. "Our Machines Now Have Knowledge We'll Never Understand." *Wired*, April 18, 2017. https://www.wired.com/story/our-machines-now-have-know ledge-well-never-understand/.

Weinberger, David. *Taxonomies to Tags: From Trees to Piles of Leaves*. New York: CNET Networks, 2005.

Weinrich, Harald. *Gibt es eine Kunst des Vergessens?* Basel: Schwabe, 1996.

Weinrich, Harald. *Lethe. Kunst und Kritik des Vergessens*. Munich: Beck, 1997.

Weitin, Thomas. "Thinking Slowly: Reading Literature in the Aftermath of Big Data." *LitLingLab Pamphlet* 1, 2015.

Welch, Chris. "Google Just Gave a Stunning Demo of Assistant Making an Actual Phone Call." *The Verge*, May 8, 2018. https://www.theverge.com/2018/5/8/17332070 /google-assistant-makes-phone-call-demo-duplex-io-2018.

Whitmore, Michael. "Text: A Massively Addressable Object." In *Debates in the Digital Humanities*, edited by Matthew K. Gold, 324–327. Minneapolis: University of Minnesota Press, 2012.

Wilding, John, and Elizabeth Valentine. *Superior Memories*. Hove: Psychology Press, 1997.

Williams, Eliza. "24 Hours in Photos." *Creative Review*, November 11, 2011. https:// www.creativereview.co.uk/24-hours-in-photos/.

Winograd, Terry A., and Fernando Flores. *Understanding Computer and Cognition*. Reading, MA: Addison-Wesley, 1986.

Wolchover, Natalie. "AI Recognizes Cats the Same Way Physicists Calculate the Cosmos." *Wired*, December 15, 2014. https://www.wired.com/2014/12/deep-learn ing-renormalization/

Woodruff, Allison. "Necessary, unpleasant, and disempowering: reputation management in the internet age." In *Proceedings of the SIGCHI Conference on Human Factors in Computing Systems*. New York: ACM Press, 2014.

Wright, Talmadge, Eric Boria, and Paul Breidenbach. "Creative Player Actions in FPS Online Video Games." *Game Studies* 2, no. 2 (2002). http://www.gamestudies .org/0202/wright/

Wrisley, David Joseph, and Stefan Jänicke. "Visualizing Uncertainty: How to Use the Fuzzy Data of 550 Medieval Texts?" Abstract for Digital Humanities, University of Nebraska–Lincoln, July 2013. http://dh2013.unl.edu/abstracts/ab-158.html.

Wu, Tim. *The Attention Merchants: The Epic Scramble to Get Inside Our Heads*. New York: Alfred A. Knopf, 2016.

Xiao, Lang, Lu Qibei, and Guo Feipeng. "Mobile Personalized Recommendation Model Based on Privacy Concerns and Context Analysis for the Sustainable Development of M-commerce." *Sustainability* 12, no. 7 (2020): 3036.

Yates, Frances A. *The Art of Memory*. London: Routledge & Kegan Paul, 1966.

Youyou, Wu, Michal Kosinski, and David Stillwell. "Computer-Based Personality Judgments Are More Accurate Than Those Made by Humans." *Proceedings of the National Academy of Sciences* 112, no. 4 (2015): 1036–1040.

Zuboff, Shoshana. *The Age of Surveillance Capitalism: The Fight for a Human Future at the New Frontier of Power*. London: Profile Books, 2019.

Zumthor, Paul. *Introduction à la poésie orale*. Paris: Seuil, 1972.

INDEX